A COMPANION TO

V.

A COMPANION TO

V.

BY J. KERRY GRANT

THE UNIVERSITY OF

GEORGIA PRESS

ATHENS AND

LONDON

© 2001 by the University of Georgia Press

Athens, Georgia 30602

All rights reserved

Designed by Betty Palmer McDaniel

Set in 10/14 Trump Mediaeval by G & S Typesetters

Printed and bound by Maple-Vail

The paper in this book meets the guidelines for

permanence and durability of the Committee on

Production Guidelines for Book Longevity of the

Council on Library Resources.

Printed in the United States of America

05 04 03 02 01 C 5 4 3 2 1

05 04 03 02 01 P 5 4 3 2 1

Library of Congress Cataloging-in-Publication Data

Grant, J. Kerry.

A companion to V. / by J. Kerry Grant.

p. cm.

Includes bibliographical references (p.) and index.

ISBN 0-8203-2250-4 (alk. paper)

ISBN 0-8203-2251-2 (pbk. : alk. paper)

1. Pynchon, Thomas. V.   2. Psychological fiction, American—History

and criticism.   I. Title.

PS3566.Y55 V234   2001

813'.54—dc21   00-032539

British Library Cataloging-in-Publication Data available

For Natalia

CONTENTS

ACKNOWLEDGMENTS

Thanks are due to St. Lawrence University for the opportunity to devote a year to this project. Sandy Hinchman once again deserves particular thanks for her careful reading of an early draft.

INTRODUCTION

As was the case with the *Companion to The Crying of Lot 49,* the present volume had its genesis in my experience of trying to introduce Pynchon to undergraduate readers. Each time I assign one of his novels, I am reminded how much of a challenge Pynchon presents to those who are encountering his work for the first time, and I find myself fending off a flurry of complaints about how obscure and difficult a writer he is. It is sometimes hard to persuade students that the game is worth the candle. With *V.* in particular, a significant number fail to finish the book, as if they are convinced that it is a labyrinth they will never find their way out of if they venture too far from the entrance.

Several factors give rise to this state of affairs, not the least of which is the novel's daunting surface. With its shifting points of view and its complex narrative structure, its cast of more than 150 characters and its extraordinarily wide range of reference, *V.* makes considerable demands on the stamina of the reader.

This companion is designed in part to overcome many of the difficulties posed by these aspects of the novel. The chapter summaries should help the reader keep a map of the main incidents in mind, and notes will resolve at least some of the perplexities caused by unfamiliar names or historical references. In addition, extracts from the work of critics who have written extended commentaries on *V.* represent the range of interpretive strategies that the novel has invited.

While making no apologies for what I hope may be the immediate and readily perceived benefits of selective reference to the Companion's several hundred entries, I would also like briefly to suggest the manner in which this particular way of supplementing the reader's experience echoes one of Pynchon's most consistently addressed concerns.

If Thomas Pynchon knows anything, and it is clear that he knows a great deal, it is the intriguing fact that, despite attack after attack on the conventional certainties enshrined in the genre, most novel readers bring with them to each text a set of remarkably conservative expectations. Despite the competing influence of a culture thoroughly imbued with the probabilistic assumptions of post-Newtonian physics, the abrupt discontinuities of its dominant medium, television, and a faith in the capacity of individuals to transform themselves from moment to moment according to the dictates of fleeting rules of "style," most novel readers continue to hope for closure, for sustained narrative momentum, and for "rounded" characters launched on a trajectory of emotional and psychological development. Pynchon has consistently made it his business to call into question both these expectations and the epistemological assumptions that inform them.

It is hardly surprising, therefore, that his first novel should in large degree be informed by a satirical intention which implicitly targets the very act of reading itself. Herbert Stencil, the argument runs, is a kind of "bogus exemplum" of the hermeneutic impulse, whose "quest becomes a selective misreading of the novel" (Hite 50). The reader is almost inevitably drawn into a quest for meaning that parallels Stencil's. "Yet in aping his practice we implicate ourselves in his plight, for it is precisely because Stencil is an inveterate hermeneuticist inured to the ordering principles of identity and causality (and thus not unlike a conventional novel reader) that he would be handicapped in reading the novel in which he appears. His and our archaeological expectation that a 'real' reconstructable story or theme lies latent in the local intractabilities of the narrative is carefully cultivated" (Kowalewski 190). Hite's formulation is very much along the same lines: "By offering the character of Stencil as a critical role model, *V.* duplicitously fosters the epistemological assumption that experience is somehow a story that will yield up its significance when it is given, as Robert Musil's Man Without Qualities puts it:

'a unidimensional order: the stringing upon one thread of all that has happened in space and time'"(49). *Caveat lector*, it is clear, is the novel's persistent subtext.

At the same time, however, we recognize in the person of Benny Profane another role model to avoid, for if Stencil allows himself to be too easily seduced by the signifying power of *V.*, Profane in the end occupies an opposite extreme. As Seed has noted (*Fictional Labyrinths* 74), he enters and leaves the novel dressed in identical outfits, having failed (by his own admission) to derive any meaning whatsoever from the experiences he has undergone. "Offhand," he tells Brenda Wigglesworth, "I'd say I haven't learned a goddamn thing" (PC491.1).

If Stencil may be said to have learned too much, and Profane to have learned too little, one might well ask what ground the novel offers for the reader to occupy. Alert to the potential for seduction, we can perhaps recognize and thus sidestep the text's many opportunities for hermeneutic excess, but we are surely still reluctant to conclude that beneath its richly complex surface there lies the same "Nothing" that Hugh Godolphin claims to have discerned beneath the Antarctic ice (PC215.28). Inevitably, then, we are inclined to seek out some middle ground, and in doing so, I believe, we enter familiar Pynchonian territory. The polarization between Stencil's overdetermined *V.*-world and the meaningless perpetual motion of Profane's existence exemplifies a thematic concern that is central to Pynchon's work in general and to *V.* in particular. As Schaub has pointed out (11), this theme finds its most succinct expression in Sidney Stencil's rueful recognition of the "intolerable double vision" that informed the political behaviors of the twentieth century and in his reluctant acceptance of the "obsolete" nature of "the real present . . . the once-respectable Golden Mean" (PC506.25). Schaub also cites Schoenmaker's recognition that "correction—along all dimensions: social, political, emotional—entails retreat to a diametric opposite rather than any reasonable search for a golden mean" (PC104.3).

At the level of character and incident, and in its commentary upon the human condition in the middle of the twentieth century, the novel as a whole bears out Stencil's and Schoenmaker's pessimism. Readers who hope to find the object of Schoenmaker's "reasonable search" in the novel's gestures toward a positive vision of human possibility are likely to be poorly rewarded for their efforts. Fausto Maijstral's oscillations bring him to what seems likely to be a temporary equilibrium between the abstractions of his youth and the rock-like inertness of the war years, while McClintic Sphere's "Keep cool, but care" (PC394.3) attempts only the most minimalist of negotiations between absence and excess of feeling. Rachel Owlglass can only fleetingly maintain the "twin envelope of peace" (PC396.2) within which Profane can supposedly find safety from both his street-level aimlessness and his potential recruitment into the hothouse world of the Crew, while Paola Maijstral's middle ground turns out to be a resumption of her marriage to the abusive sailor Pappy Hod. It is surely part of the novel's purpose to demonstrate how such tentative and/or perfunctory efforts are inevitably drowned out by the sometimes slapstick, sometimes solemn parade of human weakness, wickedness, and folly that informs the bulk of both incident and insight on almost every page.

At another level, however, the novel is remarkable for its exuberance and for the degree of exhilaration it affords the reader who tunes in to its most postmodern frequencies. The interplay of tantalizing correspondences and half-fulfilled promises that embodies the novel's meta-commentary on the human need for order, is not, of course, the solid ground from which the reader might achieve a single perspective; rather, it is perhaps equivalent to what Katherine Hayles has identified as the "quantized field" that some scientists have come to think of as a more useful designation for the fundamental component of physical reality (16). Within that field, the reader is constantly alert to the inadequacy of the extremes represented by Stencil and Profane, and hence in a permanent state of openness to the provisional nature of language's relationship with such a reality.

In that regard, the notes which follow may be thought of as a series of accretions around individual "energy knots" (the phrase is Hermann Weyl's by way of Hayles [16]) whose proper context is the total quantized field of Pynchon's novel. It is my hope that the reader of the *Companion* will find that each augmented fragment will resume its place in the novel's field and resonate with its surroundings in new and interesting ways.

In order to make the *Companion* a convenient tool for as wide a range of readers as possible, references are keyed to three editions of the novel: the 1999 Harper Perennial Classics edition (PC), the Perennial Fiction Library edition published in 1986 and reissued in 1990 (PF), and the Bantam edition published in 1964 (B). Page and line numbers for each appear in boldface along with the item that is the subject of the note. Cross references (in parentheses) are keyed to the Perennial Classics edition and direct the reader either to other pages in the novel or, when the citation is accompanied by an "n," to other annotations.

A NOTE ON THE TITLE

The reader's quest for meaning in the novel begins, as Olderman has noted, with the period in the title, which "leads us to believe that there is a word behind the mystery and leads us to turn random symptoms into an unholy kind of Word become flesh" (137). A similar claim is advanced by Kowalewski: "The importance of using the initial V. as a title resides not so much in what it suggests but in how it suggests it, how it shapes what a reader's response to the book will be. It is not what V. means that counts but what she or it makes the reader do, the appetite she or it creates. Pynchon makes the initial invite, accommodate, even dare exegesis while he constantly seems amused by the obsessive possibilities it makes available" (192).

The iconographic features of the title letter take on a retrospective significance once the novel itself has been read: "This figure, the V whose constituent elements seem to have a common, basic point of origin (but in fact do not), stands as an emblem of Stencil's quest" (Patteson, "How True" 301). "V. promises confluence, a coming together, an identity, a point where there is sameness. But if we move *up* the V, there is only divergence, absence of identity, absence of character" (McHoul and Wills 165).

A COMPANION TO

CHAPTER ONE

The twenty-three-year-old Catholic/Jewish ex-sailor Benny Profane arrives in Norfolk, Virginia, on Christmas Eve 1955 and connects with some of his old navy buddies. After a week of drinking, during which Profane finds himself unwillingly taking responsibility for the welfare of Paola Maijstral, he ends up in New York City, where he meets Fina Mendoza and entertains the idea of taking a job shooting alligators in the sewers. Profane is avoiding reestablishing contact with Rachel Owlglass, whom he had met in the Catskills in the summer of 1954.

PC1.1 PF9.1 B1.1 Christmas Eve The fleeting appeal of the opening words of the novel to our sense of Western religious practices and beliefs sets us up for all that follows in the way of the novel's skepticism toward anything resembling a grand unified theory. This "originating, charismatic moment in Western history" (Lhamon 72) is immediately placed in a mid-twentieth-century context, in which its uniqueness (and thus its capacity to define or shape experience) is called into question. "Every night is Christmas Eve on old East Main," after all. "The Christmas Eve of 1955, Pynchon proceeds to show, is thoroughly embedded in the advanced decline of its own tradition" (Lhamon 73).

Eddins sees in the opening passages of the novel an anticipation of a key theme: "The degeneration of the Virgin toward the Inanimate" (83). He notes in particular that "Christmas Eve in the Sailor's Grave sees a carol celebrating the Virgin birth interrupted by the 'atheist' Pig Bodine and the parodic celebration of 'Suck Hour' at a foam-rubber breast" (83). The fact that Mrs. Buffo's rendition of the carol is achieved only "within the limited range of the boatswain's pipe" is perhaps a further indication of the reduced possibility for transcendence afforded by Christian tradition. The potentially ambiguous implications of Profane's name (see PC1.1n "Benny Profane") suggest the degree to which the novel will insist on the tempering of the sacred by the stubbornly quotidian.

According to Hawthorne, the novel's preoccupation with the issue of parentage is also adumbrated in the opening: "Christmas Eve commemorates a birth in which we have a physical mother but an absent father. . . . In other words, the novel opens with the polar opposition to Herbert Stencil's condition of knowing his father's identity but not his mother" (79).

PC1.1 PF9.1 B1.1   1955   Given Stencil's conspiracy theorist tendencies, it is perhaps no accident that the present time of the novel situates its action squarely in the midst of America's obsession with the communist threat. Olderman points out that the McCarthy Hearings closed only shortly before the time of the novel's opening (136).

PC1.1 PF9.1 B1.22 Benny Profane   Pynchon will be remembered as one of the twentieth century's great onomastic provocateurs, dangling his characters' monikers before us in gleeful expectation of our surrender to the hermeneutic impulse. "Benny," via Benjamin, the lucky "child of the right hand," has its ironic resonances as the first name of an accident-prone schlemihl. Judith Chambers finds "Profane" particularly suggestive, claiming that it "implies his estrangement from things sacred, an apt association for our 'flabby'-souled antihero who avoids both earthly and spiritual connections. Besides its specifically doctrinal implications, 'profane' describes a person or thing not initiated into the inner mysteries or esoteric knowledge, as well as one who treats sacred things with irreverence" (52). She goes on to note, however, that "Benny," as a diminutive of Benjamin, invokes religious associations and cites Graves on the meaning of the name in Hebrew mysticism as a ruler with connections to the "day of the Divine Child" (52). As she says, we meet Profane on "the night before the birth of the Christian Divine Child." From this perspective, the combination is ambiguous. A character with such a name ought somehow to look two ways—in the direction of some kind of benevolence or beneficence as well as toward the absence of any such invitation to the good life as might be implied in the structures through which we seek to express our sense of the sacred, and indeed some of this doubleness does exist in the portrayal of Benny Profane. For example, almost despite himself, he manages to summon sufficient goodwill to protect Paola (particularly from the advances of Pig Bodine [PC400]), while at the same time claiming in the end not to have "learned a goddamn thing" (PC491.2). Hite embodies a version of this reading in her description of "the well-intentioned (*bene*) Benny . . . the presiding deity of a profane world" (59). Others are less inclined to find any such ambiguity, among them Richter, who suggests "thoroughly secular" as a gloss (104), and Safer, who claims that "Benny's given name calls to mind . . . the 'upper' Benzedrine" (87).

The temptation to read Profane allegorically through his name is scarcely lessened by the typically Pynchonian stinginess of his subsequent characterization. As Seed points out, his "sudden appearance in the first chapter without preamble or much reference to his past implies that Profane only has an existence in the present" (*Fictional Labyrinths* 72), and little more is to be gleaned as the novel progresses. We may be sympathetic with Rachel Owlglass's exasperation at his having turned his self-conception into a "Universal Principle" (PC413.6n), but we have scant reason not to follow his lead. Rachel may see past the soft "amoebalike" (PC31.7) surface he presents; we can rarely do so. The critics' tendency to reach outside the confines of the novel for meanings to attach to Profane is therefore understandable. He is "like Ishmael . . . a wanderer and one-time sailor" (Campbell 58); he "functions as an urbanized and Americanized version of the Parisian *flâneur*" (Simon 173); he is "a composite parody of a character in post-war literature, resembling Sarraute's 'homo absurdus,' 'a soulless body tossed about by hostile forces.' He is a mixture of the successors to the Camusian anti-hero in what Bellow called 'victim literature,' and the loosely existentialist new picaros of Kerouac in *On the Road* and Bellow himself in *The Adventures of Augie March*" (Dugdale 100–101).

PC1.1 PF9.1 B1.22   black levis, suede jacket, sneakers and big cowboy hat   "Pynchon is careful to point out that his dress is exactly the same at the end of the novel as at the beginning, thereby suggesting that he has not changed at all. Profane represents an attenuated and lethargic version of Beat mobility reduced absurdly to moving in order to fill the monotony of life" (Seed, *Fictional Labyrinths* 74). Profane is indeed dressed at the end in "suede jacket, levis and big cowboy hat" (PC488.7). Seed's observation is consistent with a number of other details in the novel, notably Profane's claim that "Schlemihls don't change" (PC413.3) and his assertion that he has learned nothing (PC491.1n).

PC1.3 PF9.2 B1.24   Norfolk, Virginia   Since 1801, when the first Continental Navy Yard was established in Norfolk, the city has been a center of naval operations. The U.S. Naval Operations Base was established in 1917.

PC2.7 PF10.13 B2.5   like a yo-yo   Hausdorff reads the yo-yo image in all its manifestations throughout the novel as a "*reductio ad absurdum*" of those "powerful industrial, technological energies" that Henry Adams (see PC58.10n) had encapsulated in his image of the dynamo (259). For Matthijs, the toy's characteristic back and forth motion is a fitting image for Profane's wanderings, which are "controlled . . . by external circumstances which merely occur and are not seen as significantly connected" (135). The two views find an echo in Kharpertian's claim that "Profane's yo-yoing represents Pynchon's form of the picaro's subjection to Fortune, but it signifies further the protagonist's pointless automatism and mechanism" (63). The seeming aimlessness associated with the image is given an ironic counterpoint by the Whole Sick Crew's insistence that there are rules which govern the practice of "yo-yoing" on the subway (PC322). A somewhat darker set of associations is generated by the presence in the novel of references to Yoyodyne, the defense contractor whose name "symbolize[s] the humble beginnings of the Chiclitz empire and . . . get[s] the idea of force, enterprise, engineering skill and rugged individualism in there too" (PC241.7). The Yoyodyne connection extends the Adamsian trope of the dynamo to accommodate the twentieth century's pursuit of increasingly destructive applications of technology, an association that is clearly marked when Stencil's follow-up of the link between Eigenvalue and Chiclitz leads him to Mondaugen, who worked at Peenemunde on the V-rockets. Stark's suggestion that "'yo-yo' is a pun on 'yaw'" (67) and that the image thus should be glossed in part through its association with the idea of "negative feedback" gains plausibility from this associative link to the technicalities of rocket control.

PC2.10 PF10.16 B2.9   a single abstracted Street   Just as every night is Christmas Eve on Old East Main, so too is every street an abstract and undifferentiated single "Street," evoking an underlying homogeneity that Matthijs identifies as a characteristic of "the profane mode of existence" (135). Bewildered by the highly differentiated reality of the "named streets" he has traveled in the past, Profane resorts instinctively to an abstract explanatory structure. In this regard, he is the double of Herbert Stencil, whose quest will come to seem like an attempt to fuse the history of the twentieth century into a single arbitrary symbol. Campbell (59) regards Profane's "Street" as a debased version of Sidney Stencil's more informed and therefore more complex image (PC506.20n), a reading that is consistent with the novel's overall delineation of a process of decline in cultural vitality. For Dugdale, the "Street" is evocative of de Chirico (PC323.17n) and hence part of a complex of allusions that provides "a continuity of atmosphere through the century" (83).

PC2.21 PF10.26 B2.22   SP   Shore Patrol.

PC2.23 PF10.28 B2.23   Hey Rube   The SP is calling for help. "Hey Rube" was originally supposed to be the rallying call of circus folk when they found themselves in a dispute with townspeople (Wentworth and Flexner).

PC2.25 PF10.30 B2.24   receding in an asymmetric V to the east "This early in the book . . . in a manner unknown to the protagonist and not yet made clear by the narrative itself, the letter 'V' makes its appearance and is identified with the east (the Old World, since this is where Stencil's quest will lead him) and with a fade-out. For Henry Adams, too, the Virgin-Venus was an old-world principle, one which had never really taken root in America" (Hausdorff 260).

PC2.29 PF10.34 B2.29   realizing he had one foot in the Grave The pun, according to Campbell, "makes the death-in-life theme more explicit" and reinforces the possible echo of Melville's sailors' tavern, "The Spouter-Inn:—Peter Coffin" (58).

PC3.15 PF11.16 B3.8   N.O.B.   Naval Operations Base.

PC3.33 PF11.33 B3.28   Ploy saw apocalypse   Lhamon finds a trace here of the novel's use of pentecostal imagery, suggesting that Ploy's obscenities are the equivalent of the "tongues" of Pentecost (73). See also PC7.11n and PC91.14n.

PC4.32 PF12.28 B4.22   DesLant   Destroyer Force, U.S. Atlantic Fleet.

PC5.2 PF12.33 B4.27   Mrs. Buffo   Claiming that the Sailor's Grave is a kind of sanctuary that "celebrates a denial of sexuality," Hawthorne reads Mrs. Buffo's name as confirmation. Her married state, he argues, reminds us of the only marriage mentioned, that of Paola and Pappy, which is no longer intact; her given name, Beatrice, evokes Dante's allegorical Beatrice, who "becomes the Mother Church that rejects unproductive sexuality," and, finally, her last name is reminiscent of the Latin "bufo," or "toad," and its derivative, "buffoon." "As toad or buffoon, Mrs. Buffo squats over her establishment, a bizarre parody of the celebrant" (79–80). Allen's view is less negative. Though she acknowledges that Mrs. Buffo is "corrupted," she nonetheless sees her as a kind of balancing female character, "at least as interesting" as her male counterpart, "the American businessman" (40).

PC5.4 PF12.35 B4.30   should call all barmaids Beatrice   "The debased condition of language as a referential medium is expressed by the common name shared by all of the barmaids who work there. The over-signification of the name creates a meaningless homogeneity by eliminating the elements of difference, the structuring principle that makes any language functionally significant" (Madsen 32). The allusive implication of Dante's Beatrice in this emptying out of significance provides an example of the novel's repeated invitation to the reader to at least call into question the likely efficacy of grand ordering structures of all kinds.

PC5.33 PF13.27 B5.16 X.O. Executive Officer.

PC6.25 PF14.16 B6.1 Paola Despite Mrs. Buffo's attempts to impose homogeneity, Paola alone seems to have escaped the fate of the other barmaids, who are all referred to as "Beatrice." This is perhaps in keeping with subsequent developments, which reveal Paola to be something of a positive figure in the novel. Noting that her name links her with "Paul" (she is from Malta, site of the shipwreck of the Apostle Paul), Newman sees her as "a foil to the religious parody that V. exhibits . . . a figure of salvation" (*Understanding Pynchon* 56), a view echoed by Kharpertian, for whom she is "a fertile antithesis to V." (69), and by Slade, who says that Paola is "a strong candidate for revitalized goddess of the waste land" (97).

PC6.30 PF14.20 B6.6 Valletta, Malta "The capital city of Malta. Built by Grandmaster Jean Parisot de la Valette on Mount Xeberras after the Great Siege of 1565 [PC331.19n]. It is situated on a peninsula overlooking the Grand Harbour on one side and Maramuscetto (Marsamxett) on the other" (Cassola 328).

PC7.11 PF14.36 B6.23 Paola knew scraps it seemed of all tongues One of many evocations of the Pentecostal motif that run through the novel. (The connection is established through the association with speaking in tongues and hence with the experience of the disciples on the fiftieth day—Pentecost or Whitsunday—after the death of Christ [Acts 2:4]). Newman observes that "the Pentecostal wind is reflected in Paola's last name, Maijstral, which is a Maltese wind. Furthermore, it is a wind that blows once every three days, thus underscoring the relation to the Trinity" (58). Paola is never in fact shown to have access to divine revelation, but her participation as a child in the disassembly of the Bad Priest (PC369.34n) and her partaking in the limited wisdom of McClintic Sphere (PC393.25n) are suggestive of her positive role.

PC7.22 PF15.12 B6.35 She looked like an East Main barmaid Although she seems to have been absorbed into the milieu of the

Sailor's Grave, Profane recognizes that Paola has in fact simply adopted a kind of protective coloring ("the prairie hare in the snow").

PC8.15 PF16.1 B7.21   Suck Hour!   Ploy's follow-up to the "militant atheist" Pig Bodine's interruption of Mrs. Buffo's carol turns what Hawthorne sees as a "eucharistic celebration" (80) into a travesty of maternal nurturing, a parody of the Virgin's suckling of the Divine Child (Eddins 83).

PC8.26 PF16.12 B7.34   the foam rubber breast   The first of many references to both literal and figurative prostheses.

PC9.26 PF17.8 B8.28   alien hieroglyphics   "From the opening scene in the bar when drunken feet move about in the damp sawdust . . . we are never far away from the feeling that there is something afoot, something going on 'beneath,' a code or clue to be deciphered, a plot or portent to be dreaded" (Tanner, "V2" 32).

PC10.5 PF17.23 B9.3   Newport News   City in Virginia across the James River from Norfolk.

PC10.6 PF17.24 B9.4   WAVE   Women Accepted for Volunteer Emergency Service (in the navy).

PC10.12 PF17.30 B9.12   Teflon had a camera   The chemical company Dupont had registered the name of its well-known non-stick coating in 1945, and commercial products using the resin came on the market in the following year. "The sailor whose main joy is to photograph his friends while they are having sexual intercourse is only one of many whose most intense relationships to reality are detached and impotent stares. . . . Voyeurism is another way of evading true selfhood and denying or avoiding the possibility of love" (Tanner, "V2" 25). Tanner's claim links Teflon with the voyeurism most fully explored in the "V. in Love" chapter.

PC11.20 PF18.31 B10.12   She taught them all a song   The song is the French novelist and songwriter Boris Vian's 1955 anti-war "complaint," "Le déserteur." The song is in the form of a letter to the French president, in which the writer explains why he is refusing to be drafted into the French army. Pynchon quotes two snatches of one version of the song, the original text of which is as follows:

Depuis que je suis né
J'ai vu mourir mon père
J'ai vu partir mes frères
Et pleurer mes enfants

. . . .

Demain de bon matin
Je fermerai ma porte
Au nez des années mortes
J'irai sur les chemins

Je mendirai ma vie
Sur les routes de France
De Bretagne en Provence . . .
(quoted in Clouzet 115–16).

"Closing the door on the dead years, for this soldier, can only mean closing the door on the historical era of colonialism" (Holton 341).

PC11.20 PF18.31 B10.12   French leave   The pun is perhaps a little labored. The deserting para is, in fact, taking his "leave" from France.

PC11.21 PF18.32 B10.13   the fighting in Algeria   See PC12.8n.

PC11.31 PF19.5 B10.24   the Piraeus   Piraeus is the port for the city of Athens. The para, judging from his song ("from the old to the new world"), is probably expecting to take ship for America.

PC12.8 PF19.15 B10.36   F.L.N.   *Front de Liberation National*, an Algerian nationalist organization formed to coordinate opposition to French colonial rule.

PC12.8 PF19.16 B10.37   Miraculous Medal   "An oval medal bearing on one side an image of our Lady standing on a globe with rays of light coming from her hands, surrounded by the words: 'O Mary conceived without sin! Pray for us who have recourse to thee'; on the reverse, a cross, the initial M, and a representation of the hearts of Jesus and his mother" ("Miraculous Medal," *Catholic Encyclopaedic Dictionary*).

PC12.12 PF19.20 B10.41   half Catholic   Slade suggests that, in the light of the dubious versions of Catholicism embraced by V., Profane's "Jewish schlemihlhood can rejuvenate the sterile rituals of the Catholic faith, and somehow turn them into viable values" (95).

PC12.20 PF19.28 B11.7   Pat Boone   The wildly popular singer (b. 1934) who was outstripped in sales of records at this time only by Elvis Presley. Known for his squeaky clean image and his cleaned up covers of "wilder" performers' songs.

PC13.17 PF20.23 B11.41   I have a dependent now   From the beginning, the novel establishes Profane's uneasiness at the thought of any kind of commitment to a woman. Of the male characters, only McClintic Sphere and Fausto Maijstral show any sign of willingness to enter into or sustain a permanent relationship and for neither of them does the relationship last. Ruby/Paola returns to her husband, while Elena Xemxi is killed by fascist bombs. Although Roony Winsome seems to wish that his relationship with Mafia could be more stable, he is quick to allow his thoughts to turn to Paola, a fact that aligns him with that least uxorious of characters, Pig Bodine.

PC13.25 PF20.31 B12.6   ships, untenanted, inanimate   No other word of comparable significance appears as often in *V.* as does the word "inanimate." This is the first of almost sixty occurrences in the novel and it initiates one of the main thematic threads that runs throughout. Profane is here seen to be projecting his own fears onto the seascape around him: from his perspective it is "*as if* there were nothing in this roads" but the inanimate ships (my emphasis). What is more, the passage contains a reminder that although the objects around him appear to be communicating with one another, the noises they are making are "nothing more" than what they are— noises. To wish them otherwise is to succumb to that desire which Fausto Maijstral calls into question (PC347.7n) to "populate" the street of our existence, to create compensatory fantasies as part of a "Great Lie" (PC349.22n).

As Chambers points out, however, even though Profane apparently fears such seascapes, "his counterphobic refusal to connect impels him to remain isolated and cold" (53). Paola's hug, for example, "[doesn't] help the scene be any less alien" (PC14.2). Profane's rejection of human connectedness has its associations with those portions of the novel (and they are many) that detail humanity's drift toward a kind of inanimateness.

Kowalewski reads the scene somewhat differently, claiming that "the bleak and haunting privacy of this moment seems to come out of a confrontation with (Stevens again) 'nothing that is not there and the nothing that is,' with the sense that the scene is simply *there*, beyond any obligation to narrative significance" (198).

PC15.4 PF22.5 B13.18   The enigma or sinister vision   For all that Pig Bodine is largely a comic character, this moment is a hint of a darker side, one that is played out much later when Pig attempts to rape Paola (PC400.3). In the immediate context, the obviously negative connotations of this dark, faceless figure are compounded through the association Profane makes with Rachel Owlglass's preoccupation with her MG. Pig too is playing with an inanimate machine.

PC15.9 PF22.10 B13.23   Rachel Owlglass   It has been noted that Rachel's last name would be "Eulenspiegel" in German, but there seems little to be gained from the implied association with the German peasant trickster of that name. Richter points out that the biblical Rachel was the mother of Benjamin (118). Despite the sexual nature of the relationship, there is nonetheless a maternal dimension to Rachel's connection with Profane (PC23.16n).

PC15.20 PF22.21 B13.35   Da Conho, a mad Brazilian   "Conho" is Portuguese for "an isolated rock in a river." It seems fair to say that Da Conho is someone who appears to come from his own private portion of the planet. Kharpertian regards Da Conho's obsession with violence as a foreshadowing of Stencil's obsession and the violence associated with V. (61).

PC15.26 PF22.27 B13.42   Parris Island   One of the Sea Islands in southern South Carolina; since 1915, a Marine Corps training center.

PC15.27 PF22.27 B13.42   Hagannah   "(Hebrew: 'Defense'), Zionist military organization representing the majority of the Jews in

Palestine from 1920 to 1948. Organized to combat the revolts of Palestinian Arabs against the Jewish settlement of Palestine" ("Haganah," *Britannica Online*).

PC15.30 PF22.30 B14.3   mezuzah   "(Hebrew: 'doorpost') . . . small folded or rolled parchment inscribed by a qualified calligraphist with scriptural verses (Deuteronomy 6:4–9, 11:13–21) to remind Jews of their obligations toward God. The parchment is placed in a metal, wooden, or glass case so that the word Shaddai ('Almighty') can usually be seen on the back of the parchment. After a special blessing is recited, the mezuzah is firmly fixed to the main doorpost of the home (to the right as one enters)" ("mezuzah," *Britannica Online*).

PC16.5 PF23.4 B14.14   the sizzle of chang music   Da Conho is probably imagining here the sound of a small dulcimer, an instrument that would have found its way to the Middle East in the hands of Russian Jews.

PC16.23 PF23.21 B14.34   Love for an object, this was new to him   Given Profane's fearfulness in the face of the inanimate, this is hardly surprising. Da Conho's obsession with the machine gun and Rachel's with her MG are in a sense merely preparatory, laying the thematic groundwork for our encounter with the more complex fetishism of the lady V.

PC16.26 PF23.24 B14.37   under the rose   Patteson asserts ("True" 306) that the phrase "under the rose" refers to the ancient custom of hanging a rose over a council table to indicate that everyone at the meeting was sworn to secrecy (hence, anything done "under the rose" was done secretly). Eddins, reading "rose" through Henry Adams as the symbol of the Virgin's promise of paradise, equates the phrase with the process of decline away from the "spirit-sustaining powers" of the Virgin in the direction of "the subhuman realm of blind entropic process that constitutes late Adamsian nature" (61). Eddins adds that the Latin phrase "sub rosa" is "thought by lexicographers to stem from the legend that a rose was used as a bribe to keep the indiscretions of Venus—another aspect of Adams's Eternal Feminine—from being revealed." According to Brewer, images of roses were "sculpted on the ceilings of banqueting rooms, to remind the guests that what was spoken *sub vino* was not to be repeated *sub divo*" ("Sub rosa").

PC17.28 PF23.26 B14.41 It nearly ran him over For Kharpertian, this encounter is a "parody of the love-at-first-sight encounters of mass-market romances" (61).

PC17.13 PF24.8 B15.19 He was not sure whether he meant Rachel or the car Profane's uncertainty reflects more upon his inability to acknowledge the true humanity of others than on Rachel. A few pages later, after all, he is thinking of her as a "succubus" (PC23.24).

PC18.3 PF24.31 B16.1 hostile objects The stakes quickly get higher. From a kind of generalized fearfulness in the face of the inanimate (PC13.25n), Profane has already moved on to the possibility of a deadly hostility.

PC18.3 PF24.32 B16.2 schlimazzeled Perhaps Pynchon's own coinage, from "shlimazel . . . A chronically unlucky person; someone for whom nothing seems to go right or turn out well" (Rosten 347).

PC18.21 PF25.13 B16.20 the Five Towns Kharpertian characterizes as "incidental" the social satire intended by the paragraphs that follow (62). Pynchon's own Long Island upbringing no doubt contributed much to the portrait.

PC18.26 PF25.18 B16.25 a kind of geographical incest Incest, with its implications of enclosure and lack of variety, is a common motif of Pynchon's, tying in closely with his use of the concept of entropy, which is pressed into the service of a critique of a culture in which energy in the form of new ideas is less and less available, just as genetic variety is reduced in the case of incest. The idea is reinforced with the reference to the imprisoned Rapunzel.

PC19.5 PF25.31 B16.39 Ed Sullivan Edward Vincent Sullivan (1901–74), host of the television variety show that bore his name from 1955 to 1971.

PC19.22 PF26.11 B17.15 with some intention of pissing on the sun Profane's ambition here is to hasten the fulfillment of the predictions of those nineteenth-century cosmologists who foresaw the heat death of the universe. His dimly perceived strategy of revenge upon the inanimate has the ironic effect of aligning him, if only comically, with the process of decline, which he believes is exemplified in Rachel's affection for her car.

PC20.11 PF26.34 B17.39   Isn't that the world?   Rachel's question is odd, considering her role in the novel as one of only a few characters who are able to sustain any kind of faith in and commitment to the possibility of love. Her apparent belief that the human is merely a kind of surface skim over the underlying reality of inert but enduring matter is scarcely consistent with her behavior throughout.

PC20.18 PF27.4 B18.3   Your boy's road   Rachel is as much aware of the gender constraints that limit her possibilities as she is of the class influences (Holton 329).

PC20.20 PF27.6 B18.5   west of Ithaca and south of Princeton   The boundaries of the Ivy League—Cornell in the west and Princeton in the south. Rachel's sense of the limits of her world is consistent with the summer dating history she shares with Profane; although she wants to escape from the Five Towns of her childhood, she nonetheless dates only "upperclassmen attending Ivy League colleges" (PC18.16).

PC20.26 PF27.12 B18.12   nothing but MG-words   "In this world there is very little chance of any genuine communication. Language has suffered an inevitable decline in the mouths of these stencillized and objectified figures. Rachel Owlglass, the figure who more than any other seems to harbor a genuine capacity for love, is reduced to speaking to her car in 'MG words'; while Benny Profane, who seems to want to love, feels his vocabulary is made up of nothing but wrong words" (Tanner, "V2" 24).

PC21.9 PF27.29 B18.31   her world—one of objects coveted or valued   And yet the fact remains that, with the exception of the incident with the car (PC22), what we learn of Rachel from now on lends little credence to Profane's depiction. We are perhaps being told more about Profane's fear of the inanimate here than about her.

PC22.29 PF29.9 B20.4   to fondle the gearshift   Chambers seems to read this rather literally, describing Rachel as "losing her virginity to an MG automobile gearshift" (60). Rachel's own explanation that she is simply "tak[ing] out her virginity on something" (PC413.26) allows for a less Profane interpretation. McHoul and Wills also seem to align themselves with Profane rather than with Rachel when they claim on the basis of this scene that "there is little wonder that the eventual description of their sexual intercourse is a peculiar combination of the biological and the mechanical" (McHoul and Wills 174)

PC23.5 PF29.19 B20.15 He felt like the Angel of Death Whether deliberately or by oversight, Pynchon muddies the waters thoroughly here, mixing the story of the first Passover (when the Israelites marked their doors with blood so that the Lord would pass over their houses in the process of destroying the firstborn of Egypt [Exodus 12:12–13]) with the Jewish practice of nailing a box containing verses from Deuteronomy on their doorposts (see PC15.30n). What is more, the fact that the condoms now have holes in them, making them symbols of potential generation, makes Profane's comparison with the Angel of Death seem metaphorically as well as factually inaccurate.

PC23.16 PF29.30 B20.28 umbilical tug A reminder of the maternal dimension to Rachel's relationship with Profane (see PC15.9n). Matthijs regards this metaphor as "a restatement of the schlemiel–Jewish mama stereotype" (Matthijs 131).

PC23.24 PF30.1 B20.36 succubus The fact that Profane evidently thinks of Rachel's psychic intrusion as equivalent to a nightmare of sexual possession by a female demon forewarns us of the unlikeliness of any permanent bond being forged between the sometime lovers.

PC24.8 PF30.17 B21.13 Depuis que je suis né See PC11.20n.

PC24.17 PF30.26 B21.23 I was born in a Hooverville "Hooverville" was the name coined for any temporary shantytown put together during the Great Depression. Slade argues that Profane's birthplace makes him "the proletarian of the novel, the Sancho Panza to Stencil's Don Quixote, the citizen of the secular world that his name indicates" (93). Profane's point is that he too has been witness to human suffering—to the deaths of fathers, the departure of brothers,

the tears of children. He began life among that group of outcasts from
the mainstream whom Pynchon comes to identify as the preterite,
or those passed over for salvation. Slade suggests a more or less paro-
distic role for Profane: "[He] represents the exhaustion of that liberal
tradition which exalted the proletarian in America. Nostalgic references to the thirties in V. are numerous, and are usually sabotaged
by humor, so that Pynchon can evoke the nostalgia without catering
to modern anarchic sympathy for the underprivileged. Profane is the
proletarian hero manqué, having adopted the stance not as protest
but as goal. He is capable of hard work only when he cultivates the
image of the drifter, the Okie, the dispossessed; he sentimentalizes
his own exploitation, by which he justifies his scrounging, adds
clumsiness, which he persuades himself is his fate, and enjoys his
own insincere guilt, which he rationalizes by continuously apolo-
gizing for the authentic emotion he allows to seep out. The perfect
schlemihl is also T. S. Eliot's 'hollow man'" (112).

PC24.19 PF30.28 B21.24   Being born. That's all you have to do
Paola's pessimism here reaches its nadir. By the end of the novel she
will have recovered enough equanimity to offer Pappy Hod at least
the possibility of a lasting marriage.

PC25.22 PF31.27 B22.21   Kilroy   "During World War II, the
phrase 'Kilroy was here' was found written up wherever the Ameri-
cans (particularly Air Transport Command) had been. Like CHAD in
Britain its origin is a matter of conjecture. One suggestion is that a
certain shipyard inspector at Quincy, Mass. chalked up the words on
equipment he had inspected" ("Kilroy," *Brewer's Dictionary*). "The
ubiquitous graffito of soldiers and sailors, Kilroy, an image of the
schlemihl, will reappear in the novel [see, particularly, PC470], and
here suggests that Profane is a weak deity" (Slade 95).

PC26.17 PF32.19 B23.11   the guts of something inanimate   The
contradictory juxtaposition of "guts" and "inanimate" may be read
as an instance of that instinctively anthropomorphizing tendency
which Profane evinces in his effort to fend off the fullest effects of
his confrontations with the inanimate.

PC26.18 PF32.20 B23.12   You can't ever be alone   But earlier

(PC13.25) we have been informed that Profane is in fact afraid of being alone in the presence of the non-human.

PC27.14 PF33.14 B24.2   THE PHANTOM   A comic-strip character created in February 1936 by Lee Falk, the Phantom was the forerunner of superheroes such as Superman and Spiderman.

PC28.17 PF34.16 B25.1   run neither by Greyhound nor Trailways   The "long-haul bus" that the homeless are waiting for is a metaphor for opportunities to escape from their plight. Because their homelessness is in some sense a product of the economic forces that govern mainstream society, they must wait for some alternative to the powerful monopolies.

PC28.20 PF34.18 B25.3   except for an internal voice   This seems confusing. In what sense could a voice which urges the son to "Come home" be regarded as "prodigal"? Surely the reverse would be the case, making Profane the prodigal son for disowning the voice that invites him home. Note that when Profane does respond to the voice, his parents are absent (PC408) and the fatted calf in the form of all the food that is in evidence turns out only to be the usual consequence of his mother's compulsion to feed.

PC29.21 PF35.15 B25.41   Slab   "Pynchon probably took Slab's name from *Philosophical Investigations* where Wittgenstein hypothesizes a minimal language between a builder and his assistant which would consist of nouns like 'block' or 'slab'" (Seed 75). This assertion is perhaps reinforced by the later indication that Rusty Spoon talk consists largely of proper nouns (PC317.9).

PC29.23 PF35.18 B25.43   The Whole Sick Crew   Slade repeats R. W. B. Lewis's speculation that "Pynchon modified the name from 'the sinful crew,' a term in Michael Wigglesworth's *The Day of Doom*, a long Puritan apocalyptic poem written in 1662" (98). Some critics identify the Crew with the decline of Western culture in the twentieth century. As practitioners of "the three major branches of the arts: literature, painting, and music" (Richter 116), its members represent "the dead end of romantic art" (Golden 8). Slade notes that, in comparison with the intense passions of V., "the Crew's are bloodless . . . almost harmless in their ineptitude and adolescent in their lack of imagination" (98). Dugdale, however, reminds us that, while "the Crew are degenerate representatives of their era, . . . postwar culture proper consists of their heroes, who are either mentioned by name in the text (Varèse, Ionesco, de Kooning, Wittgenstein, Sartre, Beckett) or alluded to through parody (Pollock and Rauschenberg via the visual artists, Coleman and Coltrane via Sphere)" (101). Hawthorne finds a sexual pun in the name, asserting that the Crew are indeed "a 'hole' sick crew" (83).

PC30.2 PF35.29 B26.15 apocheir From the Greek, "away" and "hand."

PC30.21 PF36.10 B26.35 The word doesn't mean anything The novel would appear to bear Profane out, providing nothing much to help the reader retain any faith in the concept.

PC31.6 PF36.32 B27.16 Still a great amoebalike boy, soft and fat Hawthorne points out that this is in effect the description of an infant and goes on to argue that Profane is a kind of Peter Pan: "In fact, as long as he can pretend to be a boy by engaging in boyish activities such as going Under the Street to hunt for alligators, he can avoid adult masculinization" (88).

PC31.11 PF36.37 B27.21 Streets . . . had taught him nothing And of course the last thing we learn from Benny is that nothing else has taught him anything, either (PC491.1).

PC31.16 PF37.5 B27.26 his only function to want Profane's vision of himself as a combination of consumer and infant is a telling one.

PC31.34 PF37.21 B28.1 being a schlemihl Profane as schlemihl is a somewhat limited case, being not so much the victim of circumstances, of forces beyond his control, but of "the symbols of our technological society," inanimate objects (Matthijs 127). Matthijs argues that Profane transcends his schlemihlhood to become an absurd hero, someone who "holds on to individuality, personal freedom and personal responsibility in opposition to a reality which is deterministic" (131). Slade has a similar take, arguing that "schlemihlhood is a method of preserving the self—of defining it—by reaching a kind of accommodation with a world always trying to violate that self"

(91–92). Seed, on the other hand, insists that Profane uses the label as a way of "reducing himself to an amoeba-like passivity" (73). Rachel's exasperation at Profane (PC413.6) is more consistent with this view than with Matthijs's.

PC32.11 PF37.32 B28.15   like a littered beach   "Although the beach image suggests that the bums and old ladies have actually gone somewhere, Pynchon assures us that they have not. Instead, their power to impose the definition of what Sidney Stencil would call 'The Situation' [see PC199.3n] has been eclipsed: the affluent have 'filled the limits of that world,' that is, defined it according to their own limited experience, then moved on without even having recognized the existence of an alterity whose definition of 'The Situation' it has occluded" (Holton 329).

PC32.18 PF38.1 B28.22   the coming on of a falling season   Simon picks up on the suggestion here of a decline—the movement from a world filled with "a sense of summer and life" to one which anticipates winter (174). He further connects Profane's "subway yo-yoing . . . to the decadent and fragmented world of the Whole Sick Crew and to the terrifying world of V." While the idea of a falling away from vitality is central to the novel, however, one might wonder if Pynchon is really equating the hordes of business commuters who fill the subways with a genuine sense of liveliness.

PC34.13 PF39.28 B30.7   Walking on a street at night   Profane's dreamscape provides one of the novel's many evocations of de Chirico's "Mystery and Melancholy of a Street," a painting whose enigmatic surrealism is re-rendered here in the form of the suggestive manhole covers and neon signs that leave no trace on the conscious mind (Dugdale passim; Seed, *Fictional Labyrinths* 30). The painting is referred to later in the novel (PC323.17n). We should probably regard the manhole covers as an anticipation of the temporary escape from street-level reality that Profane achieves via his descent into the sewers.

PC34.20 PF39.35 B30.15   a golden screw   Anticipatory of the sapphire in Veronica Manganese's navel, the removal of which from the navel of the Bad Priest contributes, presumably, to the death of

V. (Simon 174). Safer sees the story of the golden screw as a parody of an American tall tale, a debased version of the lively exaggerations that celebrate the scope and novelty of the American experiment (84).

PC34.35 PF40.12 B30.31　his ass falls off　Dugdale (84) reads this as the answer to the question raised by Pip in chapter 99 of *Moby Dick:* "'unscrew your navel, and what's the consequence?'" Perhaps this is the origin of the joke as a whole, but little seems to be gained from the association of the golden screw with the doubloon that Ahab nails to the mast of the Pequod.

PC35.2 PF40.15 B30.34　the fact of his own disassembly　Profane's nightmare of his own deconstruction finds its literal enactment in the clinical disassembly of the Bad Priest by the children of Malta (PC369.34).

PC36.6 PF41.15 B31.32　Luis Aparicio　Kook is oddly prescient in his choice of baseball heroes. The Venezuelan shortstop's rookie year for the White Sox was 1956.

PC36.14 PF41.22 B31.40　her quiet field of force　Profane's temporary recognition of the possibility that safety can be found in the form of human connectedness carries all the more weight in light of his usual reaction to the threat of closeness. This moment in a sense comes back to haunt Profane when Fina spits on him in the airport (PC391.34) and he is obliged to admit responsibility for having failed her. See also the reference to the "twin envelope of peace" (PC396.2), which Rachel has tried in vain to preserve.

PC38.16 PF42.34 B33.5　under the Street　Profane's mistrust of the "single abstracted Street" (PC2.10) which has come to symbolize the narrow confines of his schlemihl's world has already prepared us for this moment when he envisages the possibility of an alternative domain beneath the surface of the dream street. Like most of the novel's other motifs, however, this opposition of the two realms is not without ambiguity. Although Fausto Maijstral identifies the world under the street with the kingdom of life (PC348.28n) and Profane may indeed use a shotgun there without killing himself, we would do well to remember the possibility that Fausto's distinction holds good only "in dreams," and that Profane's time in the sewers is of limited duration. Tanner acknowledges that "the sewer or under-the-street (also compared to under the sea) is that area of dream, the unconscious, perhaps the ancestral memory, in which one may find a temporary oblivion, and into which the artist must descend" ("V2" 31), and in this he is echoed by Campbell, who regards the various manifestations of this subterranean territory—the subway, the sewer, the bomb shelter—as "the territory of the unconscious, of sleep, of fantasy, or of escape from danger" (60). But Tanner also sees an element of parody of Jungian elements in the "dark farce" of the tale of Benny and the alligators and in the fact that the sewer world at least is a place "where fantasy can run so rampant that you may start seeing rats as saints and lovers if you remain down there too long" ("V2" 31). Certainly Pynchon's use of urban folklore as the grounding of Profane's descent into the underworld could be seen as yet another of the twentieth century's debased simulacra of hitherto powerful sustaining mythologies (see also PC146.28n). Furthermore, there is some justice to Hawthorne's claim that Profane is using his boy's adventure among the alligators as a way of avoiding the adult responsibilities which threaten him at street level (88). Slade is even more negative in his reading, noting that the fact that "undergrounds are symbolic graves becomes steadily more obvious as Profane moves even deeper under the street" (111).

CHAPTER TWO

Rachel Owlglass goes to the office of Schoenmaker, the plastic surgeon, to pay the bill for her roommate Esther's nose job. At a party that evening, she stands with her back to Herbert Stencil, whose obsessive quest for V. we learn about for the first time. Stencil is at the party at the invitation of Esther, in whom he appears to be interested by virtue of her association with Schoenmaker. We are introduced to various members of the Whole Sick Crew. While the party winds down, jazz saxophonist McClintic Sphere is playing his last set of the evening at the V-Note. Paola Maijstral and three other members of the Crew are in the audience.

PC39.16 PF45.2 B34.37 Shale Schoenmaker, M.D. One of Pynchon's more obvious names ("schön" is German for "beautiful"). As Allen points out, Schoenmaker's profession (and in particular its most stereotypical depiction in the painful and extended description of the nose job) is a clear satirical target in a novel that calls into question our preoccupation with surfaces (43). "Such characters express the belief that intrinsic value does not exist; that all things possess only a literal significance and that this can be changed" (Madsen 33). Esther's nose and Irving's freckles are the most egregious manifestations of Schoenmaker's cynical belief in the mutability of human appearance and may perhaps be the outcome of his need to sublimate his homosexual adoration of Evan Godolphin (Hawthorne 83).

PC40.2 PF45.7 B34.42 some associative freak This raises the question of whose set of associations has come into play here. Irving's parents would appear to be the most logical first choice, but there is some suggestion, surely, that Schoenmaker has created a new name for his secretary/receptionist/nurse, just as he has given her a new appearance. In either case, just what the relevant associative freak might be is far from clear.

PC40.12 PF45.16 B35.9   The office was crowded   Rachel fears as she leaves that this gathering of "the imperfect, the dissatisfied" may represent "a sort of drawing-together or communion" (PC44.13). As Madsen points out, "It is a communion based upon a common faith in, and preference for, the cosmetic and the exterior" (33), so it is hardly surprising that one of the few characters in the novel who actively seeks connectedness in the form of human warmth and affection should be apprehensive.

PC40.31 PF45.35 B35.29   a turn-of-the-century clock   Dugdale is reminded of Tenniel's illustration of Alice passing through the looking glass (84), though in fact the clock on Tenniel's mantelpiece is an elaborate ormolu timepiece enshrined in a glass dome. Stark finds evidence in the description of the clock and the mirror of Pynchon's use of the notion of feedback. In the endless duplication of images of oscillation created by the reflection in the mirror of the clock's spinning disc and the tree branches' "ceaseless" back and forth motion, he sees an apt parallel with Esther Harvitz's situation: "The 'negative feedback' caused by the disparity between her actual and desired conditions 'overloads' her so that she can barely cope. She has come to this office for plastic surgery and, although she does not know it, she will soon begin an unfortunate affair with her doctor" (67).

PC41.17 PF46.18 B36.8   cancelling one another exactly out   This "node" may be conceptually linked with the "dead center of the carousel" where Godolphin finds the frozen spider monkey (PC216.26). Perhaps the "half understood moral purpose" that is served by the cancellation of time in the room is similar in kind, if not in degree, to the purpose that Godolphin supposes to be served by the startling image under the ice. Whatever insight is afforded in either case appears to depend upon the suspension of the norms

of everyday experience, whether of the inexorable forward march of
time or of the motion imparted by the earth's spin. Godolphin claims
to have been given a glimpse of the existential abyss; in Rachel's
view, Schoenmaker's patients are actively seeking what amounts to
the annihilation of the self beneath the trappings of cosmetic surgery.

Cain sees the clock as "a metaphor for the closed system. . . . The
clock, as a mechanism of redundancy operating along rigidly defined
and controlled lines, is designed to record time through a fixed scale
of twelve hours, creating an artificial order Pynchon terms a perpetual 'mirror-time' [PC41.26], time as merely repetition, a reflection
of that which has already been, not a process toward something new
or different. When robbed of energy, either electrical or mechanical,
the clock loses organization and slips into disorder, the eventual end
of all closed systems, whether biological, mechanical, or social" (74).

PC43.1 PF47.35 B37.26 Lamarck   Jean Baptiste Pierre Antoine
de Monet, Chevalier de Lamarck (1744–1829). Lamarck is best
known for his assertion that acquired traits can be inherited, a claim
that Darwin's theories refuted.

**PC43.5 PF48.2 B37.30 Nothing . . . is going to change the noses
of her children**   Schoenmaker is simply continuing his resistance to
what he mistakenly assumes is a Lamarckian argument by Rachel
against his lucrative trade in altered noses.

PC46.17 PF51.8 B40.26 Nothing but proper nouns   Opinions
are divided on how to read Paola's tendency to ignore the world of
things in favor of a focus on the human. Tanner, for example, suggests that "this quaint linguistic limitation offers the possibility of
an enviable immunity from the tendency towards a reification of
people which is inherent in the prevailing language" ("V2" 24), while
Bianchi invokes Wittgenstein in support of a less positive reading:
"According to Wittgenstein's theory, nouns correspond to objects,
not even facts. And Paola does not even command all nouns, but only
proper nouns, indicating that her level of communication must be
very low indeed" (10). Tanner's position is more consistent with the
novel's generally positive portrayal of Paola. Her participation in
the disassembly of the Bad Priest, her relationship with McClintic

Sphere, and her promise to wait, Penelope-like, for the return of her seafaring husband, all suggest her status as a character who has been able to resist the tendencies of her age.

PC47.16 PF52.1 B41.16   to repeat in mirror-time   Another evocation of the notion of redundancy as represented by the clock's repetitive designation of time's passing.

PC47.20 PF52.5 B41.20   The party . . . unwound   The image reinforces the idea of the clock as a definer of a closed system (PC41.17n) and of course is a reminder of the entropic tendency of such systems when no energy is brought in from the outside. As Seed notes, "The insistent 'would . . . would . . . would' sequence underlines the predictability of the party as if it is unwinding towards some point of equilibrium. Certainly parties figure again and again in the 1956 chapters and they never carry any connotations of festivity" (78).

PC47.35 PF52.20 B41.37   Young Stencil the world adventurer   The rather quaint tone of this description effectively links Stencil with his father via an echo of the Buchanesque nature of Stencil père's profession. "Young" also reminds us that Stencil is preceded by "old" Stencil, each of them, in Chambers's view, "a two-dimensional copy" of their respective forebears (48). Stencil's name of course is entirely appropriate for someone who seeks to impose structure on the potential chaos of experience. Stencil *is* what he does—he is "quite purely He Who Looks for V." (PC239.32)—and so he is capable of perceiving nothing except those portions of reality that appear within the interstices of the schematic grid of his quest. "This dedicated pursuer and collector of notes towards a supreme fiction" (Tanner, "V2" 20) is thus "an ironically modified questing hero" (Hite 47). Dugdale finds an origin for "Stencil the conspiracy-theorist" in Freud's case history of "The Psychotic Dr. Schreber" (115), while Slade looks to a literary parallel: "Stencil conceives of history much as would a Rosicrucian or a mad Mason, and indeed, he resembles Tolstoy's Pierre Bezukhov, who, having joined the Masonic Order, clutches at manifestations of the apocalyptic Beast 666" (52).

Matthijs is almost alone in championing a more positive view of Stencil. Drawing on Eliade's concept of "le temps sacré," a time "characterized as cyclical and recurrent," he suggests that Stencil's search qualifies him as a "sacred man [who] creates Cosmos out of Chaos" (141). "The V.-quest changes Stencil's view on the world, makes it 'sacred.' He picks out certain periods from the homogeneous flow of time, i.e. this homogeneity is disrupted—the disruption being the intrusion of the sacred" (Matthijs 138).

PC48.10 PF52.29 B42.4   1901, the year Victoria died   "Let's not forget good old Queen Victoria (died 1901) and the entire Victorian age, replaced/superseded by Modernism, (remember Einstein augmenting Newton?). It seems when the priest/V is dismantled, an old mechanist world-view is dismantled, replaced by a statistics/relativity/quantum theory based view—even more insidiously in Their service, but not as easy to 'grip.' Stencil jr, born 1901, chronicles the death/dismantling of V, and the Victorian world, and of course also helps to establish continuity, and shows what does *not* 'die'" (Hartwin A. Gebhardt, Pynchon List, December 30, 1995).

PC48.11 PF52.30 B42.5   the century's child   Cooley is reminded of this passage from *The Education of Henry Adams:* "The child born in 1900 would . . . be born into a new world which would not be a unity but a multiple. Adams tried to imagine the education that would fit it. He found himself in a land no one had penetrated before; where order was an accidental relation obnoxious to nature; artificial compulsion imposed on motion; against which every free energy of the universe revolted; and which, being merely occasional, resolved itself back into anarchy at last" (quoted in Cooley 317). Cooley goes on to point out that Stencil's singular view of history indicates that his education is not that of the new century.

"If [Stencil] is the 'century's child,'" Tanner argues, "then he is by the same token searching for the century's 'mother' or, more generally, who or what it was that gave birth to the twentieth century and caused it to move so rapidly towards world wars, genocide, nuclear bombs—a whole arsenal of events and inventions, and dehumanizations—which would indeed seem to be accelerating the approach of total entropy" (*TP* 45).

PC48.11 PF52.30 B42.5   Raised motherless   Both Tanner (*TP* 45) and Dugdale (78) suggest that Stencil's quest is in part to find or invent a mother for himself. Dugdale adds the possibility that Stencil is trying to "recreate his father."

PC48.16 PF52.35 B42.11   which is available   The use of the present tense implies the momentary intrusion of the narrator as biographer. The correspondence is available not to Stencil in this formulation, but to the diligent researcher who seeks it out in order to give the reader the truth about his subject. The effect is transient and possibly accidental.

PC48.18 PF52.36 B42.12   the June Disturbances   "These have gone down in Maltese history as the *Sette Giugno*. On 7 June 1919 British troops opened fire on the thousands of people demonstrating in Valletta. Three people were killed and a fourth victim died on 8 June as a result of injuries" (Cassola 331).

PC48.20 PF53.2 B42.15   Margravine di Chiave Lowenstein   "'Wife of a margrave,' and 'key' or 'clef' plus 'stronghold of lions,' with the full meaning of 'the woman who holds the key to the lion's cage'" (Harder 78).

PC48.22 PF53.3 B42.17   Mallorca   One of the Balearic islands off the east coast of Spain. Stencil has come to Mallorca from Toledo (PC57.32), following leads generated out of his suspicion that V.'s "natural habitat [is] the state of siege." Having presumably learned of the passing of Toledo back into Christian hands in 1085, Stencil has come to another site of contestation between Spain and Moorish invaders. Mallorca was captured from its Moorish rulers in 1229 after James I of Aragon laid siege to what is now Palma (Abulafia 7). Given the Lady V.'s apparent liaison with the "mad Irredentist" (PC447.29n), we might suppose that Stencil is wondering whether in some earlier incarnation she was drawn to the Muslim irredentists who briefly and futilely took to the Mallorcan hinterland to avoid James's army.

PC49.2 PF53.19 B42.32   Whitehall   London street where a number of government offices are located; hence, by extension, government in general.

**PC49.5 PF53.22 B42.35   Envoys from the zones of human cru-
cified**   An anticipation of Victoria Wren's ivory comb (PC174.2),
which later turns up in the possession of Paola Maijstral.

PC49.12 PF53.28 B43.1   a number of manuscript books   "The
concrete form of [Stencil's] legacy is a set of books written in various
European cities in the years before 1919. Stencil receives them in
1922, the *annus mirabilis* of Modernism. In so far as he is a story-
teller, his inheritance is the culture of the period between 1895–
1925" (Dugdale 77).

**PC49.15 PF53.31 B43.3   Under "Florence, April, 1899" is a sen-
tence**   One might well wonder what Sidney means by this enigmatic, if somewhat melodramatic entry. By the time we have fin-
ished chapter 7, we are inclined to wonder what motivates Sidney's
reluctance to give an official identity to the unnamed horror that
lies "behind and inside V." The "Situation" to which the reader has
access in the Florence chapter is far from the ominous symptom of
Armageddon that Sidney seems inclined to discern from his limited
spy's perspective; it is, instead, an absurd collocation of misunderstandings and coincidences, largely comic in their unfolding. Herbert appears to follow Sidney's lead in his myopic insistence on V.'s
connection during that Florence spring with a grand conspiracy
(PC161.26) and so the reader is left alone in supposing that the por-
tentousness of Sidney's cryptic note to himself may be the mark of
an ironic intention on Pynchon's part. In terms of what we know to
have happened in Florence, Sidney is evidently building his own pile
of inferences on a very small foundation—his awareness of Victoria
Wren's affinity for riot and propensity for violence (PC527.30).

PC49.23 PF54.3 B43.13   The question is ridiculous   Not so ridiculous as to have been set aside by readers, a few of whom assert that
V. is indeed Stencil's mother (Cowart, Poirier) and many of whom
acknowledge the possibility (Hite, Kharpertian, Slade, Eddins, Richter). If the facts are taken at face value, the chronology is off. In the

winter of 1919, Sidney recalls being seduced by Victoria Wren in Florence "twenty years ago" (PC528.20). Even supposing that Herbert was not conceived until eight months after Sidney meets Victoria for the first time, the young world adventurer would have had to linger in his mother's womb for more than a year in order to be born in 1901. Eddins steers a middle ground between the literal and the figurative in this matter, claiming that Victoria's "seduction of Sidney in 1899 is close enough to Herbert's birthdate to provide a significant maternal analogue, and the ominous gestation of the century to come" (83). The only other possibility is that Sidney's "twenty years" represents the convenience of a round number or the fuzziness of memory. Hawthorne is presumably making this assumption when he maintains that "the epilogue *implies* that Sidney and Victoria remained together at least long enough for her to conceive a child that was born some twenty months later after the riots in Florence. . . . In other words, if V. is, indeed, Herbert's mother, his reply to [the] Margravine that V. is not his mother is as a classic denial in which the adult son rejects his mother as a result of his mother's 'rejection' of him as a child" (76).

PC50.4 PF54.17 B43.29   that interregnum between kingdoms-of-death   The kingdom of death appears in a number of contexts throughout the novel. Fausto will identify the world of the street as the kingdom of death, both in dreams (PC348.28n) and in reality (PC354.18n). Its purposes are served both literally by the likes of Lothar von Trotha and his successors and figuratively by such manifestations of the power of the object as fetishism (PC443).

PC50.10 PF54.23 B43.35   He didn't particularly care to wake   This anticipates Stencil's recognition of a horrifying version of himself in Fergus Mixolydian, "the laziest living being in Nueva York" (PC52.2).

PC50.13 PF54.26 B43.37   He was sent to North Africa   "Stencil's experience of the North African campaign is shared with the hero of Camus' *La Chute* (1956) and Oran is the city of *La Peste* (1947). The 'Florence journal' of April 1899 seems in context to glance at Rilke's Florentine Journal, based on a visit of spring 1898.

The quest of Stencil, the author-surrogate, would thus appear to be a parody and a displacement of Pynchon's own desire to return from a time of absurdist writing to the culture of the early years of the century" (Dugdale 79).

PC50.29 PF55.4 B44.12   if not vitality   A reminder that Stencil's quest is unlikely to restore him to full humanity. It is "grim, joyless," giving him at best "a sense of animateness," rather than the real thing.

PC51.2 PF55.12 B44.21   To sustain it he had to hunt V.   "Posing this sort of attraction for Stencil, V. clearly represents 'the very essence of what is strange in woman and of all that is eternally fugitive, vanishing, and almost hostile in a fellow human being' that De Rougemont [*Love in the Western World* 244] discovers in Iseult. Like Iseult, V. is 'that which indeed incites to pursuit, and rouses . . . an avidity for possession so much more delightful than possession itself'" (Graves 66).

PC51.11 PF55.22 B44.31   an Egyptologist named Bongo-Shaftsbury   The idea of the son following in the father's footsteps has some resonance in the light of Stencil's quest.

PC51.24 PF55.33 B45.2   Chiclitz the munitions king   Clayton "Bloody" (as in, "Do you want a mouthful of bloody Chiclets?") Chiclitz is the president of Yoyodyne, "an interlocking kingdom responsible for systems management, airframes, propulsion, command systems, ground support equipment" (PC241.4). The epithet "munitions king," with its nineteenth-century overtones, seems only quaintly applicable to this twentieth-century defense contractor. It serves as an indication of Stencil's tendency to adopt his father's linguistic point of view, with its corresponding picture of the world.

PC51.24 PF55.34 B45.2   Eigenvalue the physician   As with Chiclitz, Stencil adopts an epithet for Eigenvalue that reflects his father's cultural perspective rather than that of the mid–twentieth century, when a dentist would scarcely be thought of as a "physician." The word "eigenvalue," according to Merriam-Webster's *Collegiate Dic-*

tionary, is defined as "a scalar associated with a given linear transformation of a vector space and having the property that there is some non zero vector which when multiplied by the scalar is equal to the vector obtained by letting the transformation operate on the vector; esp: a root of the characteristic equation of a matrix." Pynchon perhaps came across the word during his freshman year at Cornell, but it seems unlikely that one needs to go much further than its etymology to make at least a stab at its relevance to this particular character. "Eigen" in this context means "own" in the sense of "peculiar to" or "characteristic." Following David Milne's reading (Pynchon List, March 1995) of Eigenvalue's first name, Dudley, as suggestive of "zero," we might conclude that Dudley Eigenvalue is someone who has no value in and of himself but, like so many other characters in the novel, assumes value in Stencil's eyes as a potential lead in the quest for V.

PC52.1 PF56.9 B45.15   Fergus Mixolydian the Irish Armenian Jew   Harder suggests that this "universal man" is a symbolic Everyman, "being Irish Armenian Jew, with a Scots forename and 'mingling mode' for the surname" (75). Slade finds a possible origin for the name in Joyce's *Ulysses* and asserts that the Greek mode the name evokes is "associated with the Renaissance conception of the 'Music of the Spheres'" (251 fn). He further supposes that the same thinking might have led Pynchon to name his jazz musician McClintic Sphere. Note that Mafia Winsome tells Profane (PC237.19) about "a young actor . . . who claims to be an Irish Armenian Jew."

PC52.6 PF56.14 B45.20   ready-made   Vella ("French Surrealists" 33) identifies Mixolydian's ready-made as an echo of Marcel Duchamp's "Fountain" (the urinal that he signed "R. Mutt" and entered in the first exhibition of the Society of Independent Artists in 1917).

PC52.16 PF56.23 B45.31   an ingenious sleep-switch   This device has its much more sinister counterpart in the switch that Bongo-Shaftsbury has sewn into his arm and which he uses to scare Mildred Wren (PC78.24n).

PC52.20 PF56.26 B45.35   an extension of the TV set   The literal connectedness of Fergus and his television is figuratively echoed in the dependence of the Whole Sick Crew on the mass media for their ideas (PC52.33).

PC52.24 PF56.31 B45.40 a Catatonic Expressionist The oxymoronic qualities of Slab's self-designation add to the force of Pynchon's satirical treatment of this and other members of the Whole Sick Crew. Vella nonetheless places Slab in good company, associating his endless cheese danish paintings with De Chirico's paintings of pastries ("French Surrealists" 31), and connecting him with the action painting of Pollock and Rothko via "the important liberating factor of automatism for the abstract Expressionists" (32).

PC52.28 PF56.35 B46.1 Romanticism in its furthest decadence "Tracing the degeneration of erotic passion through successive stages in his characterization of V., Pynchon locates its lowest ebb in the morally slack and pseudo-artistically effete society of Profane. This narrative progression is thematically congruent with De Rougemont's conclusion that the history of Western society, as revealed in European and American literature, is the history of successive and increasingly more pronounced 'profanations' of the erotic myth" (Graves 68).

PC52.29 PF56.36 B46.2 an exhausted impersonation Pynchon's comments about his generation's cultural apprenticeship in the introduction to *Slow Learner* finds an echo here: "Unfortunately there were no more primary choices for us to make. We were onlookers: the parade had gone by and we were already getting everything secondhand, consumers of what the media of the time were supplying us" (9)

PC53.1 PF57.5 B46.9 a hothouse sense of time Although the idea of the hothouse (as opposed to the street) assumes greater complexity later in the novel—particularly in Sidney Stencil's formulation (PC506.20n)—at this point the reader may need to make of this phrase only what common sense analogy might suggest. Stencil seems to be invoking the closed-system connotations of the hothouse image, suggesting that the Crew have an illusory sense of their immunity from the flow of time and therefore of their lack of susceptibility to the entropic decay that affects all such systems. The later association of the hothouse with the commitment of the political Right to recuperating and preserving the past does not seem to come into play here even in retrospect.

PC53.10 PF57.14 B46.19   Schoenberg's quartets (complete) The four string quartets of Arnold Schoenberg (1874–1951), Austrian-American composer famous for his creation of atonal music.

PC53.16 PF57.19 B46.25   a kind of love feast or daisy chain The sexual daisy chain is echoed later in darker mode when Stencil imagines the Crew as being linked "by a spectral chain" in a version of the medieval Dance of Death (PC315.20).

PC54.19 PF58.26 B47.23   hangs at the edges of the Whole Sick Crew Brad's attempt to straddle the two worlds of the mainstream and the counter culture (Holton 329), while it reflects Pynchon's serious interest in cultural oppositions, is ironic in that Brad is likely to experience only a simulacrum of counter cultural attitudes via his peripheral exposure to the Crew.

PC55.6 PF59.5 B48.5   McClintic Sphere Seed maintains that Sphere is modeled on Ornette Coleman (81). There would seem to be some justification for the claim: "'I believe music is really a free thing,' said Ornette Coleman, 'and any way you can enjoy it, you should.' When Coleman burst upon the jazz scene in 1959, there were two reasons for the sensation he caused. First, there was the intensity of the unrestrained melody and compelling, crying sound that poured from Coleman's white plastic alto saxophone. Second, there was his shocking, free approach to improvising; he abandoned the fixed harmonic patterns that had been the basis of jazz structure for its entire previous existence. 'He's a fake,' said some listeners; 'He's a genius,' said others; and the controversy over the jazz revolution that Coleman began continued into the 1990s" ("Book of the Year [1994]: Biography: Coleman, Ornette" *Britannica Online*). Sphere "blew a hand-carved ivory alto saxophone with a 4½ reed and the sound was like nothing any of them had heard before" (PC55.12). Pynchon may also have recalled that Thelonious Monk's middle name was Sphere.

PC56.5 PF60.1 B48.42 Downbeat magazine Actually, Down Beat. "American bi-weekly magazine founded and edited by Jack Maher in 1934. Intended initially for the professional dance band and jazz musician, it continues to have interest for a wider readership of enthusiasts by virtue of its good jazz coverage and its yearly awards" ("Down Beat," Gammond).

PC56.11 PF60.6 B49.5 Charlie Parker Charles Christopher Parker Jr. (1920–1955). "American alto saxophonist, composer, and bandleader who is considered by many to have been the greatest improviser in jazz history and the father of the modern jazz style known as bebop. His first recordings with trumpeter Dizzy Gillespie during the mid-1940s set the pace for the jazz of the next two decades" ("Parker, Charlie," *Britannica Online*).

CHAPTER THREE

After a brief prelude, the chapter fragments into eight parts, in each of which Stencil assumes a different narrative persona. As P. Aïeul, a waiter in a cafe in Alexandria in 1898, he eavesdrops on a meeting between two Englishmen, one of whom is called Porpentine and the other of whom is later identified as Porpentine's partner, Goodfellow. Picking up only on portions of the conversation, Aïeul/Stencil speculates about the possible back-story that has brought these two men together, imagining various permutations of relationships among the people he hears being discussed—Victoria Wren, Sir Alistair Wren, Bongo-Shaftsbury.

In his second "impersonation," Stencil assumes the identity of Yusef, employed for the evening to serve punch at a party at the Austrian consulate. Yusef is aware of a diplomatic crisis that is brewing in the Nile Valley, where British and French colonial interests are threatening to clash. Among those present are Porpentine and Goodfellow, the two men whose encounter at the cafe has just been recounted from the perspective of the waiter, Aïeul. Yusef recognizes in both the reflexes of professional men of violence and wonders what has brought them to the party. A man with blue eyeglasses appears to be connected with the underlying sense of menace that Yusef identifies. Victoria Wren, her father, and her sister Mildred are also at the party.

As persona number three, Stencil takes up the point of view of Maxwell Rowley-Bugge, a former music-hall performer whose pedophilic interest in young girls has forced him into exile as a professional cadger. He makes contact with a group that has just left the consulate across the street and finds himself in the company of Porpentine, Goodfellow, Victoria, and Mildred. They are joined by Hugh Bongo-Shaftsbury and by Lepsius (evidently the man with blue eyeglasses from the consulate party), the two of whom appear somehow to be at odds with Porpentine and Goodfellow.

Stencil next becomes Waldetar, the Portuguese conductor on the Alexandria to Cairo express. As the train makes its way to Cairo, Waldetar witnesses Bongo-Shaftsbury frightening Mildred Wren with his claim to be an electro-mechanical doll. Porpentine is disgusted with him. Waldetar later sees Goodfellow disable an Arab with a vicious kick to the throat. The Arab is seen talking to Lepsius.

The fifth Stencil is Gebrail, the cynical atheist former farmer who has lost his land to the encroaching desert. He is now a Cairo carriage driver who has spent the afternoon driving Porpentine to various assignations all over the city. Gebrail has discussed the impending meeting of Kitchener and Marchand (see PC63.13n) at Fashoda with a friend and is idly conscious that Porpentine's comings and goings might be of some political significance.

As Girgis the mountebank/burglar, Stencil imagines Porpentine's clumsy attempts to confirm his suspicion that Goodfellow and Victoria Wren are having sex in his hotel room. Porpentine mistakes Girgis for his enemy Bongo-Shaftsbury.

In the last of his identifiable personae, Stencil becomes Hanne Echerze, barmaid in a German beerhall in Cairo and lover of Lepsius. Hanne overhears fragments of conversation that suggest a connection between Fashoda and a possible assassination plot. She also contrives to eavesdrop on a conversation in which Victoria Wren appeals to Porpentine for his understanding regarding her relationship with Goodfellow.

The final section of the chapter is narrated by a disembodied voice, witness to the death of Porpentine at the hands of Bongo-Shaftsbury at the Cairo opera house. Victoria Wren has left the theater with Goodfellow just prior to a struggle between Porpentine and Lepsius, during the course of which Bongo-Shaftsbury intervenes and shoots Porpentine.

PC57 PF61 B50   eight impersonations   See summary above.

PC57.1 PF61.26 B50.21 As spread thighs are to the libertine . . .
"The threefold comparison of Stencil to a devoted bird-watcher . . . a
rake, and a machinist suggests that Stencil intends to study V. metic-
ulously and to use her sexually and cavalierly as a tool for keeping
his own robot life humming along with relative smoothness. . . .
Once the hunter, V. is now the hunted; once the supreme power, she
is now an object. The narrator refers to her as 'obsolete,' 'bizarre,'
and 'forbidden' because her power has been dramatically effaced by
several thousand years of patriarchy" (Chambers 58–59).

PC57.7 PF61.31 B50.26 *The Golden Bough* or *The White Goddess*
The reference is to Sir James Frazer's *Golden Bough: A Study in
Comparative Religion*, published between 1890 and 1915, and to
Robert Graves's *White Goddess: A Historical Grammar of Poetic
Myth* (1948). These "adventures of the mind" have in common their
attempts to discover and articulate large-scale systems by means of
which human history can be brought into some kind of ordered form.
Frazer traced what he claimed to be the evolution of human thought
from the magical through the religious to the scientific, while Graves
sought to demonstrate the existence of a religious tradition based
on goddess-worship that predated and in part survived the rise of
Christianity.

Pynchon's intention in invoking these two particular texts is difficult to judge. The use of the word "merely" to describe the "scholarly
quest[s]" that led to their creation may be taken to suggest their distance from the world of real human interactions and consequences
and hence to support the claim that Frazer and Graves are satirically
employed as prototypes of the misguided Stencil. Yet Stencil's dream
that he is dreaming the reality of the quest is seen in counterpoint to
the "tiresome discovery that it hadn't really ever stopped being the
same simple-minded, literal pursuit" (PC57.9). The dream, in this
light, is given a positive spin—to be engaged in a scholarly quest is
preferable to the "tiresome" business of pursuing some empirically
observable phenomenon.

On the whole, critics have tended to ignore the reference to Frazer,
focusing instead on the symbolic resonances sounded by the allusion

to Graves's goddess. Frequent mention is made of the way in which the novel plays off its images of decadence and decline against Graves's central image. "Of the two [texts], Graves's is the more important for Pynchon, because it focuses on what the writer believes is the principle archetype of our culture. . . . With Adams's Virgin, Pynchon entwines Graves's symbol—with an ironic twist. The Virgin or Venus in *V.* has been almost wholly perverted" (Slade 53). "The novel *V.* documents Graves's argument that the shift to a patriarchal culture has made the need to know, to dominate, and to control the informing principle of action. What is lost is the ability to accept mystery and paradox" (Chambers 46).

PC57.10 PF61.35 B50.30   V. ambiguously a beast of venery   Venery is both "the practice or sport of hunting beasts of game" and "the practice or pursuit of sexual pleasure" (*OED*). Pynchon employs the double meaning of the word to communicate Stencil's uncertain response to his self-imposed quest. On the one hand it has the legitimacy of the hunt but at the same time it *feels* somehow perverse. The association of V. with a variety of forms of sexual expression, many of which might be termed "forbidden," reinforces this side of the ambiguity.

PC57.13 PF61.37 B50.83   clownish Stencil   Stencil's mocking self-characterization as the fool serves as our warning not to be too hasty in following his lead. As readers we are quite aware of being engaged in a quest not dissimilar from Stencil's, and Pynchon typically wants us to think about the implications of our need to make sense of the multiple strands of meaning that the novel spins for us to follow.

PC57.18 PF62.4 B50.38   Mallorca   See PC48.22n.

PC57.18 PF62.5 B50.38   Toledo   Stencil is presumably drawn to Toledo by tales of the months-long siege of 1084–85, when Alfonso VI, emperor of Leon and Castile, returned the city to Christian control after three hundred and seventy years of Islamic rule (Fletcher 141–42). No explicit link to V. is made, but the fact that the Moorish ruler of Toledo had Alfonso's Jewish emissary crucified has at least an echo in the crucifixions depicted on Victoria's ivory comb.

PC57.19 PF62.6 B50.39 alcázar The fortress in the heart of the old city.

PC58.1 PF62.9 B50.43 as respectable and orthodox as spying Once again we are reminded that Herbert's activities are cast in a less favorable light than his father's before him.

PC58.10 PF62.16 B51.10 Henry Adams in the *Education* Henry Brooks Adams (1838–1918), the American historian, records his difficulties in coming to terms with the twentieth century in his autobiography, *The Education of Henry Adams.* This single reference has provided readers with a broad range of allusions upon which to draw in the effort to make sense of Stencil's quest. Slade (52) claims that "Pynchon is deliberately mocking Adams" in his portrayal of Stencil, whose approach to history is a parody of Adams's "rational and sophisticated" inquiry. Other critics, less inclined to see Pynchon's intentions as parodic, suggest that the object of Stencil's obsession is a symbolic extension of the process of decline which Adams represents in his twin motifs of the Virgin and the Dynamo, the first "the avatar of a spiritual norm, a protectress who gave meaning, focus, and redemption to human experience and reconciled this experience to the rest of nature" (Eddins 52), and the second an image of the breakdown of human unity in the face of the impersonal "force" of industrial and technological advance. "V. is an archetypal Terrible Mother who fulfills the entropic prophecies of Henry Adams for the Twentieth Century. . . . V. unites both the Dynamo and the Virgin, rendering the creative powers of the divine Feminine destructive" (Newman 35). According to Eddins, those "entropic prophecies" are embodied in "the metamorphosis of the life-affirming Virgin into the life-negating dynamo. Pynchon's stroke of inspiration is to personify the latter as a grotesque simulacrum of the former, a mechanized apostle of disorder and death" (Eddins 52).

PC58.13 PF62.19 B51.13 Forcible dislocation of personality "Stencil's technique of 'forcible dislocation of personality' allows him to maintain a smug sense of superiority because he detaches 'Stencil' from most of what he does. The real self remains private, but fades away; the plastic self takes action. Such dissociation relieves 'Stencil' of responsibility and involvement, so that it becomes an equally artificial concept, an 'other' removed from the experience of the self.

"If Stencil represents one extreme of identity—its complete fragmentation—then Profane represents the other. He remains 'himself' throughout the novel, but also refuses commitment and purposeful action" (Campbell 63).

Kharpertian sees in this phrase a parody of Eliot's description of poetry as "an escape from personality." The result of Stencil's extreme version of the modernist formulation is seen in the "comically alien" clothing, food and shelter that he is obliged to accept (72).

PC58.22 PF62.27 B51.23   a nacreous mass of inference   Eddins (86) quotes a relevant portion of *The Education of Henry Adams:* "As history unveiled itself in the new order, man's mind had behaved like a young pearl oyster, secreting its universe to suit its conditions until it had built up a shell of *nacre* that embodied all its notions of the perfect." Once again the point is made that the "Stencilized" version of the Adamsian metaphor is a debased, negative formulation: "If the pearl of Adams's oyster is a myth that orders existence as a living, fecund unity and makes humanity possible, the pearls of Stencil's 'scungille farm' constitute a myth of disorder, of the dissolution of humanity into the 'supersensual chaos' [the phrase is Adams's] from which its unifying constructs had once differentiated it" (Eddins 86).

PC58.26 PF62.31 B51.27   scungille   Merriam-Webster lists the word as "scungilli" and defines it as conch used for food.

PC59.2 PF63.5 B51.39   Gordons   A Scottish regiment.

PC59.13 PF63.13 B52.6   Porpentine   The word "porpentine" is a variant of "porcupine." Pynchon has identified his source for the name as *Hamlet* I.v (*Slow Learner* 19). Since Porpentine is clearly the most humane of the quartet of agents whose rivalry is somewhat murkily set forth in the chapter, the association with the traditionally prickly qualities of the "fretful porpentine" seems inapposite.

PC59.13 PF63.14 B52.7   the duello   The rules or conventions of dueling. Porpentine and Bongo-Shaftsbury's rivalry is only loosely a duel and certainly they are not literally dueling in the corridor of the summer theater, where Bongo-Shaftsbury shoots Porpentine as the latter struggles with Lepsius. The word invokes an older era of honor between enemies and stands in ironic contrast to the actual circumstances of Porpentine's death.

PC59.22 PF63.22 B52.16   The rest was impersonation and dream "Some of these narrative centres actually correspond to characters in *The Secret Agent:* the anarchist Yusef (section ii); the cab driver Gebrail, from the grotesque with 'the steed of apocalyptic misery' in Conrad's Chapter 8 (v); the barmaid Hanne, lover of a German agent, who is given the initial placidity and incuriousness of Winnie Verloc (vii). Others are also taken from literary sources: the cafe waiter playing the role of a waiter (i) from a famous example in Sartre's *L'Être et Le Néant;* the mountebank Girgis (vi) from the acrobats in the fifth of Rilke's *Duineser Elegien* (henceforward *Duino Elegies*). Additionally, some of the minor characters are recollections from reading— the girl Alice (Carroll), the Coptic mistress of the British Embassy official (Durrell's *Alexandria Quartet*), the pimp Varkumian (Youkoumian in Waugh's *Black Mischief*). Victoria, the girl tourist of the Egypt and Florence chapters, could come from Forster or James, but the idea that she is a 'balloon-girl' [PC63.30n] tends to associate her with the latter's image of the romance as liberation of a balloon. A further connection here is that the narrative centres, with their restricted information and need to infer, are comparable to James' protagonists of the period (*In the Cage, The Turn of the Screw, What Maisie Knew*), although the multiple narrator technique derives from the Conrad of *Nostromo* and Durrell" (Dugdale 86).

Noting Levine's claim that each of the narrative personae adopted by Stencil is one of the preterite whose interest in the activities of the spies is secondary to his own private concerns, Cooley acknowledges the momentary effect that is achieved of placing otherwise marginalized figures at the heart of this tale of imperialist maneuverings. He goes on to suggest, however, that Stencil's "vignettes are, in many ways, mere expansions of the stereotypes of imperialist fiction, popular and canonical" (312).

PC59.30 PF63.29 B52.25   P. Aïeul   The first of Stencil's assumed identities. "Aïeul" is French for "grandfather."

PC59.31 PF63.30 B52.27   an Englishman   Porpentine.

PC59.32 PF63.31 B52.27   because his face was badly sunburned
The peeling skin, repeatedly referred to, of course provides the means
for the reader to keep track of Porpentine in his various appearances
throughout the chapter. At the same time, given the novel's preoccupation with skins or surfaces, it is tempting to read the peeling
off of Porpentine's skin as a symbol of his (dangerous) shedding of the
armor of indifference so essential to the successful spy.

PC60.2 PF63.35 B52.32   they're usually not tourists   Tourists (as
the novel frequently and variously illustrates) seek to appropriate the
superficial characteristics of the landscapes through which they pass,
lacking both the talent and the inclination for the kind of integration
into the reality of a place that Porpentine achieves so quickly.

PC60.9 PF64.6 B52.42   Baedekers   Detailed guidebooks, published by the German firm of Karl Baedeker (1801–59). Pynchon
acknowledges his debt to Baedeker in the introduction to *Slow
Learner* (17). The "Karl Baedeker of Leipzig" to whom the novel refers (PC441.3) was the son of the founder of the firm, which moved
to Leipzig from Koblenz in 1872.

PC60.10 PF64.6 B52.42   a Pharos   One of the Seven Wonders
of the World, the lighthouse built in about 280 B.C. in Alexandria
harbor.

PC60.10 PF64.7 B52.43   picturesque but faceless Arabs   The inhabitants of this tourist destination are mere features of the landscape, deprived of their humanity by the failure of the invading
hordes to go beyond the surface characteristics to which their guidebooks draw their attention.

PC60.26 PF64.22 B52.15   hat fingan kahwa bisukkar, ya weled
Arabic for "Bring me a cup of coffee with sugar, boy."

PC60.28 PF64.24 B53.15   Merde, Aïeul thought   Aïeul's response ("Merde" = "shit") could be prompted by a number of things,
the most straightforward of which would be his resentment at having
his "philosophical reflections" interrupted. It is also possible that he
is reacting to Goodfellow's automatic assumption that Aïeul is an
Arab, thus confirming his sour recognition of his own inertness in
the eyes of the tourists.

PC61.1 PF64.32 B53.27   This fat one was out to seduce the girl
Aïeul's series of speculations about his customers and their doings
begins with this rather accurate assessment of Goodfellow's intentions (PC86.18n). He is more fanciful in the guesses that follow.

PC61.4 PF64.35 B53.30   macquereau   French "maquereau" =
pimp.

**PC61.14 PF65.7 B53.41   Fat and Tweed would enter their con-
sulate**   See PC91.4n, where Aïeul's idle speculation finds partial and
surprising vindication.

PC61.18 PF65.12 B54.2   like a clockwork doll   In light of Porpentine's subsequent indignation at Bongo-Shaftsbury's frightening
claims to Mildred Wren that he is an "electro-mechanical doll"
(PC78.16n), this comparison is ironic.

PC61.22 PF65.16 B54.7   Pazzo son! . . .   Porpentine is singing
part of the aria from Puccini's *Manon Lescaut* in which Des Grieux
begs to be transported along with Manon. "I am insane," he sings.
"Look at me. How I weep and implore. . . . How I plead for pity"
(Cowart 65).

PC61.35 PF65.28 B54.20   avare!   Miser!

PC62.3 PF65.31 B54.23   How many times   We are reminded of
Stencil's presence behind the impersonation as his privileged awareness of Porpentine and Goodfellow's real profession shows through
these parenthetical musings. Despite Aïeul's shrewdness, we can
hardly suppose him to have divined, *in propria persona*, what has
brought the two men to this spot ("object of political assassination"
is a little too near the mark to be plausible except as part of Stencil's
overarching consciousness). At the same time, these reflections are
consistent with Aïeul's own sense of displacement and his evident
dislike of Alexandria.

PC62.10 PF66.1 B54.31   any statue's face   That Porpentine and
Goodfellow might be obliged to find confirmation of their own humanity by way of contrast with the inanimate statues of any tourist city is suggestive of the novel's exploration of that decadence
which Itague will define as "a falling-away from what is human"
(PC437.11).

PC62.28 PF66.18 B55.6   Yusef the factotum   The second of Stencil's impersonations. A factotum is a man of all work (*OED*).

PC63.10 PF66.35 B55.25   Sirdar Kitchener   "Sirdar" in this context means the British commander-in-chief of the Egyptian army (*OED*). Lord Kitchener (1850–1916) assumed the post in 1892.

PC63.11 PF66.36 B55.26   recently victorious at Khartoum   A somewhat inaccurate designation. The reference is in fact to the victory in September 1898 at Omdurman of the Anglo-Egyptian army under Kitchener's command over the forces of the Islamic fundamentalists who had been in control of the region since the fall of Khartoum thirteen years before (see PC83.3n, PC179.1n).

PC63.12 PF67.1 B55.27   down the White Nile   "Up" would be more accurate.

PC63.13 PF67.2 B55.28   General Marchand   Either Pynchon or the rumor mill has exaggerated Marchand's military status. Jean-Baptiste Marchand was in fact only a captain in the French army when he set out from Gabon in West Africa in 1896 on the expedition that would earn him his place in the history books. His role in the encounter with Kitchener at Fashoda (see PC83.25n) led to his promotion to the rank of major (Giffen 73).

PC63.15 PF67.4 B55.29   M. Delcassé . . . would as soon go to war as not   This seems to attribute a more bellicose attitude to Theophile Delcassé than was likely to have been the case. Delcassé had inherited the Marchand expedition from his predecessor and was anyway mindful of France's position in Europe generally and her relations with Germany in particular. Nevertheless, it is a fact that once Kitchener and Marchand had met and the incident had become public knowledge, the French public (and the British) was certainly ready to resort to armed conflict to resolve the dispute. Warlike gestures in the form of the mobilization of the French fleet and the stockpiling of stores and ammunition in the channel ports were made and part of the British fleet headed for Alexandria to protect the Suez Canal (Theobald 246).

PC63.30 PF67.17 B56.1   A balloon-girl   Yusef/Stencil's characterization of Victoria is yet another link in the chain of associations that binds V. to the idea of conflict. Yusef comes to his designation via the English colloquialism "Up goes the balloon" (PC63.22), an indication of the outbreak of hostilities. The epithet is repeated by Sidney Stencil in the Epilogue in his recollection of Victoria in Florence (PC528.19n). The effect is perhaps also to remind us of the manner in which most of what we read about V. is somehow filtered, literally or figuratively, through Herbert Stencil's consciousness, a point that is reinforced by Fausto Maijstral's use of the phrase to characterize Paola (PC355.16n).

PC63.35 PF67.21 B56.6 muezzins A "public crier who proclaims the regular hours of prayer from the minaret or the roof of a mosque" (*OED*).

PC64.3 PF67.25 B56.10 Leltak leben Pittas-Giroux suggests that Victoria's is a typically "mangled" tourist's Arabic, a conflation of two phrases drawn from Baedeker: *Leiltak sa 'îda:* "May your night be happy," and *Naharak Lâbân:* "Thy day be white as milk" (76).

PC64.7 PF67.30 B56.14 An older man Presumably Sir Alistair Wren. The fact that he resembles "a professional street-brawler" suggests that he too may be connected with the shadowy world of espionage.

PC64.10 PF67.32 B56.18 Named after her queen Note the pun that doubles the association: "Wren/*reine.*" The name "bestows on her all the pretensions and aggressiveness that characterized Queen Victoria" (Chambers 64), "the practitioner of divisive colonialism" (Newman 45). Anticipating Victoria's meeting with Hugh Godolphin, Chambers notes that "the mainland region of Antarctica . . . is called Victoria land." She also cites Graves's observation that in Celtic myth the wren was sacred, adding that "in Greek myth the wren is associated with the winter solstice" (64). Victoria, she finally notes, is the Latin name for Nike, the goddess of victory. Tanner wonders if the last name echoes that of Sir Christopher Wren, the seventeeth-century architect (*TP* 44).

PC64.25 PF68.9 B56.33 Count Khevenhüller-Metsch . . . M. de Villiers As Pynchon acknowledges in *Slow Learner* (17), these were the real holders of the diplomatic posts he mentions.

PC65.4 PF68.22 B57.4   a chubby blond man   Goodfellow.

PC65.7 PF68.25 B57.7   a young girl of eleven   Victoria's sister, Mildred.

PC65.8 PF68.26 B57.8   another man whose face looked sun-burned   Porpentine.

PC65.23 PF69.3 B57.25   Tewfik the assassin   Pynchon's source for this name may have been the port of Tewfik near Suez, or he may have remembered from his reading on the Fashoda incident that the Mahdist steamer which attacked Marchand's troops and which brought news of his presence in Fashoda to Kitchener was called the *Tewfikia* (Theobald 238).

PC65.31 PF69.11 B57.36   a false nose   Exemplary of the chapter's mixed tonal mode. Lepsius's weak eyes are made the emblem of a kind of moral sickliness that has its more sinister counterpart in the switch in Bongo-Shaftsbury's arm (PC78.24). Together with the implications of very real diplomatic crisis which infuse the chapter, they convey a somber message that is nonetheless undercut by such details as Lepsius's false nose, that cliche of disguise, and Porpentine's account of his visit along with Goodfellow to the British consulate disguised as Irish tourists (PC91.4n).

PC66.19 PF69.33 B58.17   The Fink restaurant   Another of Pynchon's gleanings from Baedeker.

PC66.23 PF69.37 B58.22   Maxwell Rowley-Bugge   Schulz sees him as a parody of Nabokov's Lolita-obsessed Humbert Humbert (80).

PC66.31 PF70.8 B58.31   Baedeker land   A seemingly casual indication of the notion, central to the novel, that the world occupied by tourists is at best a superficial version of the places they visit, mediated through guidebooks, and at worst, a separate reality, brought into being by those books. The concept has a bearing on our understanding of Stencil's quest, for it may be that he is simply trying to construct a guidebook to his century, one that might obscure more than it reveals.

PC66.33 PF70.10 B58.33   a young Lochinvar   The reference is to the story of young Lochinvar's daring arrival at the church where his beloved is about to marry an unworthy man. Sir Walter Scott's *Marmion* most famously retells the story:

> "O, Young Lochinvar is come out of the west,
> Through all the wide Border his steed was the best . . .
> So faithful in love and so dauntless in war,
> There never was knight like the young Lochinvar"
>   (Canto v)

Clearly, Maxwell Rowley-Bugge can only ironically be regarded as a young Lochinvar, though an early ballad tells of the sexual exploitation of a young farm girl by the laird of Lochinvar, providing a more likely parallel ("The Laird of Lochinvar—The Broom of Cowdenknows").

PC67.2 PF70.15 B58.38 Alice Pynchon's choice of name here may have been influenced by speculations regarding the creator of *Alice's Adventures in Wonderland* and his relationship with the children to whom he told his stories and whom he photographed.

PC67.13 PF70.25 B59.7 Lardwick-in-the-Fen Erstwhile home, we discover, of Victoria Wren (PC173.1), who is, when Max encounters her in Alexandria, "About the age Alice would be, now" (PC69.21). Stencil's fertile imagination creates the very strong possibility that Alice and Victoria are one and the same, but, typically, we are not allowed any degree of certainty in this as in other possible connections that Pynchon distributes wholesale throughout the text. Alice's Anglicanism is stressed in clear distinction to Victoria's Catholicism (PC70.14).

While "Lardwick" sounds Yorkshire enough (cf. Withernwick, Keswick), "in-the-Fen," or some version of it, is more likely to appear in a Lincolnshire or Cambridgeshire place name (cf. Mareham-le-Fen).

PC67.26 PF70.35 B59.20 the other automata As with his two previous impersonations, Stencil-as-Max characterizes himself as if from the point of view of the tourists who usually fill his world. Aïeul is "inert" (PC60.12), while Yusef "might as well be a fixture on the wall" (PC64.34). Madsen identifies the tourist perspective as part

of "the V-metaphysic" that informs the novel, "the selective perception of the world which accounts only for literal appearances and
substitutes a set of mechanical relationships for a moral order" (34).

PC69.19 PF72.21 B61.1   white Vöslauer   The wine Victoria is
drinking is Austrian, appropriately enough, since she has just come
from a party at the Austrian Consulate (where she has been drinking
chablis punch). Vöslau is more noted for its red wine.

PC69.21 PF72.23 B61.3   About the age Alice would be, now   See
PC67.13n.

PC69.26 PF72.27 B61.7   She was Catholic   The characterization
of Victoria's early religious experience that follows lays the foundation for subsequent indications of the increasingly private and perverse nature of V.'s appropriation of Catholic dogma, which culmi-
nates in her assumption of the role of the Bad Priest of Malta.

PC70.3 PF73.1 B61.20   wonderful yarns   Dugdale associates the
stories told by Victoria's uncle with the tales about Australian ab-
origines, "which formed the basis for Frazer's theories of totem-
ism" (87).

PC70.5 PF73.4 B61.23   a colonial doll's world   The novel's repeated invocation of tourism as an analogy for western colonialism,
combined with the direct and disturbing accounts of literal colonialism in Mondaugen's story make this early tendency of Victoria's
imagination particularly significant.

PC70.10 PF73.8 B61.28   an aboriginal Satan   "This fantasy of
imperialist oppression as the divine logos suggests that the natural
(aboriginal) order is evil and that it must be suppressed by an artificial white empire that arrogates to itself cosmic sanction for its dominion" (Eddins 60).

PC71.19 PF74.13 B62.33   Literally Horus on the horizon   Bongo-
Shaftsbury is identifying Harmakhis as one of the many epithets for
the Egyptian sun god Horus.

PC71.26 PF74.20 B62.41   Grébaut   Eugène Grébaut was director
general of the antiquities service in Egypt from 1886 to 1892. Bongo-
Shaftsbury may well be "reciting from the pages of his Baedeker," as

Maxwell Rowley-Bugge suspects (PC71.32). His reference is to what was known as "the second Deir-el-Bahri find," to which Grébaut was conducted by the real discoverer, Mohamed Abd el-Rassul (Leca 265). Baedeker does indeed name the prominent European official as the discoverer, rather than the "faceless" Arab.

PC71.29 PF74.23 B63.1   Mr. Flinders Petrie   William Matthew Flinders Petrie (1853–1942), British archaeologist and Egyptologist whose early interest in the origin of units of measurement led him to conduct detailed surveys of the pyramids at Giza. He was knighted in 1923.

PC71.29 PF74.23 B63.2   sixteen or seventeen years ago   Petrie began his work on the pyramids in 1880.

PC72.5 PF74.34 B63.12   Duplicity is against the law   The tourist realm is characterized by its order—its governing document is the timetable. Anything that threatens that order, therefore, is suspect. The cliché that in Mussolini's Italy at least the trains ran on time lurks somewhere behind the connection between "Baedeker land" and the right-wing politics of V.'s world.

PC72.13 PF75.5 B63.19   Lepsius   Pynchon no doubt came across the name in the course of his Egyptological browsings. Karl Richard Lepsius (1810–84) was a German Egyptologist.

PC72.13 PF75.5 B63.19   the climate in Brindisi   Brindisi is a seaport on the southeastern Adriatic coast of Italy. Lepsius's particular reason for having been in Brindisi is not apparent, though one can assume that the city, like nearby Bari, was affected by the widespread unrest that swept across southern Italy in 1898. The failure of Italian colonialist expansion in Ethiopia and its embarrassment at the hands of Mahdist forces at Adwa in 1896 had long been the source of public outcry and, by 1898, dissatisfaction with the government had reached its peak (Seton-Watson 191). Lepsius's appearance in Alexandria on the eve of the Fashoda crisis suggests that his job is connected to the monitoring of European colonialist activities and their aftermath.

PC72.27 PF75.17 B63.34   this soiled South   Lepsius's distaste for things southern foreshadows Mondaugen's meditation on "south-sickness" (PC243.2) and is linked by anticipatory association with the Nazi obsession with Aryan purity.

PC72.28 PF75.18 B63.36   Unless you go far enough south   As in his earlier exchange with Bongo-Shaftsbury (PC71.23), Porpentine is using the seemingly general drift of the conversation to make veiled reference to the current colonialist sparring in the Sudan. His invocation of "civilized" European values in contrast to Lepsius's "law of the wild beast" is actually somewhat ironic in the light of the claims Britain was making to possession of the territory around Fashoda "by right of conquest" (Giffen 60).

PC73.11 PF75.36 B64.15   to favor the clean over the impure   Again, the anticipation of Nazi eugenicist policies and practices is unmistakable (see PC72.27n).

PC74.17 PF77.3 B65.14   The Alexandria and Cairo morning express   Pynchon's account of the journey is closely modelled on the description offered by Baedeker. See, for example, the following from the English version of the guide to Egypt of 1908: "Beyond Hadra . . . and Sîdi Gâber . . . our line diverges to the right from that to Rosetta. . . . We cross the Mahmûdîyeh Canal . . . by a drawbridge, and the triangular sails of the boats which appear above its banks enable the eye to follow it for quite a distance" (Baedeker 27).

PC74.23 PF77.7 B65.20   Gaze's   A tour guide service, recommended in the 1897 Baedeker for Egypt, along with Thomas Cook's.

PC74.27 PF77.12 B65.25   The train itself ran on a different clock   The implication is that the inanimate world does not conform to the ordering principles by which human beings attempt to keep chaos at bay.

PC74.32 PF77.18 B65.30   the hothouse of his fellow Sephardim   "The Jews, or their descendants, who lived in Spain and Portugal from the Middle Ages until their persecution and mass expulsion from those countries in the last decades of the 15th century. The Sephardim initially fled to North Africa and other parts of the Ottoman Empire. . . . The transplanted Sephardim largely retained their native Judeo-Spanish language (Ladino), literature, and customs" ("Sephardi," *Britannica Online*).

PC74.34 PF77.20 B65.33 Scenes of specific persecution Such as the one he witnesses between Bongo-Shaftsbury and Mildred Wren (PC78).

PC75.2 PF77.22 B65.36 Ptolemy Philopator The fourth of the Ptolemaic dynasty of Egyptian kings (c. 238 B.C.–205 B.C.).

PC75.18 PF78.1 B66.10 Why put it down to God's intervention? "Waldetar's assessment points up the larger concern of the novel: the necessity to believe in some historical pattern, call it deity or Zeitgeist" (Slade 58).

PC75.32 PF78.15 B66.25 Merely train's hardware See PC67.26n.

PC76.2 PF78.20 B66.30 a grand joke Is this aside, with its somewhat bitter sarcasm, reflective of Stencil's position, and thus an indication of *his* critique of the V. world he is encountering? Or does it represent the position of an overriding narrative persona— "Pynchon" himself?

PC76.4 PF78.23 B66.33 the vocal Memnon of Thebes "In Egypt the name of Memnon was connected with the colossal (70-foot [21-metre]) stone statues of Amenhotep III near Thebes, two of which still remain. The more northerly of these was partly destroyed by an earthquake in 27 BC, resulting in a curious phenomenon. Every morning, when the rays of the rising sun touched the statue, it gave forth musical sounds like the twang of a harp string. This was supposed to be the voice of Memnon responding to the greeting of his mother, Eos" ("Memnon," *Britannica Online*).

PC76.15 PF78.32 B67.2 a German with blue lenses for eyes Confirmation of Lepsius's nationality.

PC76.17 PF78.35 B67.5 Eleusis The site that Waldetar notes from the train is of an ancient suburb of Alexandria, which bore the same name as the Greek city of Eleusis, where the earth goddess Demeter is said to have gone in search of her daughter Persephone. The desert landscape is here seen in grim contrast to the fertile environs of the Greek city and to the implied associations with fecundity that accompany the mention of Demeter.

PC76.23 PF79.2 B67.9   Mahmudiyeh Canal   A forty-five-mile-long canal built in 1820 to connect Alexandria to the Nile.

PC76.26 PF79.5 B67.13   a man-made Flood in 1801   Napoleon's armies had occupied the city in 1798 but were forced to surrender by a British Indian army contingent. At the orders of General Hutchinson, British engineers cut a canal between the dry lake bed of Mareotis and the sea at Abuqir in order to isolate Alexandria from the possibility of relief from the east. Holton finds in Pynchon's brief account "a quiet but powerful, even lyrical, sense of historical pathos," which he contrasts with E. M. Forster's Eurocentric discussion of the incident (239). Pynchon's source for this information is likely to be the Baedeker he admits to borrowing from, which contains an account of the lake's formation.

PC76.30 PF79.8 B67.17   fellahin   "A peasant or agricultural laborer in an Arab country (as Egypt)" (Merriam-Webster's *Collegiate Dictionary*).

PC77.20 PF79.31 B67.43   Suez   Southern terminus of the Suez Canal on the Gulf of Suez.

PC77.27 PF79.37 B68.7   Iberian littoral   Waldetar is remembering his life on the Portuguese coast.

PC78.16 PF80.23 B68.31   An electro-mechanical doll   "Pynchon mimics Dryden's depiction in The Medall of the Earl of Shaftesbury. . . . Dryden satirized Shaftesbury as 'Tapski' and played with the fact that he had a faucet installed in his abdomen to drain ill humors" (Newman 43).

PC78.24 PF80.30 B68.39   sewn into the flesh   Reminiscent of Fergus Mixolydian's sleep-switch (PC52.16n), this device anticipates V.'s incorporation into her body of pieces of inert matter. The implication is that the switch is somehow the means of bringing under control the unpredictable Jekyll and Hyde polarity of the human consciousness.

McHoul and Wills see the image as a starting point for the novel's preoccupation with the inanimate: "From the switch on Bongo-

Shaftsbury's arm, to the murder of 60,000 Hereros [PC259.23n], to SHROUD's reference to the similarity between concentration camp corpses and car bodies piled up in a wrecker's yard [PC314.16n], there runs a straight line with reference to which the differential increase in the inanimate can be plotted, like a V on its side" (171).

PC79.3 PF81.7 B69.10 General principles again Bongo-Shaftsbury's contemptuous dismissal of Porpentine's appeal to a generalized code of behavior contributes to the complexity of the novel's moral and epistemological vision. On the one hand, the reader is invited to share Bongo-Shaftsbury's mistrust of systematic approaches to reality—Stencil's quest for order is somehow "clownish," after all—and yet at the same time, given the proleptic associations of the Lepsius/Bongo-Shaftsbury team with the spirit, if not the fact, of National Socialist views on "cleansing," Porpentine must be seen to be in some sense on the side of virtue, and his willingness to allow humanity to color his professional judgment as a spy cannot be dismissed as a weak surrender to "general principle."

PC79.6 PF81.10 B69.13 The moment you forget yourself This threat is not long in being carried out. Porpentine's death at the summer theater represents the playing out of this moment's tensions (PC93.26n).

PC79.10 PF81.14 B69.17 Humanity is something to destroy Setting aside the somewhat stage-villain melodrama of Bongo-Shaftsbury's laugh (one almost expects to learn that he is twirling his mustache as he speaks), this assertion represents perhaps the fundamental principle that informs the novel's working through of the V. motif. "Humanity"—in the sense of some set of beliefs and attitudes that distinguishes human from other—is a messy and unpredictable inconvenience and the sooner it is eradicated the better.

PC80.10 PF82.9 B70.10 sakiehs A system of buckets and pulleys used to raise water from wells.

PC80.10 PF82.9 B70.10 The point of the green triangle "The two V's are both here: the tiny inner V of lush, life-sustaining farmland and an encompassing, contiguous V of inanimate wastes. This bivalent figure is the very model of gnostic parody, a simulacrum of creativity and growth that ultimately serves death. Cairo's position at the apex makes the city the unavoidable endpoint of encroaching sterility, the urban cul-de-sac of twentieth-century decline" (Eddins 62).

PC80.32 PF82.28 B70.33   no hostility in the desert   Gebrail's fatalistic take on the invasion of his land by the desert is most interesting in its contrast with Stencil's more frequently evinced tendency to assume the presence of a hostile animus in the events that constitute his V.-construct. The "forcible dislocation of personality" that enables Stencil to inhabit the consciousness of this Cairo carriage driver also permits him to adopt an epistemological stance that runs counter to his own inclinations.

PC81.3 PF82.33 B70.39   the Angel's trumpet   The trumpet which, according to the Qur'an, the angel Israfil (Pynchon's "Asrafil") sounds to announce the day of resurrection.

PC81.12 PF83.4 B71.7   lower half of an hourglass   "The inversion from whose sterility we suffer was, Pyncheon [sic] seems to argue, the nineteenth century's, which turned the potentialities of our experience upside down by writing history with the ABC's of Alice, Baedeker, and Colonialism (and Dentistry, Englishmen, Fashoda)" (Greenberg 63).

PC81.21 PF83.13 B71.17   like many not on any guidebook's map   Like Queequeg's island home, which "is not down in any map; true places never are" (*Moby Dick,* chapter 12). The "truth" of Gebrail's home in "Arabian Cairo" lies in its being invisible to the gaze of the tourists who consume the surface features of a city given to them only as Baedeker sees fit.

PC81.34 PF83.25 (omitted from Bantam ed.)   Gebel, Gebrail   The reflection spurred by the bitter irony of the similarity of Gebrail's name to the word for the soulless invader of his farmland is of some relevance to the novel as a whole. If the desert (and the inanimate tourist city represented by its most famous hotel, Shepheard's) and the angelic source of the wisdom of the Koran are more or less identical, then Gebrail is justified in his nihilist views and some credence can be given to Hugh Godolphin's nightmare vision of nothingness.

PC82.32 PF84.20 B72.23   the Mahdists   Followers of the Mahdi (see next note).

PC83.3 PF84.25 B72.30   Mohammed Ahmed, the Mahdi of '83
It was in fact in 1881 that Mohammed Ahmad Ibn Al-Saiyid Abd Allah first confided to his followers and then to the leaders of a number of tribes in western Sudan that he was "al-Mahdi al-Muntazar, the Expected Guide," whose task it was "to bring righteousness to a world filled with iniquity" (Theobald 32). His effectiveness as a leader was demonstrated convincingly in 1883, when his forces successfully laid siege to the city of El Obeid. He died suddenly two years later, shortly after the fall of Khartoum to his armies. Mahdist control of the Sudan lasted until 1898, when Kitchener destroyed the Mahdist army at the battle of Omdurman ("now that the movement was crushed" [PC82.33]). The belief that the Mahdi was "sleeping not dead" is consistent with Shi'ite Muslim doctrine: "Some associate the coming of the Mahdi with the second coming of Isa or Christ; others [believe] that he will be the precursor of the end of the world, and will defer his appearance until that date" (Theobald 32).

PC83.6 PF84.28 B72.34   Dejal the antichrist   Ad-Dajjal. "(Arabic: 'The Deceiver'), in Islamic eschatology, the Antichrist who will come forth before the end of time; after a reign of 40 days or 40 years, he will be destroyed by Christ or the mahdi ('rightly guided one') or both, and the world will submit to God" ("Dajjal, ad-," *Britannica Online*).

PC83.25 PF85.8 B73.11   Fashoda   In 1898 Fashoda was an abandoned outpost of the old Egyptian government in the Sudan on the banks of the White Nile, four hundred miles south of Khartoum. It was renamed Kodok as part of the settlement of the dispute between England and France that erupted in September 1898 and that returns again and again as a leitmotif of this chapter. The fig-hawker's prediction of an impending battle and subsequent apocalypse is a reminder of the level of intensity that Franco-British affairs reached during the incident, which in fact had its genesis in the launching two years before of an expedition under the command of a French army officer named Captain Jean-Baptiste Marchand (PC63.13n). Marchand had been instructed to push across the African continent from his starting point in Gabon and to establish French title to territories in the upper Nile region. He reached his objective on July 10, 1898, repulsed an attack by a Mahdist steamer, and settled down to await the consequence of his having raised the French flag over his encampment. These were not long in revealing themselves, and on September 19, Kitchener, recently responsible for the final defeat of the Mahdists at Omdurman, steamed upriver to confront the Frenchman in the name of prior British claims to the region. As accounts of the meeting became public, feelings ran high (PC63.15n) and there appeared to be a very real threat of war between the two powers.

The crisis, Eddins notes, "is just the sort of seedbed of apocalypse that V. will be drawn to for the rest of her life, as she moves from being a voyeur of the Inanimate and its forces to being its active agent" (60).

PC84.7 PF85.22 B73.29   As if a great lie were finally to be exposed   The "great lie" is presumably identical to Fausto Maijstral's (PC349.22n). The stars, one might suppose, provide powerful evidence in support of the argument from design theory of God's existence. Their absence from the sky, therefore, represents the nihilist void that Gebrail's experience has taught him is the true state of affairs and that poets like Fausto dutifully seek to conceal from view behind the cloak of "comfortable and pious metaphor."

PC86.18 PF87.24 B75.29   Goodfellow and the girl   Cowart notes that "according to Eric Partridge's Dictionary of slang and unconventional English, 'goodfellow' is Covent Garden slang for 'a vigorous fornicator'" (68). Eddins sees Goodfellow's seduction of Victoria as part of the complex of images deriving from the novel's allusion to Adams: "Both symbols . . . , the Virgin and the rose, together with their promises of harmony and grace, undergo simultaneous degeneration in the deflowering of V. by an agent devoted to sub rosa activities. It is apropos, in this connection, that the phrase 'sub rosa' itself is thought by lexicographers to stem from the legend that a rose was used as a bribe to keep the indiscretions of Venus—another aspect of Adams's Eternal Feminine—from being revealed" (61).

PC86.21 PF87.26 B75.32 Margate A popular English seaside resort.

PC86.28 PF87.33 B75.40 in 'love' with him Porpentine is by instinct no sentimentalist and has as little faith in love as most of the other characters in the novel; nevertheless, when he asks "Do you think I care?" we have to wonder why, if the answer is expected to be negative, he has just risked his limbs, if not his life, by climbing up to spy on Goodfellow and Victoria.

PC86.35 PF88.3 B76.4 We all have a threshold Porpentine recognizes that he is nearing the limit of his capacity for cool objectivity. He is directly harking back here to his earlier exchange with Bongo-Shaftsbury on the train (PC79.3n). When he assures the listener in the shadows whom he assumes to be Bongo-Shaftsbury that Victoria "is still faceless," he is insisting that the moment has not yet arrived when he has "admit[ted] another's humanity" (PC79.7) and thus rendered himself vulnerable to his more cynical rival.

PC87.20 PF88.21 B76.25 so German "The north European tourists who create a *bierhalle* in Egypt 'in their own image' which results in 'a parody of home,' are only revealing the tourists' flight from reality even while in the act of travelling; they too live among illusions, inhabitants of their own stencillings, or the stencillings put out by Baedeker" (Tanner, "V2" 31).

PC89.16 PF90.12 B78.10 a certain leitmotif of disease One that will play itself out in particular in Mondaugen's story of Foppl's siege party.

PC89.27 PF90.23 B78.21 Roughly triangular This V-manifestation, which appears and disappears in tantalizing fashion, adds to the network of associations that link Victoria, Fashoda, and the activities of the spies in Stencil's creative amplification of the "veiled references" of the journal. The stain on the plate, which may or may not be real, is an apt image of the possibility of moral darkness that Stencil half believes is at the heart of his Conradian quest. Tanner regards the description of the stain as a "miniature" statement of the novel's central concerns. "The problem of the book is here in miniature. Perhaps the changing shapes we see on the external blankness are the shifting projections of our own 'headaches' or subjective pressures; on the other hand there might actually be a stain on the plate. The description of the shape in geometric terms is of course deliberate; throughout the book we constantly come across specific angles, intersections, details of linear arrangements and numerically charted positions. It is one of the most enduring of human dreams (or needs) to feel that we live among geometry. Rather than confront shapeless space, we introduce lines and angles into it. Surrounded by the desert, man builds a pyramid. That would be another way of saying what V. is all about" ("V2" 34).

Dugdale sees a parallel with Dimmesdale's inability to escape the letter *A* in the "Minister in a Maze" chapter of *The Scarlet Letter* (87).

PC90.17 PF91.8 B79.6   Varkumian   A play on the German word for "dissolute," or "squalid" (Harder 68).

PC90.19 PF91.10 B79.8   Lord Cromer   Evelyn Baring, first earl of Cromer, had been British consul general in Egypt since 1883. Cromer was an immensely powerful and very visible administrator. Pynchon seems to be speculating about the likely effect of his death on the outcome of diplomatic negotiations over Fashoda.

PC90.30 PF91.20 B79.19   Bongo-Shaftsbury will try   To assassinate Cromer, presumably.

PC90.34 PF91.24 B79.23   *Manon Lescaut*   The Puccini opera. Goodfellow has told Porpentine that he is taking Victoria to the opera (PC84.2). Presumably this is the performance in question.

PC91.4   PF91.29   B79.29   Irish tourists   Stencil-as-Aïeul (PC61.14n) was evidently not far off in his imaginative speculation regarding Porpentine and Goodfellow. Their clowning has the serious purpose of demonstrating to their satisfaction at least that security measures at the embassy are woefully inadequate.

PC91.14 PF92.1 B79.39   like a tongue on Pentecost   The fragments that Hanne overhears as she passes through the bierhalle constitute an ironically rendered glossolalia, informed by the unholy spirit of intrigue and hence unlikely to be the source of revealed truth. In Sidney Stencil's trinitarian version of political history (PC510), the Paraclete, or Holy Spirit, is envisaged as "Apocalypse." At the same time, though, Paola Maijstral's association with Pentecostal imagery is more positive in its implications (PC7.11n).

PC92.13 PF92.33 B80.31   Your father was in a German church this afternoon   Porpentine seems to be implying that Sir Alastair's political leanings are reflected in his cultural tastes, and that he may know about her affair with Goodfellow because he has had some hand in bringing it about. Victoria's insistence that she has only "guessed" at the true state of affairs (PC92.22) seems to be prompted by some such hint on Porpentine's part and by her desire to disabuse him of the idea. While we learn later that she had in fact "seduced" Goodfellow (PC173.8), we also learn that the affair resulted in her being alienated from her family, so Porpentine's assumptions may indeed be misplaced. Her request for his understanding (PC92.25) probably reflects her fear that he might act against her father—hence Porpentine's exasperated question: "Is your whole family daft?"

PC92.27 PF93.9 B81.4   men can get killed   Porpentine is no doubt recalling Bongo-Shaftsbury's threat (PC79.3) and realizing that any acknowledgment of Victoria's claims on his sympathy may well prove fatal.

PC93–94 PF93–94 B81–82   Section VIII   Stencil's eighth impersonation differs from the others in that here he has no identity; he is only a "field of vision" (PC93.26). The dispassionate objectivity of the voice underscores the contrast with the subjectivity of the multiple points of view adopted in the preceding sections, which Patteson likens to the work of Faulkner or Durrell ("Stencil" 32).

PC93.5 PF93.21 B81.18   The corridor runs   "The corridor at the Opera House is one of many transformations of [de Chirico's] *Mystery and Melancholy of a Street*, with its arcade of four boxes, its 'indeterminate color . . . probably orange' (93–94), its girl, its statue, its killer who appears only as a shadow" (Dugdale 85).

PC93.26 PF94.3 B81.40   The fat man follows   Goodfellow's exit with Victoria here leaves Porpentine without protection from Bongo-

Shaftsbury. Presumably Porpentine has allowed his sympathy for the lovers to overcome his professional instincts. "Porpentine is destroyed, like Des Grieux in [*Manon Lescaut*], by misguided chivalry; misguided because he serves, in Goodfellow, a careless Lothario, and in Victoria, a woman whose morals alienate her family to the point of abandonment" (Cowart 68).

PC93.29 PF94.7 B82.1   The pistol smokes   Nothing in the chapter helps to explain why Porpentine has fired his pistol in the theater, unless we are to suppose that Bongo-Shaftsbury has made his move against Cromer and that Porpentine has retaliated before engaging in his struggle with Lepsius.

PC94.9 PF94.21 B82.17   Vision must be the last to go   "The description of [Porpentine's] death points to a threshold which is a crucial one for the figures in the book. . . . Death is the moment when that line is irrevocably crossed, but the book shows innumerable ways in which that line is crossed while the body is still technically alive, thus producing a mobile object which reflects but does not receive" (Tanner, "V2" 23).

"Porpentine, the representative of the British Empire, can be seen as a parody of the ageing sacred king, murdered by his successor; Frazer's example is the Shilluk kings of the Fashoda region" (Dugdale 87).

CHAPTER FOUR

Esther Harvitz pays a visit to her lover, the plastic surgeon Shale Schoenmaker. We are given the etiology of Schoenmaker's commitment to reconstructive surgery in the form of an account of the fate of Evan Godolphin, a World War I pilot who is badly disfigured in a crash. The rest of the chapter is devoted to a (literally) blow-by-blow description of Esther's nose job.

PC95.1 PF95.1 B83.1 the crosstown bus Kowalewski sees the opening paragraphs of the chapter as a "functional passage . . . in that it seems sublimated to a narrative purpose: moving Esther from one place to another. But it is not where readers are being taken that matters here, but how they were being led, through what alien country the narrative is directing us. . . . The scene refers, and this is characteristic of Pynchon more generally, to what is largely invisible. There is a density of verbal fragments which, though charged with visual energy, are not confidently visualized by the reader. The effort of moving from one visual increment to the next involves an intensity of 'almost seeing.' This semi-invisibility makes the surreal a part of the created effect. . . . There is an intensified sense of the unknown, the literally but not imaginatively unseen" (201–2).

PC95.3 PF95.26 B83.22 *The Search for Bridey Murphy* Written by Morey Bernstein and published in 1956 by Doubleday, this runaway best-seller detailed the case of Virginia Tighe, who under hypnosis appeared to assume the character of a nineteenth-century Irish girl named Bridey Murphy.

PC95.13 PF95.36 B83.32 Tchaikovsky's Romeo and Juliet Overture The "syrupy" quality of the music and the cliché implications of its title remind us that love is rarely treated without either irony or pessimism in the novel.

PC95.21 PF96.7 B83.40 the eternal drama of love and death The fact that the drama is "given life" by the inanimate workings of the radio system and that it is "entirely disconnected from this evening and this place" suggests that Esther's journey is taking her to an assignation without any promise of real human connectedness.

PC96.28 PF96.31 B84.27 unsyncopated tango The dance of the imps is regulated by the constraints of the clock's mechanism and therefore lacks the element of passionate fierceness that the jumpy rhythms of the tango impart. Esther "felt home" here—a comment on the nature of her relationship with the clock's owner, no doubt.

PC97.2 PF97.6 B84.40 Tagliacozzi Gasparo Tagliacozzi was the sixteenth-century inventor of the "Italian method" of using skin from the upper arm to perform plastic surgery on the nose ("Gräfe, Karl Ferdinand von," *Britannica Online*).

PC98.6 PF98.4 B85.37 TDY Temporary Duty.

PC98.11 PF98.10 B85.42 break champagne glasses The whole passage is highly reminiscent of Jean Renoir's 1937 film *La Grande Illusion.*

PC98.20 PF98.18 B86.9 the Flanders Fields poem in Punch The poem ("In Flanders Fields," by Lieut.-Colonel John McCree), which appeared in the December 8, 1915 edition of *Punch,* reads as follows:

> In Flanders Fields the poppies blow
> Between the crosses, row on row,
> That mark our place, and in the sky
> The larks, still bravely singing, fly
> Scarce heard amid the guns below.
> We are the Dead. Short days ago
> We lived, felt dawn, and now we lie
>   In Flanders fields.
>
> Take up our quarrel with the foe;
> To you from failing hands we throw
> The torch; be yours to hold it high.
> If ye break faith with us who die
> We shall not sleep, though poppies grow
>   In Flanders fields.

The poppy, which grew prolifically on fields churned up by battle, became the symbol of World War I.

PC98.30 PF98.28 B86.19   the battle of Meuse-Argonne   Actually a series of battles fought on the Western Front in September and November 1918.

PC99.15 PF99.12 B86.41   Thiersch grafts   Named after the German physician Karl Thiersch (1822–95). "A very thin skin (split-skin graft) which, unlike the thicker 'flap' does not need to retain its own blood supply during the period following transfer to the new site" (*Oxford Companion to Medicine*).

PC99.25 PF99.21 B87.9   Profane would see some of them   The realm beneath the street is the refuge of only some of these victims of the culture's failure to heal its wounded. The street itself—the Street of the twentieth century?—is populated by others. Again Pynchon's sympathy for and interest in the passed-over members of society surfaces in a passage of marked poignancy.

PC100.1 PF99.32 B87.21   AEF   American Expeditionary Force.

PC100.2 PF99.33 B87.22   Halidom   The word signifies something held sacred, perhaps referring to the young doctor's "ideas of his own."

PC100.2 PF99.33 B87.22   allografts   The more accurate word would be "xenograft." An allograft is a graft from a donor of the same species as the recipient, which in fact is what Schoenmaker offers.

PC100.2 PF99.33 B87.33   the introduction of inert substances   A clear anticipation of V.'s "bodily incorporating little bits of inert matter" (PC528.9).

PC100.26 PF100.21 B88.5   CP   Command Post.

PC101.4 PF100.34 B88.20   This mineral period   The phrase renders almost explicit a connection between Schoenmaker and Fausto Maijstral III, whose affinity with the inanimate rubble of his bombed island home arises out of a similar wartime tragedy (PC327).

PC101.21 PF101.12 B88.37   a sympathetic beginning   Schoenmaker's rage at Halidom's misguided enthusiasm for the inanimate does indeed mark him, in the novel's terms, as one of the Good Guys. The "deterioration of purpose" (PC102.7), which has rendered him vulnerable to Rachel's attack, is part of the novel's overall depiction of the "used-upness" of all kinds of human energies and of that "falling-away from what is human" that Itague offers as the definition of decadence (PC437.11n).

PC102.12 PF101.37 B89.22 Stencil, pursuing a different trail Different from what? The trail in question is presumably the one that begins in Florence in 1899.

PC103.32 PF103.19 B90.40 Like they all wanted Pittas-Giroux suggests that Pynchon may be echoing David Riesman's *The Lonely Crowd,* citing the following passage:

> The extreme case of self-exploitation for reasons not necessarily associated with economic or social advance is plastic surgery of the sort which, unlike straightening children's teeth or removing a mole, actually alters the person's Gestalt, so that he is no longer visually the *same person.* As the beggar exaggerates deformity to excite pity, and by that very fact shows how hard the world bears down on him, so the person who normalizes his looks to the point of change of Gestalt shows the degree of pressure put on the physiologically and psychologically underprivileged by the personality market of leisure and work. (quoted in Pittas-Giroux 101)

PC104.2 PF103.26 B91.3 his private thesis Pynchon's own mistrust of binary extremes is reflected in Schoenmaker's theory. See also PC506.20n.

PC105.35 PF105.17 B92.34 Stick it in . . . pull it out "The sexuality of Esther's nose job is a comic inversion of the usual joke about men and the length of their noses, demonstrating a vaguely unhealthy reversal of role-playing" (Olderman 129).

PC110.2 PF109.2 B96.13 She was sexually turned on "Fulfilling the male image of the sexually desirable woman, [Esther] lets herself be trapped by her own body. Unable to penetrate beyond its surface, she does not evolve and thus remains a fetish that lacks the ability to develop into full adulthood" (Hawthorne 84).

PC111.1 PF109.34 B98.1 No "Esther's nos: that says it all. . . . Once nos can be repeated there is no saying whether the nos are simply repeats, differences, or contraries. And if no cannot even be preserved from yes (the truth-tables overturned), what hope for the sanctity of the animate?" (McHoul and Wills 175).

PC112.4 PF110.33 B98.2 Jacobean etiology Stark argues that "Jacobean" represents for Pynchon a low point on the sine curve of history, as manifested by brutality and decadence (113).

CHAPTER FIVE

Profane has been working in the sewers of New York for two weeks. He pursues an alligator into Fairing's Parish, thus providing the occasion for a history of that curious domain and its creator. Pig Bodine shows up at Rachel Owlglass's apartment in search of Paola, where an afternoon of beer-drinking is interrupted by a phone call from Stencil, who has been hit in the buttocks by a shotgun blast while pursuing the V-thread into Fairing's Parish.

PC113.1 PF111.25 B99.22 This alligator The targets of the alligator hunts as parody are variously identified. Seed notes three possibilities—"American war movies, American hunt narratives, and missionary colonialism" (79)—while Kharpertian adds the dragon-slayings of medieval romance (63).

PC114.9 PF112.15 B100.9 Walter Reuther American union leader (1907–70). President of United Automobile Workers from 1946 to 1970 and president of the Congress of Industrial Organizations before its merger with the American Federation of Labor.

PC114.21 PF112.26 B100.21 the next winter day you happen to be overpassed Pynchon injects a wry irony into this address to the reader via an implied pun on the concept of preterition. We are the elect, only temporarily "passed over" by the concrete span of the highway above our heads. The bums who take shelter are permanently "overpassed" by society.

PC114.29 PF112.33 B100.30 Hickey-Freeman and like-priced suits The Hickey-Freeman company was founded in Rochester, New York, at the beginning of the twentieth century to produce superior quality ready-to-wear men's clothing.

PCI14.34 PFI13.2 BI00.35 Oswiecim The Polish name for the town that became the site of Auschwitz-Birkenau.

PCI14.34 PFI13.3 BI00.37 Mikolaj Rej While I have been unable to ascertain whether Pynchon has fabricated this particular ship, there is no doubt that 1949 was the year for defections from Polish vessels in the United States. On February 9, the SS *Batory* sailed from New York minus nineteen of its crew, and on March 2, sixty-one men went missing from the *Sobieski.*

PCI15.13 PFI13.16 BI01.9 the Great Sewer Scandal of 1955 "5 In Queens Guilty in Sewer Scandal" was the headline of the lead story in the *New York Times* for June 10, 1955. A contractor and his son were convicted along with three borough employees after a two-mile section of brand new sewer in Laurelton, Queens, had to be replaced. The trial lasted almost fourteen months and was then the longest criminal trial in the nation's history.

PCI15.23 PFI13.25 BI01.20 under the summer streets of Brownsville Brownsville is a neighborhood in Brooklyn, but Richter wonders if this is "a veiled reference . . . to the 'Brownsville Affray,' in which a company of black soldiers was accused of armed riot on the summer streets of Brownsville, *Texas,* also on the thirteenth of August, but in 1906" (129).

PCI16.8 PFI14.9 BI01.41 Speedy Gonzales Best known as the Looney Tunes cartoon mouse from Mexico, Speedy Gonzales had his origins in a salacious joke that was originally about a Mexican man who suffered from premature ejaculation. The punchline Pynchon reproduces here, though, is from the rather different version that was going the rounds in the early fifties. Here it is, as told to William Anthony Nericcio:

> An Anglo husband and wife find themselves forced to share a hotel room with a Mexican fellow by the name of Speedy Gonzales. The worried husband notices his wife and Speedy exchanging suspicious glances. The husband decides that there is only one way to keep anything from happening between them

and that is for him to stick his finger into his wife's vagina and keep it there all night. Sometime during the night the husband has to sneeze and brings his hand to his face as he does so. Immediately afterwards, the husband returns his finger to wife's vagina. . . . Suddenly, Speedy Gonzales's voice is heard saying "Señor . . . your feenger . . . eeets up my ahhhssshole." (218)

The allusion loosely anticipates, through the suggested connection between the joke and the cartoon rodent, the "apocrypha" regarding Father Fairing that "dealt with an unnatural relationship between the priest" and Veronica the rat (PC124.2).

PC116.16 PF114.17 B102.6   FCC   Federal Communications Commission. Regulatory agency established by the Radio Act of 1937.

PC117.21 PF115.20 B103.8   AF of L   The American Federation of Labor.

PC118.26 PF116.19 B104.9   Bung the foreman   Reading the alligator hunt as "a political allegory both of Weberian charisma and rationalization and of domination of the preterite by the elect," Kharpertian suggests that "dehumanizing power is represented and satirized in the foreman Bung" (64).

PC119.7 PF116.36 B104.25   Chinga tu madre   Fuck your mother.

PC120.8 PF117.33 B105.20   Fairing's Parish   "This interpolated story performs three functions: first, it causes Profane and the reader to question the relation between 'history' and 'fiction,' between 'fact' and 'myth'; second, the novel's record of a record further blurs the distinction between reality and fiction within the novel; and third, the first two functions have a leveling effect, serving as a reminder that Profane himself is a fictional creation and making the reader wonder whether there are in fact levels of reality at work in the novel. Pynchon uses this same principle to create the major symbol of the novel, V." (Campbell 60–61).

PC120.22 PF118.9 B105.35   Baltimore Catechism   A catechism is a manual of instruction in matters of the Catholic faith, often

couched in the form of questions and answers. The Baltimore Catechism was published in 1885.

PC120.23 PF118.11 B105.37   Knight's *Modern Seamanship* Critics have noted the similarity of this enigmatic text to the copy of *An
Inquiry into Some Points of Seamanship* that Marlow finds in *Heart
of Darkness*. The "honest concern for the right way of going to
work" that Marlow discerns in the book he finds is shared by Fairing
and recorded in the earnest pages of his journals, but of course in a
thoroughly debased and parodied fashion. Booker finds the oblique
allusion more generally significant: "The link to Conrad suggests a
powerful ideological complicity between the Christian drive to convert 'heathen' peoples and the drive for imperial domination that informs *Heart of Darkness*" (23).

PC120.28 PF118.14 B105.41   between 86th and 79th   "The ex-
actitude with which the narrator identifies the locale attests, it is
being suggested, to his veraciousness, his sensitivity to rat demogra-
phy" (Kowalewski 199).

PC122.3 PF119.20 B107.1   shortly after sext   The noon canonical hour during which prayers are traditionally said in the Roman
Catholic church.

PC122.29 PF120.7 B107.29   Iona   One of the Inner Hebrides islands off the west coast of Scotland. In A.D. 563, Saint Colomba arrived from Ireland to christianize Scotland. Fairing is likening his
sewer parish to the monastic community founded by Colomba.

**PC123.10 PF120.21 B108.3   The stories . . . were pretty much
apocryphal**   A reminder of the manner in which the novel calls all
stories into question.

PC123.14 PF120.24 B108.7   It is this way with sewer stories
"This is as close to any kind of apologia as one is ever likely to get
from Pynchon. It is a cocky, protected assertion that leaves wary
readers optionless; indeed it makes us appear presumptuous. We are
dealing with an author who freely admits to writing and loving sewer
stories because they just *are*" (Kowalewski 200).

PC123.28 PF121.1 B108.23   a dark stain shaped like a crucifix

Reminiscent of the stain on the plate that troubles Hanne the barmaid (PC89.26).

PC123.33 PF121.5 B108.27   Veronica   McHoul and Wills read "Veronica" as "true image" (164), while Harder suggests the plant or Saint Veronica as possible origins or associations (68). Lhamon weaves a complex skein of allusions in relation to Veronica Manganese (PC511.10n), some of which presumably come into play here.

PC124.3 PF121.11 B108.32   a kind of voluptuous Magdalen   The reference invokes the three women whom tradition has associated with the name Magdalen—Mary of Magdala, from whom Christ is said to have purged seven devils (Luke 8:2), Mary of Bethany, who annointed Christ's feet with perfume and wiped them with her hair (John 12:3), and the unnamed prostitute who also wiped Christ's feet with her hair (Luke 7:38).

PC124.8 PF121.16 B108.28   scapular medal   *Scapular:* "1 a: a long wide band of cloth with an opening for the head worn front and back over the shoulders as part of a monastic habit b: a pair of small cloth squares joined by shoulder tapes and worn under the clothing on the breast and back as a sacramental and often also as a badge of a third order or confraternity" (Merriam-Webster's *Collegiate Dictionary*). *Scapular medal:* "a medal worn in place of a sacramental scapular" (Merriam-Webster's *Collegiate Dictionary*).

PC124.21 PF121.27 B109.10   V. has expressed a desire to be a sister   Victoria Wren had briefly entertained a similar desire (PC69.28).

PC125.30 PF122.32 B110.13   the gift of tongues   The novel makes at least half a dozen references to Pentecost (see, particularly, PC7.11n), not all of them consistent with any single symbolic pattern. At a stretch, one might see the possibility of the alligator's being infused with the Holy Spirit as an indication of Profane's instinctive desire for the redemption of the preterite. At the same time, the miracle is just one of three that Profane envisages, and the other two—the resurrection of the crazy Father Fairing and the intervention of the rat Veronica—do not lend credibility to the first.

PC126.2 PF123.1 B110.21   mainspring and escapement   An echo of Profane's nightmare (PC35.6) in which he fears that his "clock of a heart" may be "left behind to litter the pavement."

PC126.13 PF123.12 B110.35 catechumen *Catechumen:* "1: a convert to Christianity receiving training in doctrine and discipline before baptism 2: one receiving instruction in the basic doctrines of Christianity before admission to communicant membership in a church" (Merriam-Webster's *Collegiate Dictionary*). "Fairing's treatment of the rats . . . resonates with the hints in *Heart of Darkness* that Kurtz may have descended into cannibalism" (Booker 23).

PC126.27 PF123.22 B111.6 "Roony" Pittas-Giroux claims that "the nickname derives from *The Education of Henry Adams:* William Henry Fitzhugh 'Roony' Lee, the son of Robert E. Lee, was a classmate and friend of Adams's at Harvard" (108).

PC128.34 PF125.22 B112.42 His wife was an authoress Mafia seems to be a somewhat broadly drawn caricature of Ayn Rand, whose novels also expound a theory of how "the world can . . . be rescued from certain decay." Kharpertian sees a broader target in "the writers of popular romances" (68).

PC129.6 PF125.29 B113.7 It wasn't much of a Theory "As women are characteristically shown during this period, [Mafia] has no capacity for the ideal; her 'vision' sinks to an absurd level of physicality, a mockery of the ideal which men like Herbert Stencil are still able to envision" (Allen 43).

PC131.8 PF127.24 B114.4 Dashiell Hammettlike Richter (130) wonders if readers are being invited to remember the opening of Hammett's *Maltese Falcon:* "Samuel Spade's jaw was long and bony, his chin a jutting v under the more flexible v of his mouth. His nostrils curved back to make another, smaller, v. . . . The v motif was picked up again by thickish brows rising outward from twin creases above a hooked nose."

PC132.15 PF128.28 B115.43 had taken a Brody Steve Brodie is reputed to have jumped from the Manhattan side of the Brooklyn Bridge on July 23, 1886, to win a two-hundred-dollar bet. The sense of the expression "to take a Brody" is thus to take a suicidal leap.

PC134.29 PF130.35 B118.8 Sartre's thesis Pig's question works

on a number of levels. The sheer comic incongruity of such a reference coming out of Pig's mouth is the most obvious effect achieved,
though of course it is immediately normalized by the explanation
that occurs to Rachel—he has been "hanging around the Spoon"—
and that affords access to the broader implications of the allusion.
Most fully dramatized in La Nausée, Sartre's position is that people
tend to adopt the most readily available "identity" offered by their
culture, rather than performing the hard work of creating their own,
unique selves. The novel characterizes the Whole Sick Crew as being
made up of individuals who have constructed their identities almost
wholly from components offered by the mass media.

PC134.32 PF131.1 B118.11 they talked proper nouns Among
the finite number of "building blocks" out of which the Crew construct their vision of the world. Eigenvalue will note the dangers of
dependence on such a closed system of communication (PC317.15).

PC135.12 PF131.14 B118.25 Stencil's just been shot at Tempting as it is to try to explain this incident by assuming a connection
with our last glimpse of Profane, the fact that Stencil dodges a second
shot (Profane fires only one) leaves the usual room for the possibility
that his paranoia is justified.

PC136.14 PF132.13 B119.22 especially irregulars The oxymoronic aspect of an "organized body" of "irregulars" captures some of
the spirit of Stencil's quest. This fascination with what amounts to
the imposition of order on chaos leads Eigenvalue to think of Stencil
as someone who goes through life "grouping the world's random caries into cabals" (PC159.17).

PC136.33 PF132.30 B119.42 Collecteurs Généraux Literally
translated, this would mean "General Collectors." The nomen-
clature is somewhat puzzling as applied to a person, though, since
"collecteur" can be used as a word for "sewer," as in "grand collecteur," or "main sewer."

PC136.35 PF132.33 B120.2 with an amazing memory The
reader is surely intended to be amazed indeed that the man is able
after more than thirty years to recall a single person among many
from one group of tourists among many.

PC137.12 PF133.7 B120.14   But had found them waiting   This uninflected assertion forces us temporarily into alignment with Stencil's conspiratorial vision, inviting us to share in the possibility that mysterious opponents are indeed following him around with the intention of cutting short his investigations. By the time the incident surfaces again when Stencil discovers the Fairing/Malta connection (PC486), we are more inclined to share Fausto Maijstral's dismissive view of the "clues" on which Stencil bases his V-structure (PC487.3).

PC137.22 PF133.17 B120.25   alter kocker   Dirty old man (Yiddish).

CHAPTER SIX

Profane finds himself obliged to fend off Fina's advances, which culminate in her claiming to want him to relieve her of her virginity. Realizing that the sewer job is winding down, Profane makes perfunctory gestures in the direction of finding different work. He leaves the Mendozas' apartment and the alligator patrol after Fina is gangraped by the Playboys.

PC138.1 PF134.25 B121.22 **like accidents** His meeting with Rachel Owlglass is a case in point (PC16). The association in Profane's mind between women and accidents is a clear impediment to anything resembling a genuine relationship—as is borne out by subsequent events.

PC139.27 PF135.34 B122.28 **inanimate calluses slapping inanimate goatskin** The music Profane is trying to dance to lacks all human warmth. Appropriately, therefore, Dolores is "halfway across the room."

PC140.5 PF136.8 B122.41 **Mierda** Shit.

PC140.7 PF136.10 B123.1 **His worst memory** It seems likely that Profane is fearful of what he may have said to Fina in the phone booth on the subject of love, a dangerous topic of conversation for someone with his instinctive reluctance to commit himself.

PC140.32 PF136.35 B123.27 **Randolph Scott** American actor (1898–1987) who acted almost exclusively in westerns.

PC141.3 PF137.4 B123.34 **nothing but wrong words** "Self-identified as 'schlemihl,' [Profane] distrusts words as protective counters. Rather words, like the man-made objects that surround him, actualize his separateness; in this, words are as hostile as objects. They limit and seek to control what he wants to find on a preverbal level where he cannot and does not distinguish between rational categories as does V. (or Stencil) but, instead, becomes a voyeur who, like Mondaugen, watches but does not act" (Hawthorne 88).

PC141.11 PF137.11 B123.41 Why did she have to behave like he was a human being Despite his mistrust of inanimate objects, Profane is quite willing to become one himself in order to protect himself from the effects of human warmth. Fausto III's retreat into nonhumanity (PC330.13n) is prompted by a similar desire to buffer the self against the intrusion of feeling.

PC141.19 PF137.18 B124.6 maricón Queer.

PC142.24 PF138.21 B125.9 the Feast of San' Ercole dei Rinoceronti The feast, that is, of Saint Hercules of the rhinoceroses. Possibly modeled on the Feast of San Gennaro, which is held on Mulberry Street in September. (The Feast of San Giuseppe, which falls on March 19, is traditionally the occasion when zeppole di San Giuseppe are served. These fried cream puff rings filled with sweetened ricotta are on the menu at Pynchon's festival too.)

PC142.25 PF138.22 B125.10 Ides of March March 15, the day of Julius Caesar's assassination.

PC142.26 PF138.23 B125.11 Little Italy An area of lower Manhattan, between Houston Street in the north and Canal Street in the south, bisected by Mulberry Street, the main drag of the neighborhood.

PC142.32 PF138.34 B125.17 zeppole A kind of cheese-filled pastry.

PC143.21 PF139.15 B125.43 He wasn't comfortable in this street Mulberry Street is just part of the "mosaic of tilted street-surfaces" through which Profane moves when he is not under the street in the sewers. The real world and his dream world have come together, and the faceless people, milling about without "logic," fail to achieve the effect of humanizing the disturbing landscape of this version of Fausto's street of the twentieth century (PC347.37n).

PC143.26 PF139.19 B126.6 shiny-machined breast- and buttock-surfaces The girls are scarcely human at all. They anticipate the automata in the Rape of the Chinese Virgins (PC427.14).

PC143.32 PF139.26 B126.13   Geronimo is a tourist And like all the tourists in the novel, he is interested only in the surface features of the "sights" he singles out for attention—the women who populate the streets of the city.

PC144.7 PF139.36 B126.24   Someplace else An odd and rather heavy-handed moment. The characters in the scene hear only the music from *Madame Butterfly*—no one is singing. In order to make the connection between the band's choice of entertainment and the exchange that has just taken place between Profane and Angel, the narrator invokes a putative performance of the opera so that he can comment on the linguistic incongruity of an American and a Japanese singing to each other in Italian (Angel has just asked Profane to speak Italian to three American girls).

PC144.7 PF139.36 B126.24   the American ensign and the geisha Benjamin Franklin Pinkerton and Cio-Cio-San, the central characters in Puccini's *Madama Butterfly*.

PC144.9 PF140.1 B126.26   a tourist's confusion of tongues See PC144.7n, and Victoria's tourist's Arabic (PC67.25n). This aside seems to be about both the opera and the projected attempt to pick up the three girls. Perhaps inadvertently the tourist motif is linked with the Pentecostal imagery that also informs the novel. The "confusion of tongues" is presumably the reverse of the clarity of communication achieved by the Pentecostal gift (cf. Genesis 11:7, "Come, let us go down there and confuse their speech, so that they will not understand what they say to one another").

PC144.14 PF140.6 B126.32   Sfacim Lucille's reaction ("I don't want to sit with any nasty mouth") indicates that this word has sexual or otherwise potentially offensive connotations, a fact borne out by its absence from the standard dictionaries. Pynchon-list contributors have argued back and forth inconclusively on the subject, confirming the difficulty posed by the presence of so many dialectal variations in Italian. Some possibilities aired on the list include the Neapolitan "fucker," the Calabrese "two-faced bastard," and the unidentified "ah, shit." The latter seems the most plausible, given the translation of "sfacimento" offered by Pynchon.

PC144.34 PF140.25 B127.12   The other could knock her up higher   "The other" is presumably Profane's darker alter ego, Benny Sfacim, accidentally named by Geronimo, but real nonetheless. This is the Profane who is possessed "off and on" by "a desire . . . to be cruel" (PC146.14).

PC145.9 PF140.35 B127.22   De Nobili cigars   Modestly priced cigars.

PC146.1 PF141.22 B128.6   WPA   Works Progress Administration or, after 1939, Work Projects Administration. A federal agency created in 1935 to provide work for the millions left without employment by the Depression.

PC146.3 PF141.25 B128.8   every 39 feet   The standard length of an American rail.

PC146.4 PF141.25 B128.9   Wars don't have my beat   "My" should probably be "any."

PC146.27 PF142.11 B128.36   they hammered together a myth   "The old myths no longer work: they no longer serve significantly to frame or 'scaffold' the contemporary world (it is worth noting in passing that in chapter 1 we hear of a seaman Ploy, who is transferred from USS *Scaffold* to a mine-sweeper named *Impulsive*—a shift that may be indicative of a desirable change in ways of living in the modern world). In their place we have temporary and transient improvisations using the ephemeral detritus of the modern street. The privileged hierarchies of significance and interpretation of the past must be abandoned, and we must look to the overlooked areas of the contemporary world for new sources of meaning" (Tanner, *TP* 55).

PC148.34 PF144.10 B130.33   A pool ball lay even with his eyes   Profane's usual luck is holding, and of course his sense of being cornered by the situation with Fina is confirmed by his finding himself literally behind the eight ball here.

PC150.8 PF145.14 B131.38   Tom Mix   Star (1880–1940) of over two hundred silent western movies.

PC151.6 PF146.9 B132.31   a stranger to the world downstairs   The possibility of escape from the street-level reality of life is temporary at best. At the psychological level, Profane's journey into the depths has hardly provided him with useful insights and he is increasingly inclined to shy away from self-knowledge.

PC151.30 PF146.30 B133.13   borrowed time   Profane's "devil's advocate" is reminding him of his affinity with the alligators. Like theirs, his time in the sewers is a kind of "peace-in-tension" before the necessary return to street level, where he seems destined to deny his own humanity.

PC151.33 PF146.33 B133.16   the most perfect shape of that was dead   The Freudian note struck by Profane's projection of this death-wish onto the alligators reinforces our sense that the journey into the sewers is—though perhaps only comically—a journey into the depths of the self.

PC152.25 PF147.21 B134.3   *The Great Train Robbery*   Credited with being the first narrative film, it was made in 1903 and directed by Edwin S. Porter. Profane seems to have a taste for the silent western (PC150.8n). Perhaps the absence of words from the scenes of derring-do appeals to Profane, whose pessimistic belief in the "wrongness" of his own vocabulary has been made explicit (PC141.3n).

PC153.16 PF148.10 B134.29   George Raft   American movie actor (1895–1980) noted for his gangster roles and his broad-shouldered suits.

PC153.31 PF148.24 B135.3   while the wind streamed bleak and heatsucking   Despite the potential protection represented by the office and its promise of a job, Profane opts to confront the wind down at street level. The hothouse/street opposition that is here literally depicted is given a more explicitly figurative spin by Sidney Stencil's journal entry (PC506.20n). Nonetheless, Profane's brief moment of eye contact with the messenger gives this scene enough of a surreal quality to ensure that we do not dismiss his change of heart about the job as simple laziness on his part. The messenger has the credibility associated in Profane's mind with the world beneath the street and with the world inhabited by those whom contemporary American society has marginalized.

PC155.23 PF150.11 B136.25   pingas   Pricks.

PC156.20 PF151.4 B137.15 Behind them the street was chaos
The natural condition that prevails in the exposed territory of the street.

PC156.26 PF151.10 B137.22 Her eyes had become hollowed
The chain of associations here finds its terminus later when Fina makes it clear that she holds Profane accountable for her fate at the hands of the Playboys (PC391.34n), an accusation that Profane seems to acknowledge as just. The fact that Fina has come to resemble the barely human Lucille, with whom Profane *was* willing to have sex, suggests that he has sent the message that the only bond that can be forged between men and women is through the most mechanical and meaningless of couplings. Eddins sees Fina as a victim of the street's power to destroy symbols of potential redemption (83).

PC157.5 PF151.23 B137.36 the dream-street In both Profane's and Fausto's formulations, this is dangerous territory. Profane's dream-street contains the threat of disassembly (PC35.3), while Fausto's is the kingdom of death (PC348.29).

CHAPTER SEVEN

Stencil visits the soul-dentist Dudley Eigenvalue and is prompted to talk about his father's first encounter with Victoria Wren. We are transported to late-nineteenth-century Florence, where the young Evan Godolphin has just arrived in response to a message from his explorer father. Elsewhere in the city, Rafael Mantissa and his accomplice Cesare await the arrival of the Gaucho, whose assistance Mantissa has sought in a plan to steal Botticelli's *Birth of Venus* from the Uffizi Gallery. Victoria Wren, whom Evan Godolphin has briefly flirted with from his cab, encounters Hugh Godolphin in a church. He tells her of his discovery of a place called Vheissu, which has come to haunt his dreams, and she insists that she be permitted to help him. Evan is arrested after nearly being killed in a fall at his father's apartment and eventually ends up in the same cell as the Gaucho, who is arrested at the request of Venezuelan diplomats who believe him to be part of a plot to foment unrest in Caracas by staging demonstrations in Florence. The Gaucho is questioned by Sidney Stencil, who asks him, not about Venezuela, but about Vheissu. When police attempt to arrest Hugh Godolphin, he escapes and finds refuge, coincidentally, with Mantissa, whom he has known from years before. Sidney Stencil, the Venezuelan authorities, and the Italian secret police are all embroiled in the mix-up over Vheissu/Venezuela, which is comically complicated by the fact that the florist who sells Mantissa the Judas tree in which he intends to smuggle the Birth of Venus out of the gallery is named Gadrulfi. Victoria Wren goes to meet Evan Godolphin upon his release from prison. The Gaucho's followers march on the Venezuelan Consulate, where a riot breaks out, witnessed with fascination by Victoria. Mantissa stops

Cesare as he begins to cut the Boticelli from its frame and escapes with Hugh and Evan Godolphin to the river, where they commandeer a barge to make good their escape.

PC158 PF152 B138 *She hangs on the western wall* "The chapter title . . . constitutes an explicit link between [*The Birth of Venus*'s] position in the Uffizi and the placement of the Virgin's image on the western wall of Chartres" (Eddins 64).

PC158.5 PF152.25 B138.19 **Eigenvalue** See PC51.24n.

PC158.6 PF152.27 B138.24 **He had seen the original sponge** Pure titanium is produced by the reduction of titanium tetrachloride (obtained from a variety of crude ores) through the addition of sodium or magnesium in an argon atmosphere. The result is a porous material (sponge), which is then crushed and further refined. The fact that the narrator appears to provide confirmation of the recent origin of at least one component of the dentures (Eigenvalue had seen the sponge only a year ago), and Eigenvalue's own assertion that he made them, prepare us to share in the soul-dentist's ruminative dismissal of Stencil's conspiracy-theory outlook.

PC158.8 PF152.31 B138.26 **Clayton ("Bloody") Chiclitz** See PC51.24n.

PC159.10 PF153.17 B139.10 **a distal amalgam** A surface filling. Perhaps it takes a "conscious effort" for Eigenvalue to think of Stencil's fantasy in this way because he is aware that to do so is to acknowledge the possibility that there might be a modicum of truth alloyed with the generally illusory nature of the world-adventurer's "clues." The reflection that follows suggests that Eigenvalue is not persuaded by his own simile.

PC159.17 PF153.24 B139.16 **grouping the world's random caries into cabals** The belief that Stencil is engaged in little more than assembling a "concatenation of purely accidental details" (Hite 61) is not confined to Eigenvalue. Much of what we have learned thus far of Stencil's quest encourages us to side with the dentist. And yet, as Eddins points out, there is some danger that too ready a dismissal of Stencil's "vignettes of cabalistic intrigue" causes them to "collapse into fodder for a rationalistic debunking of the very notion that history might be shaped by conscious, premeditated agency, and the book's essential mystery is dissipated into rather flaccid satire" (51). The novel depends rather heavily upon our willingness to sympathize with the impulse that lies behind Stencil's pursuit of V., even as we retain a degree of skepticism regarding the actual V-structure that he brings into being in the process.

PC159.28 PF153.35 B139.27   the Situation   Stencil's adoption of his father's vocabulary (cf. "Chiclitz the munitions king" [PC51.24n]) is one of many indicators of the presence in the novel of a thematic strain focusing on parents and children—the two Godolphins, Fausto and Paola Maijstral, Mélanie L'Heuremaudit and her father, in addition to Sidney and Herbert Stencil.

PC160.6 PF154.11 B139.43   intimate with the details of a conspiracy   Stencil's reasons for believing this are mysterious, to say the least. The reader does not know what has led him to Eigenvalue in the first place. It is not until May that the dentist introduces Stencil to Chiclitz (the present conversation is taking place in mid-April), so the V-rocket connection that is established via Mondaugen has yet to be made; why, then, does Stencil regard Eigenvalue's association with Chiclitz with suspicion? He hasn't seen the dentures, though perhaps he has heard about them from one of the Crew (Charisma is seen groaning over an Eigenvalue root canal [PC131]). The whole tenor of the chapter's opening is a salutory reminder of the way in which the reader is drawn into Stencil's frame of reference through a barely sustained set of guilt-by-association connections and coincidences.

PC160.16 PF154.20 B140.11   Prosthetics   At the most literal level, Stencil presumably chooses the last "field" on Eigenvalue's list because he knows about the dentures and is merely trying to provoke the dentist into some kind of admission. By this time, however, we have been sufficiently alerted to the figurative significance of the displacement of the organic by the inert to recognize that, despite our willingness to share Eigenvalue's dismissive attitude toward Stencil's random groupings, we are drawn once again into a degree of complicity with his attempt to make meaning. Fergus Mixolydian's sleep-switch, Bongo-Shaftsbury's electric switch, and Evan Godolphin's experience at the hands of the opportunist Halidom are all called to mind in support of Stencil's "surprising" choice.

PC160.23 PF154.25 B140.17 Fauchard Pierre Fauchard, eighteenth-century French dentist and author of the textbook *Le Chirurgien Dentiste*, of which Eigenvalue possesses a first edition.

PC160.24 PF154.27 B140.18 Chapin Aaron Harris American dentist (1806–60) and author of *Principles and Practice of Dental Surgery* (1845); one of the founders of dentistry as an organized profession.

PC161.8 PF155.8 B140.39 only the poor skeleton of a dossier "He's trying to find out what there is of V. outside of V.-text. Of course there is nothing—only the dossier, this history, his story of V., the totality of just more V-text. Nothing but noting" (McHoul and Wills 167).

PC161.9 PF155.9 B140.39 Most of what he has is inference A key admission, which adds considerably to the wariness with which we are beginning to evaluate everything we "learn" about V. The primary means by which Stencil attempts to bring his quarry to light— "impersonation," "dream," "inference," "forcible dislocation of personality"—are responsible for much of the novel's epistemological slipperiness. And yet, short of concluding that the novel intends *only* to make fun of Stencil's overanxious meaning making, a strategy that, as Peter Cooper points out, runs the risk of "eviscerating" the novel (quoted in Eddins 55), we are obliged to match the text's disruptive strategies with a willingness to suspend our instinctive desire for certainty and the closure it can bring.

PC161.23 PF155.22 B141.10 any of a thousand Great Paintings The generality of this admission gives way in the actual narrative of events in Florence to the details of Mantissa's obsession with the Botticelli Venus, reminding us yet again of Stencil's ability (and his compulsion) to render specific what in fact has clearly remained blurred and indeterminate.

PC161.26 PF155.26 B141.13 one of those grand conspiracies One might argue that only in Stencil's predisposed and fertile imagination could the events with which Victoria Wren becomes "tangentially" involved be regarded as "grand." Although the comic opera machinations of the Gaucho and the Figli di Machiavelli take a somber turn in the violence of the riot, the Vheissu affair descends steadily into farce as one coincidence or misunderstanding gives way to the next. On the other hand, the chapter generates the same general aura of pre–World War I power politics as do the events in Egypt, reminding us of V.'s association with events that were far from farcical.

PC161.29 PF155.29 B141.17   the surface accidents of history Typical of the ambiguous manner in which the novel presents Stencil's quest. The clear implication here is that beneath the accidental configurations of any given moment in time there exists a kind of deep and abiding structure—"V. and . . . conspiracy"—which is the real object of Stencil's investigations. Yet Eigenvalue's subsequent musings on the gathers in history's fabric that follow invite us to question, as he does, Stencil's ability to see past the "surface accidents" that configure the particular ripple in which he is caught. Once again we are obliged to consider the possibility that Stencil in fact is unable to perceive anything other than the temporary semblances of order afforded by his own subjective engagement with the past.

PC162.1 PF155.35 B141.24   sinuous cycles This anticipates one of the early Faustos, who refers in his journal to the "regular and sinusoidal" rhythms of history (PC327.33n). Unlike Eigenvalue, however, who appears to regret that "we are . . . lost to any sense of a continuous tradition" (PC162.7), Fausto regards "continuity" as a "fiction," a by-product of our tendency to "humanize" history (PC326). While both men view Stencil's undertaking with amused skepticism, they do so for quite different reasons. Eigenvalue supposes that it might be possible to achieve a vantage point from which to recover a sense of the continuity of human experience, and therefore dismisses Stencil's conspiracy theory approach as the product of a limited vision. Fausto, on the other hand, sees it as symptomatic of the desire to create apparent continuity in a world where none exists.

PC162.11 PF156.9 B141.38 a costume too Esthetic for such a fat boy "Evan is an English chap out of Gilbert and Sullivan or late-Victorian/Edwardian fiction, but also a prodigal . . . returning to his father" (Dugdale 88). Aestheticism as a movement had its champions in the persons of such figures as Oscar Wilde, Walter Pater, and James McNeill Whistler.

PC162.20 PF156.18 B142.5 F.R.G.S. Fellow of the Royal Geographic Society.

PC162.26 PF156.26 B142.12 Dickens's Fat Boy Appears in *Pickwick Papers* as a comic, though slightly sinister figure associated with the Wardle family of Dingley Dell. "I wants to make your flesh creep," he says at one point.

PC163.3 PF156.34 B142.22 a characteristic acquired from the age Presumably the "compulsion to glory" that he has spent some time resisting.

PC163.10 PF157.3 B142.29 Dartmouth The Royal Naval College.

PC163.19 PF157.11 B142.41 a bay named Cher Ballon It is no doubt just one of those nagging coincidences that Evan is about to make the acqaintance of Victoria Wren, the "balloon-girl" of both Stencils—Herbert as Yusef the factotum and Sidney in his own person (see PC63.30n).

PC163.25 PF157.16 B143.2 Vheissu A number of readers find allusions to issues of identity in the name: "If 'Vheissu' encodes anything, it is a pun—'Wie heisst du?,' 'What is your name?'—that parodies Stencil's preoccupation with *sub rosa* identities" (Hite 54). See also Eddins (65), "The insidious message of Vheissu is: 'V.'s you,'" and Cooley (313), "One of the many possible decodings of the word Vheissu [is] *V, he is us; V, she is u.*" Cooley adds that this "amounts to an assertion that the distinction between the dark places and the civilized ones, between Kurtz's 'mad' soul and our own, is illusory, or more alarming, that the categories may be precisely reversed." Bonnie Surfus also acknowledges the implied question about naming but adds that it may be possible to read the name as another question—one that takes the implied German more literally than idio-

matically and becomes "How are you called?"—as in "How can I get
in touch with you?" Following Chambers, who finds a number of
anticipatory references in the novel to the "fat boy" atomic bomb,
Surfus goes on to argue that "the two meanings could imply very
different sentiments: one, a request to know someone's name; the
other, a kind of secret password, a way to evoke the god/gods/god-
dess. I favor the 'goddess' reading. And in both forms of the German
expression. For if Vheissu is representative of the development of
the bomb, then 'Vheissu' could express either a question—what do
we call this mystery? OR a prayer to whatever force is behind this
discovery" (Pynchon List, February 22, 1995). Heikki Raudaskoski
finds a cognate in the Sami word "viessu," which means "a mountain
hospice" (Pynchon List, July 2, 1996).

**PC163.28 PF157.20 B143.6   outlandish regions where the Estab-
lishment held no sway**   The Conradian associations that many critics have noted in other contexts are reinforced here in Evan's characterization of Vheissu as a place akin to the "region of the first
ages . . . where no warning voice of a kind neighbour can be heard
whispering of public opinion" that Marlow enters in pursuit of Kurtz
(Conrad 85).

PC164.5 PF157.31 B143.20   the author of *The Renaissance*   Walter Pater (1839–94), "English critic, essayist, and humanist whose ad-
vocacy of 'art for art's sake' became a cardinal doctrine of the movement known as Aestheticism" ("Pater, Walter," *Britannica Online*).

PC164.9 PF157.35 B143.23   a cabal grand and mysterious   The
language ensures that we remain conscious of Stencil's guiding consciousness in the account of events in Florence.

PC164.15 PF158.4 B143.30   like a parlay of horses   Like "gaggle
of geese" or "singular of boars," this has the ring of one of those
specialist terms for a group of particular animals. However, James
Lipton's *Exaltation of Larks,* surely the modern bible on the subject,
does not list it. Presumably, then, Pynchon is being somewhat literal
and suggesting that a group of horses gathered head to head as if
in conference might then act collectively in a manner not to be explained by any analysis of each individual horse's disposition.

PC165.5 PF158.28 B144.13 Signorina . . . Miss, oh, pretty lady, are you English?

PC165.33 PF159.8 B144.32 Signor Mantissa See PC167.4n.

PC166.1 PF159.21 B145.3 Cellini Benvenuto Cellini (1500–1571), celebrated Florentine goldsmith.

PC166.11 PF159.31 B145.15 for they reflected a free-floating sadness Cowart suggests that the sadness in Mantissa's eyes may derive from Walter Pater's descriptions of the melancholy of the Venus (15).

PC166.16 PF159.35 B145.19 gentle-eyed Mazzini Giuseppe Mazzini (1805–72). "Genoese propagandist and revolutionary, founder of the secret revolutionary society Young Italy (1832), and a champion of the movement for Italian unity known as the Risorgimento. An uncompromising republican, he refused to participate in the parliamentary government that was established under the monarchy of the House of Savoy when Italy became unified and independent (1861)" ("Mazzini, Giuseppe," *Britannica Online*).

PC166.32 PF160.14 B145.37 Like Machiavelli he was in exile Perhaps the reference is to the eight years between 1513 and 1521 when Niccolo Machiavelli (1469–1527), Florentine statesman and most famously the author of *The Prince* (1513), was out of favor with the governing Medici family and retreated from public life to his family's estate outside the city.

PC167.1 PF160.17 B145.41 the same patterns Stark (112) compares Mantissa's cyclical theory of history with Dnubietna's "step-function" vision of discontinuity (PC355.33n) and Fausto I's wave-function view (PC327.33n).

PC167.3 PF160.20 B146.1 that inner circle of deracinated seers Mantissa's name generates a typical doubleness of allusion. On one hand, as Newman has noted, the name derives from the Greek word for seer—*mantis* (55)—on the other, a mantissa is "an addition of comparatively small importance, esp. to a literary effort or discourse" (*OED*). From the first of these comes the association of Mantissa with figures such as Eliot's Tiresias (Newman 55, Dugdale 89). From the second comes Cowart's assertion that "Mantissa comes to be representative of the fate of his melancholy nation, reduced to makeweight status in two world wars—and almost the Germans' makeweight in both" (15). Perhaps, too, this second association is yet another of the novel's reminders about the dangers of attaching too much significance to trifles.

Cowart maintains that Mantissa's idealizing of a thing of beauty associates him with the cult of aestheticism (14), while Dugdale finds a broad range of allusions to draw on: "Mantissa is another synthesis: in his rather cloudy political past, he recalls Conrad's ineffectual anarchists, notably the angelic Michaelis; in his attempt to steal the *Birth of Venus* he is a *reductio ad absurdum* of the aesthete in the school of Pater, who gazed at the 'sinister smile' of the Gioconda, and wrote a chapter on Botticelli in *The Renaissance: Studies in Art and Poetry*. . . . As 'a man in love with Venus' [PC224] he is the self-styled 'wrinkled Tannhauser,' Henry Adams. The description of his face identifies him with the general Yeatsian idea of the mask, and with the golden form of the Byzantium poems. There are echoes of Rilke (the 'street-long festival of sorrow' of the fair in the *Leid-stadt* in the Ninth 'Duino Elegy' . . .), who wrote a poem called 'The Birth of Venus' and saw the painting in 1898; and of Eliot (of the seer Tiresias, who foresuffered all, and of the fisher King musing by the canal), reinforced by others elsewhere in the chapter ('continuous tradition' [PC162], 'family reunion' [PC197]). It is noticeable that these allusions tend to assert the continuity between the turn of the century and Modernism, transferring to the latter the Decadent sense of Europe as 'a gallery one is familiar with but long weary of, useful now only as shelter from the rain, or some obscure pestilence' [PC167]" (88–89).

PC167.6 PF160.22 B146.3 Decadents of England and France "In England the Decadents were the poets of the 1890s—Arthur Symons ('the blond angel'), Oscar Wilde, Ernest Dowson, and Lionel Johnson, who were members of the Rhymers' Club or contributors to *The Yellow Book*" ("Decadent," *Britannica Online*). In France the poets Verlaine, Rimbaud, and Mallarmé and the novelist Huysmans were among the writers who were identified with the term.

PC167.6 PF160.23 B146.4   the Generation of '98 in Spain   A group of writers and intellectuals loosely associated under this appellation, among them Unamuno, Pio Baroja, Angel Ganivet, and Ramiro de Maeztu. They were collectively influenced by the spirit of pessimism that possessed Spanish society in the wake of the Spanish-American War, when the last remnants of Spanish imperial glory were lost. Mantissa is thus associated via the image of adjacent circles with the gloom of the Spanish fin de siècle, with its sense of a present rendered dismal in the afterglow of a glorious past, and with the challenge to both literary and social convention offered by the English and French writers.

PC167.11 PF160.28 B146.10   Il piove, dolor mia . . .   My pain rains down / And still I cry.

PC167.18 PF160.36 B146.19   Vedi, donna vezzosa . . .   Behold, fair lady, this poor fellow / Always singing of love like a steamship.

PC167.26 PF161.6 B146.28   the Gaucho   Dugdale points out that "the Gaucho is a Nostromo in reverse, a Latin American come to Italy" (88). Cowart sees him as a Conradian "psychological double" of Victoria Wren and links him, via his "wideawake hat," with the German soldiers in South-West Africa and Victoria's "aborigine-suppressing uncle in Australia" (15–16). Vukimorich suggests Katherine Anne Porter's short story "Flowering Judas" as a source for the character of the Gaucho (22).

PC168.21 PFH161.33 B147.14   Be a man   The Gaucho's machismo stands in direct contrast to the aestheticism that motivates Mantissa and prepares the way for his exaggerated enthusiasm for the activist side of Machiavellian doctrine.

PC168.35 PF162.10 B147.29   Last year in Venezuela   In 1898, the government of Joaquín Crespo rigged the presidential election to secure victory for a puppet candidate, prompting the opposition candidate, José Manuel Hernández, to begin a revolution (Marsland 218). Presumably, the "they" of whom the Gaucho speaks are Crespo and his cronies.

PC169.9 PF162.18 B147.39   the lion and the fox   Mantissa may well be forgiven for favoring the cunning approach. In chapter 18 of

The Prince, Machiavelli is fairly clear where he stands: "You must know there are two ways of contesting, the one by the law, the other by force; the first method is proper to men, the second to beasts; but because the first is frequently not sufficient, it is necessary to have recourse to the second. Therefore it is necessary for a prince to understand how to avail himself of the beast and the man. This has been figuratively taught to princes by ancient writers, who describe how Achilles and many other princes of old were given to the Centaur Chiron to nurse, who brought them up in his discipline; which means solely that, as they had for a teacher one who was half beast and half man, so it is necessary for a prince to know how to make use of both natures, and that one without the other is not durable. A prince, therefore, being compelled knowingly to adopt the beast, ought to choose the fox and the lion; because the lion cannot defend himself against snares and the fox cannot defend himself against wolves. Therefore, it is necessary to be a fox to discover the snares and a lion to terrify the wolves" (137–38).

PC169.27 PF162.35 B148.15   the last chapter of *Il Principe* Chapter 26, "An Exhortation to Liberate Italy from the Barbarians."

PC169.30 PF163.2 B148.18   the Medici . . . were the foxes, and he hated them The Gaucho is overlooking the fact that *The Prince* was written in an attempt to curry favor with the Medici and that, though Machiavelli had good reason to hate the family on whose orders he had been imprisoned and tortured, he was not averse to resorting to deception in order to press the cause of Italian unification.

PC169.31 PF163.3 B148.19   a lion Cowart regards the Gaucho's approving citation of Machiavelli's call for "an embodiment of power" as an indication of the likelihood that his Garibaldean republicanism will readily shade in a couple of decades into an allegiance to Mussolini's fascism (16).

PC171.1 PF164.7 B149.20   Capo di minghe! Dickhead!

PC171.23 PF164.29 B150.1   The Judas tree A generic name for trees of the genus *Cercis*. Mantissa's gratuitous reference to the color of the tree's flowers suggests that the tree is *Cercis siliquastrum*. The

name "Judas tree" comes from the belief that Judas Iscariot, Christ's
betrayer, hanged himself from such a tree. "The 'genealogical tree' of
the Virgin is the Tree of Jesse. . . . Its parodic counterpart in V. is the
hollow Judas tree" (Eddins 64).

PC172.1 PF165.4 B150.15 Aspetti Wait.

PC172.32 PF165.34 B15.4 She is so beautiful "Pynchon's allusions to the Botticelli masterpiece make the painting an ironic emblem for the book's eponymous character at the inception of her
decadent career" (Cowart 14). Following Henkle's lead, Cowart employs a pun—"The birth of V-ness"—to link the painting with the
novel's central motif. "Whereas the goddess of love in Botticelli's
painting is born in daylight out of the breezy Aegean, V. is born at
night in the midst of tumult. As one of the most representative cultural totems of the civilization whose decline the advent of V. inaugurates, the Birth of Venus stands for all that is endangered by the
new dispensation embodied in V." (19).

PC172.33 PF165.35 B151.5 Davvero Truly.

PC173.1 PF166.2 B151.11 late of Lardwick-in-the-Fen, Yorks
See PC67.13n.

PC173.32 PF166.30 B151.42 beginning to detest anarchists
Victoria's budding political awareness anticipates the growing association between V. and the politics of the right.

PC173.32 PF166.31 B151.43 the Fabian Society "Socialist society founded in 1883–84 in London, having as its goal the establishment of a democratic socialist state in Great Britain. The Fabians
put their faith in evolutionary socialism rather than in revolution"
("Fabian Society," *Britannica Online*).

PC173.32 PF166.31 B151.43 even the Earl of Rosebery Rosebery was British prime minister for fifteen months (1894–95) and
headed a Liberal Party unable to agree sufficiently to overcome
strong Conservative tendencies in the House of Commons. That
Victoria should find herself detesting "even" this most ineffectual of
liberals is sufficient indication of the direction her political beliefs
are taking.

PC174.2 PF167.1 B152.7   an ivory comb   The comb shows up again in the hair of the Bad Priest (PC368.20n) and in the possession of Paola Maijstral (PC478.8n).

PC174.9 PF167.7 B152.14   the crucifixions of '83   None of the accounts of the Mahdist uprising in the Sudan that I have read, including two almost contemporary accounts by men not inclined to downplay any factor that might redound to the discredit of the Mahdi (Winston Churchill and F. R. Wingate), makes any mention of crucifixions.

PC174.10 PF167.7 B152.15   Her motives . . . may have been . . . uncomplex   Since we have every reason to associate Victoria with other avatars of V. who appear throughout the novel, we should probably be skeptical about this possibility.

PC174.24 PF167.20 B152.29   a nunlike temperament pushed to its most dangerous extreme   "Pynchon's description of her thoughts at this time calls attention to the heretical and esoteric quality of her faith: attaching no guilt to the extra-marital quality of her relationships with men, she seeks absolution because her affairs fall short of her goal of union with a metaphysical ideal" (Graves 65).

PC175.14 PF168.9 B153.13   I want to confess   "A final iconographic detail . . . may be intended by the author's having Victoria often attended by Hugh or Evan Godolphin. Their surname puns on the name of the aquatic mammal that attends the goddess in certain ancient representations, e.g. the Aphrodite of Cyrene" (Cowart 19).

PC175.32 PF168.27 B153.33   He started telling her about Vheissu   A variety of suggestions have been made as to the provenance of the Vheissu motif. Newman (54) and Berressem (passim) invoke Poe's "Narrative of Arthur Gordon Pym," Tanner suggests that it is a mixture of Borges and Conrad ("V2" 35), and New finds "elements of myth and medieval romance" (104). Both Eddins (64) and New (104) refer to Vheissu as a fantasy.

According to Berressem, the account of the journey to Vheissu "is a carefully constructed collage of several interwoven topoi. It is a stylized journey from the extreme North to the extreme South (see also Mondaugen's North/South obsession), and a journey through parts of South America mingled with exotic elements" ("Pym" 6). Madsen finds echoes of Dante: "his description of the geographical approach to Vheissu is allusive of the landscape through which Dante makes his descent into Lower Hell. The 'treacherous swampland,' for instance, recalls the Marsh of Styx, across which Dante travels to the gate of Lower Hell. . . . Godolphin's 'vast tundra' is reminiscent of the Plain of Dis, the vast plain filled with the cries of entombed heretics; the 'dolmens and temples of dead cities' are allusive of the city of Dis, where skeptics and heretics are tormented. The 'vast tundra' also recalls the sandy waste that separates the second and third circuits of the seventh circle of Hell" (46–47).

PC176.11 PF169.4 B154.5 fury-ridden The Furies were the Greek goddesses of vengeance who arose from the underworld to avenge violence committed against family members.

PC176.20 PF169.12 B154.14 You are Godolphin We may be tempted momentarily to adopt a Stencillian response to this indication that Victoria knows who Godolphin is. A few lines later, however, our suspicions are explicitly laid to rest when she says that she has read about his exploits in books and newspapers. Godolphin is clearly quite famous.

Dugdale maintains that Godolphin "is, as a hero of Empire, an amalgam of historical figures, such as Scott, Stanley and Gordon . . . , with characters in the fiction of such writers as Haggard and Kipling. . . . As an adventurer equally estranged from his own civilisation and from the primitive society he flees to, he corresponds to the central characters, Kurtz and Jim, in the tales Conrad wrote in the 1898–1900 period" (89).

PC177.1 PF169.27 B154.31 the wrong reasons Godolphin has clearly come to mistrust the jingoistic rhetoric of imperialism, haunted as he is by his sense of the more complex and private compulsions that drove him toward the Vheissu and the Pole and by his constant awareness of what he discovered in each place (PC215.28).

PC177.2 PF169.28 B154.32 the Chinese campaigns The two so-called Opium wars (1839–42, 1856–60), in the second of which Charles Gordon, later to die at the termination of the siege of

Khartoum (PC178.35n), distinguished himself sufficiently to become known as "Chinese Gordon."

PC177.4 PF169.30 B154.35   Englishmen dying in South Africa today   Godolphin is presumably referring to the Boer War, though hostilities between the British and the Boers did not break out until mid-October 1899 and this conversation is taking place in April.

PC177.17 PF170.6 B155.5   Vheissu is hardly a restful place Though the association is anachronistic, the reader may well be reminded of James Hilton's Shangri-La as a contrast to Vheissu.

PC177.30 PF170.18 B155.19   a madman's kaleidoscope   Another echo from Conrad, who gives the same simile to Marlow in *Lord Jim* (Dugdale 89). "This perpetual singularity . . . is finally the chaos and randomness of the entropic vortex no longer held at bay by such unifying symbols as the Virgin and Eden" (Eddins 65). "The colours of Vheissu, which take no meaningful shape, like a 'madman's kaleidoscope,' perhaps correspond to the semantic shape-shifting that Dante finds punished in the Inferno" (Madsen 47).

PC177.34 PF170.22 B155.23   She was taken by surprise   Victoria is momentarily disconcerted by Godolphin's presumably coincidental choice of the county of her birth for the site of his analogy. Given the circumstances of her estrangement from her family, she can be forgiven for wondering if Godolphin is hinting at his awareness of her history (which may include, of course, the incident with Ralph McBurgess in the theater in Lardwick-in-the-Fen).

PC178.6 PF170.30 B155.30   They are skin too   Godolphin's role in the novel seems to be to remind us of the possibility that beneath the surface of our public institutions and practices lies a void. In the wake of recent theorizing in the area of post-colonial studies, however, our reading of this passage is likely to be complicated by our wondering whether Godolphin's failure to find "the soul of that place" is not in part the result of his being forced to read Vheissu through the lense of British imperialist attitudes.

PC178.22 PF171.8 B156.5   a dark woman tattooed from head to toes   The image seems to be an adaptation of the scene in *Heart of Darkness* when Marlow sees the "gorgeous apparition" of the woman on the bank of the river near Kurtz's station (100). In the increasingly violent language of his extended metaphor, Godolphin aligns himself with Kurtz, upon whom "the fascination of the abomination" has worked to create an appetite for just such "abominable satisfactions" as Godolphin suggests could be found in the figurative flaying alive of the tattooed woman. "Godolphin expresses a sadistic sexuality that is one of Pynchon's dominant images for European colonialism" (New 101). Twenty-three years later, at the urging of Vera Meroving, Godolphin will be seen putting into diminished though nonetheless disturbing practice the impulses he unguardedly reveals to Victoria Wren, as he whips the hanging Bondel (PC295).

Other readings of the scene stress its contribution to the surface/depth motif that runs through the novel; "since the Romantics, writers have been fascinated by the *topos* of art as the painted veil over the abyss, the pattern obscuring the void, or, as Hugh Godolphin sees it, the tattooed skin that conceals Nothing. But this version of underlying chaos is thoroughly hyperbolic because it denies the name of order to any state of affairs short of a comprehensive 'plot'" (Hite 65). "The desire to tear into the tattooed surface of things in order to discover the soul beneath, and the desire to stand in the dead center of the carousel are in reality one and the same—the urgent need, in all human beings, to master the flux of life's variegated surface, its inexorable movement of the future into the past" (New 101).

PC178.35 PF171.23 B156.19 directly after we'd entered Khartoum Pynchon has strayed from the historical record here in order to afford Godolphin the occasion for the disgust that prompts him to take on the surveying job that leads him to Vheissu. The small British force sent to relieve Gordon at Khartoum (after months of delay caused by the indecisive policies of the British government) arrived two and a half days after the victorious forces of the Mahdi had lowered the British flag. No one from this force entered the occupied city to bear witness to the effects of the six hours of unrestrained killing and looting that followed the breaching of the defenses (Theobald 121).

PC179.5 PF171.27 B156.24 To General Gordon Against the express orders of the Mahdi, a contingent of his soldiers had stormed Gordon's command post at the palace, where they stabbed and hacked him to death before decapitating him (Theobald 121).

PC179.15 PF171.35 B156.35   Contour lines . . . blank spaces The passage has a close parallel in *Heart of Darkness:* "True, by this time it was not a blank space any more. It had got filled since my boyhood with rivers and lakes and names. It had ceased to be a blank space of delightful mystery—a white patch for a boy to dream gloriously over. It had become a place of darkness" (Conrad 33).

PC180.2 PF172.20 B157.17   espionage activities There is no indication that Godolphin is attempting to mislead Victoria by pretending to be some kind of spy, but nothing suggests that he is in Florence for any reason but to pursue his own urgent preoccupation with the memory of Vheissu. Victoria's enthusiasm for the clandestine has presumably been sparked by her affair with Goodfellow and is clearly increasing. There is no mistaking the eagerness with which she "harangues" the old explorer in an attempt to become part of whatever sub rosa dealings he is engaged in.

PC182.2 PF174.11 B159.7   carefully slit each cigarette "The discovery is so improbable, so contrived, that surely Pynchon takes an ironic stance toward it" (New 105).

PC182.34 PF175.5 B159.43   how accidental was it, really? Like so many similar questions the novel raises, either directly or indirectly, this one is never answered.

PC183.16 PF175.21 B160.17   Even one we have never heard of This implausible remark is calculated to maintain the chapter's somewhat melodramatic tone and of course provides yet another occasion for the introduction of intimations of conspiracy.

PC184.6 PF176.9 B160.43   Look at Uruguay Ratón is presumably referring to the revolution of 1897, which ended with the assassination of the country's president.

PC184.23 PF176.23 B161.18   the same continent "This cavalier explanation resembles Stencil's grasping at circumstances to discover conspiracy where none may exist" (Slade 60).

PC187.17 PF179.8 B163.39   specifically to organize the Venezue-

lan colony   Presumably in support of the revolutionary ambitions of Cipriano Castro, who had been preparing to make his bid on the presidency for a number of months (Marsland 218).

PC187.30 PF179.21 B164.10   things were quiet in Caracas   Not for long. On May 23, 1899, Cipriano Castro launched the five-month campaign that would end with his assumption of the presidency in October of the same year.

PC187.34 PF179.25 B164.14   only two years since settlement of the boundary dispute   The date is off here. A long-standing dispute between Venezuela and Britain over the latter's claim to certain portions of neighboring British Guiana had come to a head in 1895 and an appeal had been made to the United States. Grover Cleveland invoked the Monroe Doctrine in support of Venezuela and diplomatic tensions ran high. The two disputants agreed to arbitration, but it was not until 1899 that a decision was handed down (Marsland 217).

Cooley (319) regards this as an example of the novel's deliberate invocation of events that fail to materialize into crises—the Fashoda incident being a case in point. He argues that the novel "denies us the battles and political 'events' we have called history, foregrounding instead, the people, events and places that have fallen between the cracks" (319). (See PC161.26n.)

PC188.5 PF179.31 B164.22   Cuernacabrón   Perhaps a tautology—a cuckold with a set of antlers—or perhaps "a cuckolded pimp."

PC188.6 PF179.32 B164.22   Scheissvogel's beer garden   The Gaucho, "being a tedesco in spirit" (PC186.7), has chosen his favorite rendezvous accordingly. That it is also the choice of Hugh Godolphin for his meeting with Evan sounds a few warning bells and the reader is likely to wonder at the echo of the German beer hall in Cairo (PC87.20), where Hanne the barmaid is invited by her lover Lepsius to indulge in a spot of amateur espionage. Once again, we are invited to indulge our appetite for patterns of connectedness, and once again we are left with little more than speculation. Porpentine's portentous speculations about Sir Alastair Wren's enthusiasm for Bach (PC92.13n) are repeated in Sidney Stencil's supposition that the Godolphins could also be in the employ of the Germans (PC200.4), and we might be forgiven for assuming that Pynchon is using "German" as a catch-all for the darker human impulses which the novel chronicles. "Scheissvogel" might loosely be translated as "bird shit."

PC191.14 PF182.29 B167.16   compulsion to beg shrift "Like the Ancient Mariner, himself the survivor of a terrible experience at the South Pole" (Cowart 21).

PC192.33 PF184.6 B168.32   He felt isolated from a human community Having been confronted with the "hard dead-point of truth" (PC193.14), which tells him of the empty abyss beneath the surface of human culture, Godolphin not surprisingly finds himself yearning for the very community he professionally shunned during all his years as an explorer. The sense of isolation he experiences here is akin to Profane's feeling of being alone in the streetscape of his dream (PC34.13).

PC193.6 PF184.13 B168.40   the Campagna's fevers The once marshy lowland plain surrounding Rome was notoriously unhealthy. Visitors particularly ran the risk of contracting malaria.

PC193.7 PF184.14 B168.42   Ludgate Circus Thomas Cook's son and partner, John Mason Cook, presided over the company's move to enormous and rather grand premises in Ludgate Circus at the east end of Fleet Street in London in the early 1870s. Pynchon's assumption is that a Cooks tour would begin and end at the company's head office.

PC193.8 PF184.16 B168.43   a peregrine or Don Juan of cities The tourist is cast as a predator, both literally and as the sexually voracious libertine who pursues his own pleasure without any thought of the true humanity of his victims.

PC193.10 PF184.18 B169.2   that interminable Catalogue, that non picciol' libro In Mozart's *Don Giovanni*, Leporello regales Donna Elvira with a list of Don Giovanni's amorous conquests in the "catalogue" aria ("Madamina, il catalogo è questo"); the notebook in which he has kept his record is, he assures her, not a small one.

PC193.12 PF184.21 B169.5   the suicidal fact That is, the "Nothing" that he finds beneath the Polar ice (PC215.28). In wondering whether he is bound to keep silent, Godolphin reveals some kinship with Fausto Maijstral, who conceives of the poet's job as one of cloaking the mindlessness of the universe in "comfortable and pious metaphor" (PC349.28) in order to protect his fellow human beings from the truth.

PC195.24 PF186.10 B170.33 Port Said   Egyptian port that provides the entry point from the Mediterranean into the Suez Canal.

PC196.2 PF186.36 B171.19 Gadrulfi the florist   The florist's name is both sufficiently like and sufficiently unlike Godolphin's to signal clearly the comic-opera nature of the confusions and misunderstandings that ensue.

PC197.16 PF188.8 B172.29 the seeming vastness of that street   Another slightly sinister streetscape in which human endeavors seem to fade into insignificance like the "revolutionary song" that Cesare is singing.

PC197.23 PF188.17 B172.41 the current Foreign Minister   Pynchon presumably means the British Foreign Secretary Lord Salisbury, who was also Prime Minister at the time. The exact source of Sidney Stencil's irritation at his boss is unclear, though it is possible that Salisbury's reputation for behind-the-scenes diplomacy was sufficiently widespread to lead Sidney to attribute the "appalling" nature of the current "Situation" to the machinations of the Foreign Office under Salisbury's guidance.

PC198.16 PF189.4 B173.24 Later, when you're done   Sidney's masculine assumption of Victoria's sexual availability, as evidenced by his "giving" her to Demivolt, is ironic in the light of the fact that it is she who eventually seduces him, at least in his recollection (PC528.20n).

PC198.34 PF189.20 B173.42 costermongers   Fruit and vegetable sellers operating from carts on the street.

PC199.3 PF189.23 B174.3 no Situation had any objective reality   Sidney's thoughts on the subject of "Situations" reflect an ambivalence that resembles the reader's response to Herbert Stencil's various attempts to make sense of the V-phenomenon. On the one hand, we are ready to share Eigenvalue's (and Sidney's) judgment that clusters of events assume meaning only in the eyes of the beholder, but on the other, we recognize and sympathize with the urge that prompts Sidney to pursue "rapport" and Herbert to pursue connections.

PC199.6 PF189.26 B174.6 more mongrel than homogeneous "The word 'mongrel' carries here, as usual, a pejorative sense, and in *V.* with its acute awareness of race and colonialism, it carries a less abstract meaning as well—a racial mixture. Sidney Stencil's insistence on a 'degree of rapport' suggests an ethnocentrism which serves to protect his version of The Situation from epistemological and political dissolution and guarantees the exclusion of the kind of discrepant or non-synchronous experience that Said and Bloch speak of" (Holton 331).

PC199.10 PF189.30 B174.11 degree of rapport "If, as Lyotard argues, the terror and the sublimity of the event lie in part in its unrepresentability, then for Sidney Stencil there is at least safety in numbers. Truth, or knowledge, thus ultimately becomes a problem not of verification (or at least not of verification alone) but of consensus, privileging the homogeneous over the heterogeneous" (Holton 331).

PC199.19 PF190.3 B174.20 northern/Protestant/intellectual . . . Mediterranean/Roman Catholic/irrational Sidney's cultural bias is mirrored in the distrust of the South that Kurt Mondaugen shares with his countryman Karl Baedeker (PC243.33). In each case the negative sentiments are the result of a conviction that order is more likely to prevail under the governance of reason and the enforcement of dispassionate rules of conduct. For Sidney, teamwork is the key; for Mondaugen, science; for Baedeker, the timetable.

PC200.6 PF190.24 B175.1 a member of the Dreibund The Dreibund, or Triple Alliance, was a (supposedly) secret agreement among Germany, Austria-Hungary, and Italy, made in 1882 and modified from time to time over the next thirty years. Sidney's position in the Foreign Office is sufficient to explain his awareness of the existence of the alliance. He is clearly assuming that Italy and Germany are likely to be working together in a fashion hostile to British interests. This reflects official British skepticism toward rumors that the treaties explicitly expressed the desire to maintain cordial relations with Britain (Giffen 124). Recent tensions between Germany and Britain over the former's stance toward the Fashoda incident would no doubt be in the forefront of Sidney's mind.

PC200.20 PF191.1 B175.17   Deauville   Resort town on the Channel coast of France, just south of Le Havre, where Evan Godolphin has been "recuperating after two months of good-natured lechery in Paris" (PC163.17).

PC201.19 PF191.34 B176.13   a loud morra game   A game in which two players simultaneously hold out a certain number of fingers, while calling out what each guesses will be the total of fingers extended. The player who guesses the total correctly wins a point.

PC201.35 PF192.11 B176.30   Savonarola   From 1494 until his death in 1498, Girolama Savonarola was the head of a democratic Florentine government. A member of the Dominican order, he was passionately committed to the reform of the Catholic church, a mission that he pursued with enough vigor to earn the deadly enmity of the Pope. He was hanged and burned on May 23, 1498.

PC203.15 PF193.23 B177.41   So Vheissu becomes a bedtime story   The Vheissu that is depicted in Evan's recollections of his father's yarns does indeed sound like an imaginary and fabulous domain, but, apart from the "human sacrifice," it is notably different from the "feral and lunatic dominion" (PC215.34) of Hugh Godolphin's current accounts, the tenor of which Evan can only intuit from the behavior of the Italian and British authorities. Because Evan's renewed faith in his father's sanity is the product not of any concrete demonstration of the existence of Vheissu but only of a set of responses to the assumption that it does exist, we can scarcely follow his lead entirely in our assessment of Captain Hugh's reliability. Here, as in much of the rest of the novel, we must negotiate an understanding of a narrative that combines the playful with the portentous, the farcical with the metaphysical, and refuses to come to rest within any one mode.

PC203.20 PF193.28 B178.3   something that could not have been an accident   "But of course there is no reason to believe that it is not. No reason, that is, unless one has already inherited and made his own the structure of one's father, for whom there are no accidents but only patterns" (New 105).

PC203.23 PF193.31 B178.7   this condition of being just human Having been persuaded to see past his boyhood disappointment at his father's fallibility, Evan now comes to regard "being just human" as a positive attribute, thus invoking the novel's depiction of the various ways in which contemporary humanity surrenders to the inanimate.

PC203.31 PF194.2 B178.15   Call it a kind of communion   Tanner notes that the word "communion" occurs with some frequency in the novel and suggests that it invokes "notions of community (and communication)" as well as referring to Holy Communion (*TP* 52). Although sometimes ironically inflected (for example, in the "communal wine" that is circulating at one of the novel's many parties [PC453.14] and the "absolute communion" of tourism [PC441.23]), it is often, as here, the signifier of a kind of hope in the face of the possibility of extinction. Fausto uses the term in relation to the sense of identification he achieves with his island home during the bombing (PC336.24).

PC204.2 PF194.8 B178.22   Cinque, tre, otto   The successive guesses of the morra players (PC201.19n).

PC204.29 PF194.34 B179.8   Un' gazz'!   "Una gazza" = "magpie."

PC205.5 PF195.8 B179.20   the Quadruple Alliance   The joke seems rather too esoteric to be widely appreciated outside "spy circles." The Englishman can scarcely be referring to the Quadruple Alliance of 1815 among Britain, Austria, Russia, and Prussia, nor to the Quadruple Alliance of 1834, which Britain and France formed with claimants to the thrones of Spain and Portugal. Since neither of these alliances involved Italy, the joke would make no sense. Given Ferrante's musings on the Triple Alliance (PC206), it seems that the point of the joke lies in the Englishman's *anticipation* of Britain's joining the three other European powers in what would then be a quadruple alliance, an outcome that Ferrante regards as unlikely in the extreme.

PC205.12 PF195.15 B179.27 someone should assassinate Umberto I The king was in fact assassinated by an Italian anarchist on July 29, 1900. The assassination followed on the heels of the imposition of martial law and the savage repression of recent unrest in the country after the failure of Italian colonial policies (PC72.13n), and Ferrante's disgust is probably prompted by his own knowledge of and perhaps participation in the repressive tactics of the government.

PC205.28 PF195.31 B180.1 Palestrina Vogt's mother's "illusion" that she has had an affair with Giovanni Palestrina is indeed "curious" since the composer died in 1594. Note that the comic tone of this reference invites our derision, whereas we are not so quick to dismiss "Mehemet's recurring lament" that he too belongs to a distant era (PC496.34).

PC206.4 PF196.4 B180.14 Since 1882 When the Triple Alliance was formed, making Germany and Austria-Hungary allies of Italy.

PC207.14 PF197.10 B181.16 Not when a barbaric and unknown race . . . Another instance of the wildly vacillating tone of the chapter, which here once again turns farcically melodramatic. The fact that Vogt's mother's fantastic summary is a paraphrase of Sidney Stencil's supposedly secret report to his superiors is a clear invitation to the reader to surrender any vestige of credulity that might still remain regarding the reality of the so-called grand cabal, which the Italians and the British believe they are uncovering. However, although the activities of the spies are thus conclusively ridiculed, the chapter nonetheless retains a certain haunting quality, derived from Hugh Godolphin's passionate recollections of his experiences in Vheissu and at the Pole. Private nightmares are no less real because the world's affairs are conducted at a high pitch of absurdity.

PC208.13 PF198.6 B182.10 It could stand for Venus And of course, for Mantissa, Vheissu and Venus do come to stand for the same thing (PC221.25).

PC208.28 PF198.19 B182.26 Via del Purgatorio and Via dell'Inferno Florentine geography evidently conspires to provide a location that begs for allegorical interpretation. Victoria Wren, as a still young avatar of the V-principle, might be supposed to be situated on the cusp between salvation and damnation. Evan Godolphin describes it as a "still point between hell and purgatory" (PC212.9n), a phrase that has an echo in his father's description of the Pole as "one of the only two motionless places on this gyrating world" (PC216.24n).

PC209.14 PF199.2 B183.6 She overrated virtú Victoria's "private gloss" on Machiavelli, like the Gaucho's, fails to take into account the blending of force and cunning that the concept of virtú represents. "It is true that, unlike any other humanist writer, [Machiavelli] openly associates princely *Virtú* not with law (which he deems often insufficient to the combat that is ineliminable in politics), but with the abilities to dispense violence, or imitate the lion, and practice deception, or imitate the fox" (Dietz 18).

PC209.16 PF199.5 B183.8 that sort of imbalance While in one sense this identification of a fin-de-siècle falling away from cultural health has its parallel in the novel's critique of mid-twentieth-century decadence (McClintic Sphere's equilibristic recommendation—"Keep cool, but care" [PC393.25]—is relevant here), the statement of the problem as a "tilt toward . . . the less forceful" reminds us of the association that comes into being between V. and the exercise of absolutist kinds of power.

PC209.18 PF199.7 B183.10 standing stone-still at the crossroads "No longer the sacred Triple Goddess, she now supports the Trinity of Father, Son, and Holy Ghost of Catholicism, a patriarchal religion, and is implicated in the entire patriarchal shift, which has left us slouching inevitably toward the most sinister Trinity of all— the bomb" (Chambers 76).

PC209.34 PF199.22 B183.27 as some doctors of the mind were beginnning to suspect Pynchon offers few clues to the identity of these "doctors of the mind." The language of the passage that follows would appear to invoke Jungian notions of the collective unconscious, but Victoria's Catholicism can hardly have its roots in the theories of someone who had yet to begin the internship in the asylum that inspired his famous theories.

PC211.23 PF201.3 B185.5 As if something trembled below its

surface   Victoria seems to be picking up on the intelligence community's anxiety over the supposed tunneling activities of the inhabitants of Vheissu.

PC211.26 PF201.6 B185.8   Fra Angelico   Guido di Pietro (c. 1400–1455), "also called Giovanni da Fiesole, Italian painter, one of the greatest 15th-century painters, whose works, within the framework of the early Renaissance Florentine style, embody a serene religious attitude and reflect a strong classical influence" ("Angelico, Fra," *Britannica Online*).

PC211.26 PF201.6 B185.9   Titian   Tiziano Vecellio (1490–1576), a Venetian painter.

PC211.27 PF201.7 B185.9   Brunelleschi   Filippo Brunelleschi (1377–1446), "architect and engineer who was one of the pioneers of early Renaissance architecture in Italy. His major work is the dome of the Florence Cathedral (1420–36), constructed with the aid of machines that Brunelleschi invented expressly for the project" ("Brunelleschi, Filippo," *Britannica Online*).

PC211.28 PF201.8 B185.10   they say radium changes   Evan is very much up to the minute in his analogy; it was less than a year before this moment that Marie Curie had discovered radium's existence.

PC211.31 PF201.11 B185.14   Perhaps the only radiance left is in Vheissu   Victoria's rather mournful comment reflects the degree to which she has already appropriated Hugh Godolphin's experience and begun to formulate her own "private gloss" on it, as she has with Machiavelli (PC209.13). In her reappearance as Vera Meroving, her fascination with Godolphin takes a darker turn.

PC212.6 PF201.21 B185.25   guitar, violin and kazoo   The anachronistic kazoo is a Pynchon trademark. It surfaces again in the reference to the lost Vivaldi kazoo concerto (PC453.5).

PC212.9 PF201.23 B185.29   some still point between hell and purgatory   "Victoria the Forster/James girl tourist turns into Porpentine's Manon and Mata Hari. Here, meeting Evan at the crossroads . . . she becomes a parody of Dante's Beatrice and Eliot's Lady in the white gown in 'Ash Wednesday'" (Dugdale 88).

PC212.9 PF201.23 B185.29 there's no Via del Paradiso An observation whose pessimistic allegorical implications appear to be borne out by the novel as a whole.

PC212.12 PF201.26 B185.31 they seemed to give up external plans As Tanner points out, "this idyll of unpatterned emotional directness is momentary" ("V2" 33).

PC212.18 PF201.32 B185.38 the strolling chains of tourists like a Dance of Death "Also called Danse Macabre, medieval allegorical concept of the all-conquering and equalizing power of death, expressed in the drama, poetry, music, and visual arts of western Europe mainly in the late Middle Ages. Strictly speaking, it is a literary or pictorial representation of a procession or dance of both living and dead figures, the living arranged in order of their rank, from pope and emperor to child, clerk, and hermit, and the dead leading them to the grave. The dance of death had its origins in late 13th- or early 14th-century poems that combined the essential ideas of the inevitability and the impartiality of death" ("death, dance of," *Britannica Online*). The concept surfaces on three other occasions in the novel: during the dreamlike re-creation of the events of 1904 (PC278.11); in the Rusty Spoon, when Stencil is told about it by a friend of Slab's (PC315.17); in the subway, where Stencil wonders if the flow of commuters represents the "Dance of Death brought up to date" (PC323.12).

PC214.13 PF203.19 B187.22 Some Hofbrauhaus of the spirit The Höfbrauhaus beerhall in Munich was the site of the founding of the National Socialist German Workers' Party. The association of the tourists who frequent Scheissvogel's with this birthplace of Nazi politics aligns them (and tourists in general) with V.

PC214.34 PF204.3 B188.1 some truth to tell to a son "Through legacy, the interpenetrations of past and future generations, there comes about an acceptance of 'dreams of order,' or rather a participation in them, that seems to me one of Pynchon's more hopeful suggestions for the role of art in human affairs. Certainly when Mantissa speaks about it to Hugh Godolphin, he suggests at one and the same time the idealized role of father, priest, artist, critic—what it is we would like to believe we do" (New 106).

PC215.20 PF204.24 B188.25 in the mad dances called Cook's tours See PC212.18n. Although the link is with the earlier reference to the Dance of Death, the idea of the "mad dances" is more consistent with another medieval dance phenomenon known as Saint Vitus's Dance, in which mobs of dancers would fling themselves about in a violent frenzy.

PC215.22 PF204.25 B188.26 the explorer wants its heart The contrast that Godolphin expresses here, between surface and depth, is another of the novel's more or less explicit nods in the direction of *Heart of Darkness*, in which Kurtz, like Godolphin, discovers a hollowness beneath the surface veneer afforded by so-called civilization. Note, too, in Godolphin's earlier description of Vheissu as a tattooed woman, the implied lengths to which the explorer may be ready to go in order to penetrate beneath the skin of a place.

PC215.28 PF204.32 B188.34 It was Nothing I saw We have perhaps already been afforded a hint of the consequence of Godolphin's "vision of the existential abyss" (Cooley 315) in his internal response to Victoria's naive admiration for his exploits (PC177.1n). The old notions of Queen and country have come to seem like mere surface decoration, the sense of order they provide illusory at best.

PC216.3 PF205.5 B189.3 I have been at the Pole Godolphin thus beat Roald Amundsen to the South Pole by some thirteen years.

PC216.24 PF205.26 B189.25 one of the only two motionless places on this gyrating world "A familiar conceit, this actually locates what T. S. Eliot calls, after St. John of the Cross, 'the still point of the turning world'" (Cowart 20). Dugdale also cites Eliot, comparing the Antarctic to the waste land (89).

PC216.35 PF206.1 B189.38 the corpse of one of their spider monkeys "Beneath the Vheissu-like 'hard blue ice' of Cocytus where Dante sees tortured shadows, Godolphin finds the spider monkey frozen in the Antarctic ice. But Dante discovers Satan, Dis, frozen upside down in the lake of Cocytus: if the spider monkey is a 'mockery of life,' then Dis is a mockery of meaning—an infernal inversion of divine beauty, order and harmony. . . . Dante's vision of immobilized chaos is comparable to the 'dead center of the carousel' which is Vheissu" (Madsen 47). Cooley sees an "inconclusive" allusion to the leopard carcass in Hemingway's "Snows of Kilimanjaro" (319).

Chambers looks to the history of the atom bomb for a key to the allegory of the monkey: "Suffice it to say that when Godolphin penetrates the Antarctic and sees the blue-green monkey, he represents the scientist Ernest Rutherford, who penetrated the core of the atom, a penetration that would lead to the Trinity test site. . . . The blue-green spider monkey frozen in the ice at the heart of unexplored territory, like Einstein's 'energy locked into structures in a "frozen" state' tells the awesome tale of the thrilling struggle for knowledge. . . . Godolphin sees in the Antarctic the discovery of the properties of uranium" (Chambers 71,73).

PC217.2 PF206.3 B189.40   I think they left it there for me   "The response is not a logical one, but in Pynchon's world it is the expected one. . . . Godolphin is unable to rest in meaninglessness but instead is driven to a construct, however malevolent, in which the personal struggle to order life is good and diametrically opposed to the universal mystery that mocks the struggle and is therefore evil" (New 102).

PC217.11 PF206.11 B190.7   a dream of annihilation   As Madsen points out, the novel itself depends on a kind of resistance to Godolphin's insight: "Whilst a character like Hugh Godolphin or Raphael Mantissa may conceive of V—as Vheissu or Venus—as a type of void, a 'gaudy dream, a dream of annihilation,' the ongoing development of the narrative plot is directed towards the construction of a figural system in which V is the primary object of interpretation" (29). According to Dugdale, "The ideas of the Antarctic as a dream of annihilation, of colour as a disturbing mask, and of the world as nothing but surface, can all be traced to Melville" (89).

PC217.17 PF206.17 B190.14   What truth I came to   "That truth is the final product of the phenomenon of colonialism, of which Godolphin represents the other aspect, in which the imperialist seeks to possess what he has conquered, only to end by being debased by the slave's submissiveness" (Slade 62).

PC219.18 PF208.12 B192.3   He did not hear her eagerness   Victoria's taste for violence will soon find an outlet when she actually joins in the riot in front of the Venezuelan consulate (PC527.28).

PC220.18 PF209.9 B192.40   as if she saw herself embodying a feminine principle   "The riot is the birth, really, of Anti-Venus, the modern perversion of the goddess who so serenely reigns on the 'western wall' of the museum that is human civilization" (Cowart 20). "At home in the riot at the end . . . she is the woman in Yeats' 'No Second Troy,' Maud Gonne, a figure whose career has several parallels with hers" (Dugdale 88).

PC221.19 PF210.7 B193.37   What sort of mistress, then, would Venus be?   "Signor Mantissa was this Waste Land's Tiresias, knowing and foresuffering all in that single, intense moment in the Uffizi" (Cowart 22).

CHAPTER EIGHT

Profane allows his erection to determine which employment agency he will go to and thus finds himself once more in contact with Rachel Owlglass, who sends him off to a job as a night watchman. The history of Pig Bodine's adventures as the generator of pornographic radio messages is related, Roony Winsome approaches Rachel in an effort to get closer to Paola and Profane is initiated into the ways of the Crew. Stencil, who has met a German engineer called Kurt Mondaugen, begins to tell Eigenvalue the story of Mondaugen's experiences in Southwest Africa.

PC226.27 PF214.34 B198.29   Inanimate money was to get animate warmth   While Profane's mistrust of the inanimate aligns him, like the young Schoenmaker, with the "Good Guys," his somewhat cynical formulation of the relationship between money and sex is a reminder of his marginal status among the company of the righteous.

PC227.9 PF215.13 B199.4   inanimate schmuck   That Profane should think of his penis as inanimate speaks volumes about his attitude toward sex.

PC227.14 PF215.17 B199.9   a bum lying across the aisle   "Taken together, the Crew, as caricatures of alienation, and Profane's fellow victims, as very real examples of disaffection, make up the 'highly alienated populace' Sidney Stencil had prophesied in 1919 [PC506.27]" (Slade 111).

PC228.21 PF216.20 B200.11   a true windup woman   An anticipation of another fantasy of Profane's, the "all-electronic woman" (PC414.24). The image is linked with V. through the association with the clock eye worn by her many avatars. Bongo-Shaftsbury's reference to a "clockwork doll" (PC78.8) also comes to mind, as do the automata of Satin's ballet (PC427.23). Brenda Wigglesworth's poem refers to a "clockwork figure" (PC490.18).

PC229.14 PF217.8 B200.40 any sovereign . . . yo-yo A yo-yo, that is, which is not in the control of someone holding its string. Such apparent self-determination, however, is not altogether positive, since in the case of a yo-yo it leads to inertness.

PC229.23 PF217.17 B201.7 began to doubt his own animateness Matthijs argues that the yo-yo metaphor is ambiguous: "On the one hand it is opposed to 'inutility, lonesomeness, directionlessness' but on the other hand it implies determinism, having 'a path marked out' over which one 'has no control.' The latter has very specific implications for Profane: he begins to doubt his own animateness. This means that it constitutes a threat, and that directionlessness is preferable to determinism" (131).

PC231.18 PF219.1 B202.33 Knoop "His name comes from science, The Knoop Scale, 'a scale of hardness based on the indentation made in the material to be tested by a diamond point.' It was named after F. Knoop, an American chemist" (Harder 72).

PC232.20 PF219.37 B203.30 a foulmouthed louseridden boozehound While Winsome's incredulousness at the Crockett legends is well founded, his version of the truth would seem to be equally exaggerated. The historical Crockett neither rose to the heights of the legend nor sank to the depths of Winsome's characterization.

PC232.25 PF220.4 B203.36 The song invited parody Winsome's song is a parody of the 1954 "Ballad of Davy Crockett" by Tom Blackburn and George Bruns, the first verse of which is as follows:

> Born on a mountain top in Tennessee,
> Greenest state in the land of the free,
> Raised in the woods so's he knew ev'ry tree,
> Kilt him a b'ar when he was only three
> Davy, Davy Crockett,
> King of the wild frontier.

PC234.16 PF221.27 B205.14 the passive look of an object of sadism While Winsome is projecting his own feelings for Paola onto Pig, Mafia is next door "watching herself undress in the mirror." A

complex of associations links this scene with the fetishism of the
"V. in Love" chapter—the mirror, Paola's supposed passivity, Pig's
"stag-movie fantasies" (which an imaginative stretch might connect
with the ballet that is danced to the music of Porcepic, or "pig epic").

PC237.20 PF224.14 B207.42   an Irish Armenian Jew   See
PC52.1n. It is not clear whether Fergus Mixolydian and Mafia's
young actor are one and the same.

PC238.27 PF225.21 B209.6   David Ben-Gurion   Israel's first
prime minister (1886–1973).

PC238.30 PF225.24 B209.10   Grace Kelly   American movie star
(1929–82) who married Prince Rainier of Monaco.

**PC239.3 PF225.28 B209.14   his own rathouse of history's rags
and straws**   The novel's complex epistemological stance is fore-
grounded once more in this editorial aside. Although the impulse of
each of those five million New Yorkers to create his or her own version of the past seems to be under attack here, as is Stencil's whole
undertaking throughout the novel, nonetheless we are conscious of
the fact that Pynchon himself has assembled an edifice built out of
historical fragments. Holton argues that "the building of a historical
rathouse is not simply a matter of *jouissance,* of the free play of the
imagination: such a 'postmodern style of history' would, as Foster
fears, 'signal the disintegration of style and the collapse of history'"
(338). He cites the novel's numerous invocations of historical inci-
dences of anti-imperialist struggle as evidence of Pynchon's implicit
belief in the capacity of history to give rise to truths about the human
condition.

PC239.10 PF225.34 B209.21   Stencil fell outside the pattern
Evidence of the balancing act Stencil is obliged to perform between
his desire to follow through on the hints afforded by his father's journals and his fear of losing what little impetus is provided by the quest
itself. To translate his "private version of history" into direct action,
and thus to fall within the "normal distribution of types," Stencil
would presumably have to be much more energetic in his pursuit.

PC239.14 PF226.1 B209.26   this grand Gothic pile of inferences
One of the novel's most explicit reminders that we should retain a
healthy degree of skepticism toward Stencil's quest.

PC239.19 PF226.6 B209.31   the ultimate shape of his V-structure
It is, of course, of considerable importance to Stencil that his "V-structure" never assume its "ultimate shape," since that would mean his quest had come to an end.

PC239.24 PF226.11 B209.36   about drives as intellectualized as Stencil's Note the contrast with Profane, who instinctively seeks consolation in a world that at least suggests the existence of the realm of the unconscious.

PC239.27 PF226.13 B209.40   purely the century's man Stencil's claim to be the product/representative of his age is, in one sense, a protective fiction, "something which does not exist in nature." As such, it is part of the novel's questioning of our willingness to put off our individual failings and anxieties on abstractions. On the other hand, it also reminds us that Stencil is one of the central characters in a novel whose concern is precisely with "the century" and its drift toward decay and inertia. What Stencil records in the course of (re)constructing V.'s domain is a history of the twentieth century sufficiently rooted in fact to serve as social critique, and sufficiently skewed by idiosyncrasy and comic exaggeration to leave room for a meta-critique of history itself.

PC239.32 PF226.20 B210.2   quite purely He Who Looks for V.
Stencil's anxiety at the thought of bringing his hunt for V. to an end is bound up in the fact that, as this designation indicates, he has no identity beyond his role as quester after V. Hite points out that, "though Stencil defines himself as He Who Looks for V., it is the reader who keeps running into her—or it" (55), reinforcing the parallelism of the reader's own attempt to find meaning in the novel with Stencil's efforts.

PC240.8 PF226.28 B210.13   metempsychosis The passing of the soul from one body to another.

PC240.8 PF226.30 B210.14   his quarry fitted in with The Big One The fact that the point of view here so nearly aligns with Stencil's makes both the tone and the content of this passage worth attending to. The designation "The Big One" seems almost self-deprecatory in its degree of overstatement, as if Stencil is conscious of the need to distance himself from believing too literally in the existence of "the century's master cabal." The comparison with Victoria Wren's involvement in "the Vheissu plot" further suggests that Stencil recognizes the role played by coincidence in the creation of his V-structure. Even more telling is the added comparison with Father Fairing's deranged association between Veronica the sewer rat and a whole new "rat-order." If V. "fits in" to a grand conspiracy through a combination of fortuitous connection and private delusion, then possibly the grand conspiracy itself is at best a kind of metaphorical structure. The fact remains, however, that Stencil is attempting to come to terms with an undeniably real history of violence and atrocity, and so "The Big One," for all its distancing effect, at least names as a possibility the existence of an underlying pattern of human agency.

PC240.30 PF227.13 B210.37   rate and free gyros Rate gyroscopes are used for such purposes as measuring rate of turn in aircraft or roll rate in ships. Free gyroscopes, like "sovereign yo-yos" (PC229.14), must come under a degree of control before they can be used for practical purposes.

PC241.18 PF227.36 B211.19   Kurt Mondaugen "Mondaugen" = "moon eyes."

PC241.19 PF227.36 B211.19   Peenemunde A village in northeastern Germany where the V rockets used against Britain in World War II were developed and tested.

PC241.19 PF228.1   Vergeltungswaffe Eins and Zwei The V-1 and V-2 rockets. Literally, "vengeance weapon one and two."

PC241.29 PF228.11 B211.31   Stencilized "Stencil's version of Mondaugen's story is narrated with an overlay of historiographical conscience by a professed truth-teller: male violence toward women as sadomasochism; Africa as playground for European fantasies; Herero genocide as Holocaust dress rehearsal; colonialism as sex tourism; imperialism as psycho-cultural conquest" (Sanders 86).

CHAPTER NINE

Kurt Mondaugen has been posted to Southwest Africa in 1922 to conduct observations of radio waves known as sferics. He has been alarmed by inklings of unrest among the Bondelswarts people of the region and is advised by a local administrator that he would be safer if he were to seek refuge at the farm of an erstwhile German colonist. Mondaugen stays at Foppl's for two and a half months, entering an increasingly hallucinatory state of mind in which the decadent behavior of the house's inhabitants becomes mingled with recollections of the campaign of 1904, when German troops exterminated sixty thousand Hereros, and of its aftermath. Among the participants in Foppl's siege party are Vera Meroving (who appears to be Victoria Wren) and Hugh Godolphin.

PC242 PF229 B212   Mondaugen's story   "'Mondaugen's story' is an allegory, much in the tradition of *Heart of Darkness*, in which Africa is called upon to provide a space in which the European Zeitgeist can be visited by its disavowed spectral double" (Sanders 82). According to Dugdale, "the principal literary echoes are of *Der Zauberberg* (1924) [Thomas Mann's *Magic Mountain*] (the engineer arriving at an enclosed community of the sick, and becoming sexually bewitched) and *Der Steppenwolf* (1927) (the two women, the assimilation of the studious hero into decadence), with Hesse's carnival scene a point of overlap with Poe ['The Masque of the Red Death']" (92). Berressem also notes the parallels with Poe's story ("Godolphin" 4).

PC242.1 PF229.2 B212.21   the Warmbad district   Warmbad is about twenty-five miles north of the border between South Africa and what is now Namibia.

PC242.4 PF229.4 B212.23 Kalkfontein South   About thirty-five miles north of Warmbad.

PC242.8 PF229.8 B212.27   Willem van Wijk   According to Pittas-Giroux, the name is a joke. "Van Wijk . . . bears the name of one of the first tribal chiefs to sign 'protection' agreements with the European settlers. The original Willem van Wyk was a leader of the mixed-race Bastard tribe of Rehoboth District. The Bastards habitually sided with and spied for the white settlers against their fellow natives" (177).

PC242.9 PF228.9 B212.29   Windhoek   The administrative center of the South-West Protectorate and now the capital of Namibia. Windhoek is some five hundred miles north of Warmbad. Van Wijk is an official of the South African administration of the protectorate.

PC243.3 PF230.9 B213.1   depression-time in Munich   Inflation caused in part by the burden of reparation payments after World War I produced economic hardship in Germany that would lead to the total collapse of the economy eighteen months later.

PC243.4 PF230.10 B213.2   mirror-time in the South-West Protectorate   Following World War I, when South African troops defeated German colonists, German Southwest Africa was placed under the control of the Union of South Africa by a League of Nations mandate. The reference to mirror-time takes us back to the image of the clock in Schoenmaker's waiting room (PC46.18) and to the associated notion of mirror-time as a kind of repetition or recapitulation of time already passed (PC52.1). Later associations between Munich's carnival time and the decadence of the siege party reinforce this reference.

PC243.7 PF230.13 B213.5   sferics   Short for radio atmospherics—brief signals triggered by lightning strokes.

Critics have noted the metaphorical function of Mondaugen's research project, commenting on the similarity between the sferics and the fragments of information that Stencil is assembling (Campbell 65; Madsen 42). The analogy between Stencil's quest and the reader's meaning-making efforts is also noted: "The Mondaugen-sferics metaphor describes a sort of linear algebra: it seems to be a relatively

simplistic statement of the relationship between literary interpretation, which stands for the act of making meaning in an infinitely
various world-text, and all epistemology, which often seems to be no
more than listening to the atmosphere speak to itself through a jerry-
built radio" (Porush 124).

PC243.8 PF230.14 B213.6   H. Barkhausen   Heinrich Georg Barkhausen (1881–1956). German physicist best known for his discovery
of certain properties of magnetism known as the Barkhausen effect.

**PC243.23 PF230.28 B213.22   what had once been a German col-
ony**   Germany's annexation of Southwest Africa was a gradual affair, spanning the years from 1884 to about 1902. The colony passed
into the control of the Union of South Africa under a League of
Nations mandate in 1920. Mondaugen's discomfort mirrors that of
many of his compatriots back home as Germany continued to smart
under the political and economic burdens which had been growing
increasingly onerous in the years since the war.

PC243.35 PF231.3 B213.35   Fasching   Munich's equivalent of
Mardi Gras.

**PC244.15 PF231.16 B214.7   Abraham Morris has crossed the
Orange**   Morris had been living in South Africa as an employee of
the South African army. His decision to return coincided with the
growth of unrest over a dog tax, first imposed by the German administration and then quadrupled by the South Africans. "The Bondels,
who needed dogs for hunting, tried to raise the tax by selling their
stock, carting wood, and burning lime, but, living on the extreme
edge of destitution (the official report), were hard pressed to find
the money. Between September 1921 and January 1922, no less than
140 cases for failure to pay the tax were taken before the magistrate,
and one hundred men were convicted and sentenced to fines of £2 or
fourteen days' imprisonment.

"It was at this time that Morris, Christian, and a handful of followers decided to return home, although they had been denied official
permission. The arrival of a party of fifty men with women and children produced a White panic that 3,000 Nama were gathering to attack, and the police were alerted" (First 101).

PC245.7 PF232.7 B214.36 Jacobus Christian and Tim Beukes
Christian was the de facto leader of the Bondels, but Beukes had been appointed as chief by the South African administration.

PC245.12 PF232.12 B214.40 Veldschoendragers The Habobes, a Hottentot tribe.

PC245.12 PF232.12 B214.40 Witboois One of the Hottentot tribes of Namibia (also known as the Koweses), whose paramount chief Hendrik Witbooi had stubbornly resisted German incursions until his defeat at Naukloof in 1894 (Soggot 3).

PC245.30 PF232.28 B215.16 spread to the Portuguese frontier
Sanders suggests that this comment of van Wijk's is a significant interpolation by Pynchon into the language of the report on which the account of the arrest of Morris is based. He links it with van Wijk's later claim that the days of von Trotha are back (PC246.11). "The . . . report wants to hide the fear and assert rationality in terms of and by means of the law. Pynchon knows that this is futile; the fear enters in parenthesis, obliterating internal African divisions, as the local administrator's mind sets to work, not unpoetically, from the sense-data of a European geography of occupation, imagining a rumor" (90).

PC245.31 PF232.29 B215.18 Die lood van die Goevernement . . .
The language is reproduced verbatim from the 1923 *Report of the Commission Appointed to Inquire into the Rebellion of the Bondelzwarts.* For comprehensive reproductions of source material concerning the uprising of 1922, see Dewaldt.

PC246.11 PF233.6 B215.34 the days of von Trotha are back again Between the years 1904 and 1910, German troops under the command of General Lothar von Trotha systematically exterminated some 80 percent of the Herero population of Southwest Africa.

PC246.24 PF233.19 B216.3 an ordered sense of history and time Dugdale finds an echo here of Eliot's concept of myth (116).

PC247.21 PF234.14 B216.38 a flurry of gunfire Pynchon has departed from his source with regard to the timing (PC248.12n).

P247.26 PF234.18 B216.43 As usual a party was in progress
This clearly invites comparison with the lifestyle of the Whole Sick Crew.

PC247.27 PF234.19 B217.1 pargeting Ornamental plaster work.

PC248.5 PF234.33 B217.17 In here we shall hold Fasching. . . . a state of siege The retreat into merrymaking behind closed doors clearly echoes Poe's "Masque of the Red Death," while the reference to the state of siege is a forewarning of the likely reappearance of V., whose natural habitat it is (PC57.18n "Toledo").

PC248.12 PF235.1 B217.23 two and a half months Pynchon's sources indicate that the incident that sends Mondaugen scurrying for safety in Foppl's farm—the attempt by van Niekerk to arrest Abraham Morris—occurred on May 8. Mondaugen thus arrives at Foppl's on the morning of May 9. By about July 24, when he leaves, the real rebellion would have been over for almost six weeks, having come to an end with the surrender of Christian and Beukes on June 7 or 8 (the reports are contradictory on this date). Pynchon has extended the duration of the unrest in contradiction of his sources presumably in order to add weight to the siege motif that informs the chapter. He has also added details which suggest that actual gunfire was widespread from the beginning. In fact, military operations occupied only the period from May 29 until June 7.

PC248.20 PF235.10 B217.31 sealed off from the outside world "Foppl's fortress . . . stands as a . . . means . . . to arrest time, to replay history . . . an environment hermetically sealed off from the outside world, perpetuating a redundancy of movement as thorough as that of the clock" (Cain 74–75). The hothouse metaphor that comes into play later in the novel is anticipated here in the aura of nostalgia that increasingly informs Mondaugen's story.

PC248.29 PF235.20 B217.42 a tiny European Conclave or League of Nations "Pynchon's insight into colonialism in Namibia is radical in that he interprets the colonial conflict as blind impersonal and dehumanizing forces united by violence and sadism. His understanding of the relationship between metropole and frontier is in line with revisionist historiography. Pynchon connects the frontier to the metropole by placing metropolitan decadence in the desert and making it part of the wasteland it has created. The effect is of the frontier viewed through a metropolitan grid superimposed on it" (Haarhof 37–38).

PC249.31 PF236.19 B218.38 not in good taste Mondaugen's reaction to the roof garden is consistent with his "distrust of the South," and is reminiscent of Sidney Stencil's "northern/Protestant/intellectual" (PC199.19) attitude toward Italy. At the same time, however, Mondaugen's increasing alienation from the decadent world of the siege party is adumbrated in his distaste for the gamey aesthetic of the terrace.

PC250.7 PF236.30 B219.7   Vera Meroving   "The last name, Meroving, evokes the slack Merovingian dynasty [in sixth-century Gaul] which subdivided its ever shifting lands and was characterized by chronic warfare. The first name, Vera, means 'faith,' but its other connotations qualify that meaning. That is, the wood of the vera tree is used as a substitute for lignum vitae—literally, 'wood of life.' Also, the wood of the vera tree is characteristically yellow (a color which recurs incessantly in *V.*), the same color as the alloys of vanadium, for which 'V' is the chemical symbol" (Lhamon 79). Richter hears "where-am-I-roving" (109).

PC250.8 PF236.30 B219.8   Lieutenant Weissmann   "A professional Aryan even in name" (Richter 109).

PC250.16 PF237.2 B219.16   her left eye was artificial   Chambers notes that a number of books on the Goddess devote space to her "magic eye" (79). "By making this artificial eye also a watch, Pynchon suggests the shift from cyclic time to clock time. . . . If, as some myths explain, the Goddess's power is concentrated in her eyes, then the replacement of her powerful eye with an artificial one indicates her complete usurpation" (79). According to Madsen, "Victoria Wren's desire to shape historical events to the form of her own choosing [is] now reified in Vera's elaborate clock-eye" (41).

PC251.30 PF238.13 B220.28   as if Mondaugen had dreamed them   This anticipates the later passages in which the ontological status of Mondaugen/Stencil's observations is called into question.

PC251.34 PF238.19 B220.32   notes which to German ears should have remained natural   My colleague Michael Farley offers the following gloss:

Within the Western European tradition of art music (1600's up to the late-19th Century) a great deal of the drama of a work stems from a careful delineation between major and minor modes. The major/minor issue rides, in part, upon the question of whether the third degree (of a seven-pitch scale) is four half-steps (a major third) above the first degree of the scale, or three half-steps (a minor third) above. The quality (major or minor) of the seventh degree of the scale is an additional identifier. A composer/performer moves cautiously in getting from one of these modes to the other, i.e., with a great deal of respect for their dramatic potential.

In the traditional and popular musics of a number of cultures (Western European, Cuban, Slavic, Arabic, Iberian, African, African-American) which might have contributed to the formation of tango, the playful interchange of major and minor thirds and sevenths is a constant. It is not that the expressive attributes of thirds and sevenths have been lost: they are enhanced. Artists use a striking array of effects to bring the transition from one of these intervals to the other to the listener's attention (e.g., growls and other timbral distortions in combination with a gradual sliding between pitches). The stable (stuffy) fifth degree undergoes the same expressive treatment.

If we are to assume a common cultural stereotype, i.e., that Germans are the dyed-in-the-wool custodians of the Western European tradition of art music, we can assume that this kind of facile "play" in the use of major/minor intervals (that is, indeed, a notable characteristic of tango) might set German ears on edge. (Personal correspondence)

PC252.7 PF238.26 B220.43   sjambok   A strong and heavy whip made of rhinoceros or hippopotamus hide (*OED*).

PC252.23 PF239.2 B221.12   Hedwig Vogelsang   Both Stark (102) and Haarhof (35) note that the agent for Adolf Luderitz (the first and most aggressive German appropriator of land in Southwest Africa) was named Heinrich Vogelsang. Dugdale identifies Hedwig as "the generic figure of the girl temptress, exemplified by the Lulu of Wedekind, Berg and *Pandora's Box*" (92). "Vogelsang" = "birdsong."

PC252.28 PF239.6 B221.21   interior winds which could not have

arisen by accident   Evidence, perhaps, of the effect of Stencilization on Mondaugen's story. Like Evan Godolphin's speculation regarding the broken stairs (PC182.34), this casual evocation of the possible presence of a manipulative human agency is more plausibly the product of Stencil's mindset than Mondaugen's.

PC252.34 PF239.13 B221.28   long before Caprivi (some even before Bismarck)   Leo von Caprivi was German chancellor from 1890 to 1894, having succeeded Otto von Bismarck, who was chancellor from 1871.

PC253.3 PF239.17 B221.33   hung all in black velvet   Berressem ("Godolphin" 4) notes the echo here of a description in "The Masque of the Red Death."

PC253.6 PF239.19 B221.36   Foppl's own planetarium   Eddins regards the planetarium as a mirror of the process of "surrogation," which is dramatized in the events of 1904 and in the suppression of the uprising that is going on outside the gates of the farm. That process, in which "humanity systematically exterminates humanity in defiance not only of life-affirming morality but of the life principles inherent in nature," is "a cosmic usurpation." The gold leaf covering Foppl's artificial sun "is an index to the parody of nature's life-sustaining processes by dead artifice that informs the novel's structure, while the 'coarse cobweb of chains, pulleys, belts, racks, pinions, and worms' that drives the system suggests a nightmare of raw mechanical complexities replete with overtones of sadism" (Eddins 69). In Cain's view, "The planetarium, like the fortress, simulates a clock, 'parodying' in this instance the movements of the celestial spheres on which time is based" (75).

PC253.8 PF239.21 B221.38   the nine planets   A planetarium operating in 1922 would show only eight planets. Pluto was not discovered until 1930.

PC253.19 PF239.33 B222.8   having chosen the planet Venus for her partner   "It is possible to read this as a demonstration that love (or at least desire) makes the world go round. And Pynchon, with his fine sense of cliché, no doubt intends this. But the final allusion once again is to slavery, oppression. Without knowing it, Mondaugen has found the generator, albeit not the one he was looking for. . . . For the reader at least there should be less ambiguity surrounding the power generator and the generations of slaves who have powered this society as Mondaugen reaches bottom in his descent and finds, perhaps, the very slave whose place as generator on the planetary treadmill had been unoccupied" (Holton 334).

PC253.30 PF240.6 B222.19   scar tissue   "The wounds represented here as smiles and winks can be read as the inscription of the desire and power of the oppressor on the literal body of the slave— from the point of view of the torturer, a point of view that Mondaugen has passively accepted" (Holton 335).

PC254.17 PF240.28 B223.1   Foppl's response   "The most striking echo of *Heart of Darkness* is Foppl himself, a disciple of General von Trotha, who had attempted to put into practice Kurtz's prescription for Africa: 'Exterminate all the brutes!' Foppl is a parody of both the fictional Kurtz and the historical von Trotha" (Cooley 314).

PC256.13 PF242.19 B224.27   the Schwabing quarter   The Munich equivalent of Paris's bohemian Left Bank.

PC256.13 PF242.19 B224.28   The Brennessel cabaret   A nightclub in the Schwabing quarter of Munich frequented by the likes of Dietrich Eckart, "the spiritual founder of the National Socialist Party" of whom Hitler writes approvingly in *Mein Kampf* (http://www.flinet.com/~politics/antisemi/mkv2ch15.html). *Die Brennessel* (The Nettle) was the title of the Nazi humor/propaganda magazine published 1931–38.

PC256.14 PF242.20 B224.28   D'Annunzio   Gabriele D'Annunzio (1863–1938), Italian writer and political leader. "In 1919 D'Annunzio and about 300 supporters, in defiance of the Treaty of Versailles, occupied the Dalmatian port of Fiume (Rijeka in present-day Croatia), which the Italian government and the Allies were proposing to incorporate into the new Yugoslav state but which D'Annunzio believed rightly belonged to Italy. D'Annunzio ruled Fiume as dictator until December 1920, at which time Italian military forces compelled him to abdicate his rule. Nevertheless, by his bold action he had established Italy's interest in Fiume, and the port became Italian in 1924" ("D'Annunzio, Gabriele," *Britannica Online*).

PC256.14 PF242.20 B224.29   Mussolini   Benito Mussolini (1883–

1945), Italian prime minister from 1922 to 1943. (See PC256.16n "Fascisti," PC443.12n).

PC256.15 PF242.21 B224.29   Italia irredenta   Literally, "Unredeemed Italy." The name of those portions of Italian-speaking Europe under foreign rule during the period 1861–1920 ("Irredentism," *Brewer's Dictionary*). The fact that Mussolini drew inspiration from D'Annunzio's attempt to bring Fiume back under Italian rule suggests another of the novel's associations of V. with the nascent fascism of the period (PC262.26). The lady V. is rumored to have run off with a "mad Irredentist" after the death of Mélanie L'Heurmaudit (PC447.29). Dugdale notes the irony of the fact that V. dies on Malta, "victim of a mad extension of Irredentism in which the island was bombed to rubble in an impossible attempt to regain it for Italy" (111).

PC256.16 PF242.21 B224.29   Fascisti   Originally, the *Fasci di Combattimento*, or "Fighting Leagues," founded in 1919 in Milan by Mussolini. Formed into a political party, the National Fascist Party, in November 1921.

PC256.16 PF242.21 B224.29   National Socialist German Workers' Party   Better known as the Nazi party. Before 1920 it was called the German Workers' Party.

PC256.17 PF242.22 B224.30   Adolf Hitler   By this time, Hitler's aggressive leadership of the Nazi party was beginning to make him known locally.

PC256.17 PF242.22 B224.30   Kautsky's Independents   Karl Kautsky (1854–1938) was the leader of a splinter group of the German Social Democratic Party.

PC257.4 PF243.7 B225.12   it's under the League of Nations   See PC243.23n. Weissmann's response to Mondaugen's apparently naive remark is consistent with widespread skepticism regarding the efficacy of the League.

PC257.16 PF243.19 B225.26   He fell asleep and dreamed   As Hite points out, "Mondaugen's dream, which seems a 'forcible dislocation' of Mondaugen's own personality, has little direct relevance to Stencil's quest for V." (63). It serves at best to confirm the already established association between the decadence of Munich in the early twenties and the extravagances of the siege party.

PC259.9 PF245.4 B227.7 his Chinese and East African campaigns "It was about this time that Leutwein, having been declared too lenient, was superseded by von Trotha. This new commander was noted in Berlin for his merciless severity in dealing with natives. In the Chinese Boxer rebellion he had carried out his Imperial master's instructions to the letter; and no more worthy son of Attila could have been selected for the work at hand. He had just suppressed the Arab rebellion in German East Africa by bathing that country in the blood of thousands and thousands of its inhabitants, men, women and children" (South Africa 59).

PC259.11 PF245.8 B227.10 Vernichtungs Befehl Pynchon has been misled by his source. Von Trotha's August order was in fact simply the order for the disposition of troops in the impending battle of Waterburg, which was fought on August 11. The order did contain the sentence "I want to attack the enemy . . . simultaneously with all sections in order to annihilate him," (quoted in Bridgman 122), but this was not the so-called "extermination order" to which Pynchon refers here, which was issued much later, on October 2. That proclamation read as follows: "I, the great general of the German troops, send this letter to the Herero People. Hereros are no longer German subjects. They have murdered, stolen, they have cut off the noses, ears and other bodily parts of wounded soldiers and now, because of cowardice, they will fight no more. I say to the people: anyone who delivers one of the Herero captains to my station as a prisoner will receive 1000 marks. He who brings in Samuel Maharero will receive 5,000 marks. All the Hereros must leave the land. If the people do not do this, then I will force them to do it with the great guns. Any Herero found within the German borders with or without a gun, with or without cattle, will be shot. I shall no longer receive any women or children; I will drive them back to their people or I will shoot them. This is my decision for the Herero people. The Great General of the Mighty Kaiser" (quoted in Bridgman 127–28). In light of the novel's assertion that this proclamation called upon the German forces "to exterminate systematically every Herero man, woman and child they could find," it seems worth noting that von Trotha's open letter was accompanied by further instructions: "This order is to be read to the troops at quarters with the additional statement that even if a trooper captures a captain of the Hereros he will receive the reward, and the shooting of women and children is to be understood to mean that one can shoot over them to force them to run faster. I definitely mean that this order will be carried out and that no male prisoners will be taken, but it should not degenerate into killing women and children. This will be accomplished if one shoots over their heads a couple of times. The soldiers will remain conscious of the good reputation of German soldiers" (quoted in Bridgman 128). Regardless of the German general's intentions, however, the effect of his policies was as the novel records, there being general agreement among all the sources I have consulted on the numbers of Herero casualties, whether from the direct action of German troops or from the indirect effects of starvation and thirst. Pynchon's numbers are taken directly from the South African Report.

PC259.19 PF245.14 B227.18 Berg-Damaras Also known as the Bergdama. Nomadic people of central Namibia, often serving as serfs to Hereros.

PC259.22 PF245.17 B227.21 This is only 1 per cent of six million A number of critics have noted the shift in tone here. According to Hite, "The unexpectedly flip sarcasm of this remark . . . emphasizes a vertical perspective on the subsequent events of Foppl's siege party" (64), while Cooley claims that "this arresting shift in tone extracts from readers a disturbing admission—that our willingness to read about atrocities in the 'objective' language of history implicates us in those very atrocities" (310). Kharpertian argues that the sarcasm serves to signal the narrator's satirical stance toward the violence of Mondaugen's story.

According to Cooley:

Pynchon's presentation of the Herero genocide as a prelude to the Nazi Holocaust calls to mind Hannah Arendt's vision of imperialism in *The Origins of Totalitarianism*. . . . In her commentary on Gobineau and the origins of French racism, Arendt points to the myth of the Frankish (Germanic) descent of the French aristocracy. Gobineau's version of this myth makes it possible to pretend . . . that every exceptional man belongs to the "true surviving sons of . . . *the Merovings,* the 'sons of kings.' Thanks to race, an 'elite' would be formed which could lay claim to the old prerogatives of feudal families, and this only by asserting that they felt like noblemen; the acceptance of the race ideology would become conclusive proof that an individual was 'well bred,' that 'blue blood' ran through his veins, and that a superior origin implied superior rights" (Arendt 53 [Cooley's emphasis]).

These are precisely the ideas of which V. is the embodiment. (310)

PC260.17 PF246.6 B228.10 he detected a regularity or patterning The similarity to Stencil is glaringly obvious and is reinforced both by the reluctance Mondaugen feels in pursuing the decoding ("Something kept him off") and by his suspicion that the breakdown of his home-made oscillograph might not have been "quite an accident."

PC261.15 PF247.1 B229.3 the Japanese you'll remember bottled us up in Port Arthur During the Russo-Japanese war of 1904–5, Japanese forces besieged Port Arthur in southern Manchuria after Russia backed out of an agreement to withdraw troops from the region. The siege lasted from February 8, 1904, until January 2, 1905 ("Russo-Japanese War," *Britannica Online*).

PC261.30 PF247.15 B229.18 Of course you did Our first indication that Vera Meroving and Victoria Wren may be one and the same.

PC262.5 PF247.25 B229.28 Cléo de Mérode French ballet and theatrical dancer (c. 1866–1966). "De Mérode may have been the only dancer to base her career on a hairdo. Her 'bandeaux,' or hair swept back over her ears into a chignon, fit her dance act, which was basically a Greek revival or interpretive dance concert" (Cohen-Stratyner).

PC262.5 PF247.25 B229.29 Eleonora Duse Italian actress

(1858–1924) and lover of the poet and playwright D'Annunzio (PC256.15n).

PC262.10 PF247.31 B229.33   the man in fact who gave her to Europe   D'Annunzio, whose novel *Il Fuoco* is based on his relationship with Eleonora Duse.

PC262.11 PF247.32 B229.36   in Fiume   See PC256.15n.

PC262.14 PF247.34 B229.38   the Andrea Doria   Italian battleship ordered to shell D'Annunzio's palace in Fiume in order to persuade him to relinquish command of the city.

PC262.20 PF248.3 B230.4   She was past forty and in love   There is an echo here of a note Duse sent to her manager after he had asked her permission to do what he could to suppress the novel: "I did not tell you the truth a little while ago. I know all about the novel and have agreed to its publication, for all my sufferings, great though they may be, do not count when it is a question of adding one more masterpiece to Italian literature. And then—I am forty years old—and in love" (quoted in Knepler 272).

PC262.24 PF248.7 B230.7   the novel about their affair   *Il Fuoco*, which Vera has mentioned earlier (PC262.11). "*Il Fuoco* had been in preparation since 1897. [D'Annunzio] cannot have doubted the effect the book would have on Duse; she and he are the main characters in it. It was, of course, not his first novel about his own love affairs, nor was he the first writer to use such materials. But it is doubtful that any woman had ever been used so viciously as Duse in *Il Fuoco*. From the beginning, he had been taking notes on her, each day, after having left her, and set down with feverishly sensual crudity all the recollections of the hours of love" (Knepler 271–72).

PC262.27 PF248.10 B230.9   in Paris just before the war   Anticipating V.'s appearance in the V. in Love chapter.

PC262.28 PF248.10 B230.10   his supreme moment   "The occupation of the town in defiance of the treaty of Versailles (1919–20) appears in this passage only as a doomed act of folly, with no indication of its further historical significance. But an earlier conversation, between Weissmann . . . and Mondaugen points towards the connection between 1919 and 1922. . . . The unsuccessful occupation was the direct inspiration for Mussolini's so-called 'march on Rome' in 1922. D'Annunzio has the unique distinction among the artists of the period of having acted as catalyst to a revolution. His abortive intervention in politics enabled his writing to have effects in the real world" (Dugdale 110–11).

PC262.30 PF248.12 B230.13   as if hinting she'd like to be kissed The erotic component of V.'s preoccupation with violence has already been established in the Florence interlude.

PC262.31 PF248.13 B230.14   This siege. It's Vheissu   It is a little hard to determine just what prompts this remark. Perhaps Vera associates the Bondel insurgents with the "barbaric and unknown race" (PC207.14), which the intelligence services of Italy and Britain suppose to be about to invade Europe via the network of tunnels beneath the Antarctic ice.

PC263.14 PF248.30 B230.35   our Vheissus are no longer our own   "Overtly, the passage explains the attraction to political activism for D'Annunzio, or Pound, or Yeats. Reacting to the expropriation of art and fantasy by the new mass society, they seek to reverse the process by entering and altering the public world. However, the terms of the passage lend themselves to conversion into a description of a process with which the text is also concerned, in which the dream is followed by the real thing, but the dreamer is not the agent of its realization. Instead of the artist 'working out' his political hallucinations on a real human population (as at Fiume) they work out, become political fact (as in Mussolini's coup) as if through magical causation. This is the closest that *V.* comes to a formulation of the manner in which art is transformed into political reality" (Dugdale 111).

PC263.27 PF249.7 B231.5   No time for pranks. No more Vheissus.   From one point of view, this suggestion that Godolphin may have fabricated the Vheissu story as a joke is so significantly at odds with the harried earnestness of the original revelations which he shares with Victoria Wren and Mantissa in Florence as to justify Eigenvalue's apparent inference that the discrepancy is a function of Stencil's ambivalence toward the V-structure he both desires and fears to bring into focus. Perhaps, Eigenvalue is speculating, Stencil has simply amplified Mondaugen's memory of the incident in the rockery, adding Godolphin's revealing soliloquy as a counter to the overly disturbing possibility that Vheissu and all that it represents may have more than the private significance that Godolphin has attached to it. At the same time, though, the element of farce that unmistakably infuses the Florence chapter may simply find its foundation in this indication that all the scurrying around and paranoia was based on a "prank."

PC264.6 PF249.20 B231.19   Eigenvalue made his single interruption "Eigenvalue, Stencil's auditor, even interrupts, as Marlow's listeners do [in *Heart of Darkness*], drawing attention to the narrative frame. Stencil's retelling of 'Mondaugen's story' foregrounds the problems of verisimilitude and narrative authority, already significant in Conrad" (Cooley 313).

PC265.8 PF250.21 B232.15   to look like Dietrich's As Dugdale notes, though he attributes the observation to Vera Meroving (92), Pynchon is jumping the gun here. Dietrich's first starring role was in *Der Blaue Engel* in 1930. She had appeared as an extra as early as 1923, still a year away from Hedwig's prescient anticipation of her famous thin-eyebrowed look.

PC267.7 PF252.13 B233.43   The strand wolf Later identified (PC284.32) as the brown hyena.

PC268.7 PF253.8 B234.37   Realgymnasium The semiclassical nine-year German secondary school, which included mathematics and natural sciences in its curriculum.

PC269.18 PF254.16 B236.1   loup-garou French for "werewolf."

PC269.32 PF254.29 B238.15   Dreams will help you not at all "Thus, through the use of metaphorical devices, such as Dnubietna's catenary [PC350.11] and Mondaugen's dream song, Pynchon strengthens the central theme of *V.*: the conscious plots of mankind, whether cabals or cables, serve as metaphorical illusions or delusions that mask the only truth of man's existence—accident" (Kozlowski 4).

PC270.7 PF255.5 B236.30   some of it could have been dreamed
The deliberately ambiguous status of the fragments recounting
events during the von Trotha campaign is a complex extension of the
effect generated by the chapter's already questionable provenance.
Not only is the whole story "Stencilized," but portions of it are further removed from any controlling principle of verisimilitude by the
possibility that they may have been the product of scurvy-induced
dreams.

PC270.11 PF255.8 B236.34   herrenschaft   Power, dominion.

PC270.21 PF255.18 B237.1   It's an old dispute   Christian was
shot on October 25, 1903, during a scuffle with German soldiers who
were attempting to arrest him. The ambiguity about who fired the
first shot is not reflected in Pynchon's source, which quotes the German administrator Leutwein's claim that Christian was killed by in-
discriminate rifle fire from his own people and then goes on to dismiss that claim in favor of an eyewitness report indicating that a
German soldier shot Christian (South Africa 93).

PC271.17 PF256.9 B237.34   makoss   A long whip. From "mak
os," Afrikaans = "tame oxen" (Ware).

PC271.23 PF256.14 B237.39   You'll make him go   Perhaps Vera
is referring to Godolphin's intention of trying for the Pole once more
(PC255.8) and is hoping that Mondaugen will encourage the old
explorer.

PC271.31 PF256.22 B238.6   counter-crepitating   The rattling
noise caused by the roulette ball's contrary rotation to that of the
wheel.

**PC271.33 PF256.24 B238.8   precisely the dynamic uncertainty
she was**   Kowalewski identifies this "dynamic uncertainty" as "the
most unintimidated and liberating" characteristic of the language of
the novel (193).

PC273.10 PF257.32 B239.16   the nightfall of ambiguity   The
reader is likely to recognize in this striking phrase an apt metaphor
for her or his own experience of the novel.

PC273.15 PF257.36 B239.21   I know what your interest is   Mondaugen is presumably referring to his suspicion that Weissmann is collaborating with Vera Meroving in her ill-defined plan regarding Godolphin.

PC273.21 PF258.4 B239.27   ground his teeth solicitously   It is hard to imagine how teeth grinding could sound solicitous.

PC274.18 PF258.35 B240.19   He was given a lovely mare   The shift of narrative focus here is so abrupt as to leave the reader wondering just who "He" is. The effect is to embed in the narrative structure the uncertainty that increasingly overtakes Mondaugen about whose story is being told. While some critics have assumed without question that the "He" is Foppl, others prefer the less exact designation of "Firelily's rider." Slade is among the latter group, claiming that "the soldier has no name in Pynchon's novel because he is part of that collective impulse toward the inanimate which is the principal theme of the book" (66).

PC274.21 PF259.1 B240.23   Bastard servant   Basters, from Afrikaans "baster" = "bastard," are a racially mixed group of Namibians, the descendants of Dutch and French men and Nama women ("Baster," *Britannica Online*). They remained loyal to the Germans during the 1904 rebellion of the Hereros.

PC275.4 PF259.17 B240.41   Freyr   Norse god of peace, fertility, rain, and sunshine.

PC275.32 PF260.7 B241.28   since hearing about the Treaty of Versailles   The treaty, signed on June 28, 1919, contained two particularly harsh provisions according to which Germany was to pay reparations for the financial hardships caused by the war and to accept its guilt for the war. A commission established the amount of the reparations at a staggering $33 billion ("Versailles, Treaty of," *Britannica Online*).

PC275.34 PF260.10 B241.30   They'll drain his juices   Mondaugen associates Vera Meroving and Weissmann with the hyenas howling outside the gates.

PC276.2 PF260.12 B241.33   the Kiel revolt   A mutiny among German sailors of the Kiel-based fleet, November 1918.

PC276.9 PF260.19 B241.41   nostalgia forced on him   The poli-

tics of the hothouse world of the siege party are defined largely by
Foppl, the presiding "demon" of the place (PC271.1), and by Weissmann and Meroving. They are the politics of nostalgia and become
increasingly anathema to Mondaugen.

**PC276.10 PF260.20 B241.41   something he was coming to look
on as a coalition**   The traces of Stencil's habitually paranoid frame
of mind can be seen at moments such as this, when Mondaugen begins to reveal a similar tendency.

PC277.3 PF261.10 B242.29   little black sjambok   A two-way critique—of Weissmann's sadomasochistic racism and of the underlying imperialist assumptions upon which it is built—results from the
pun on *Little Black Sambo.*

PC277.13 PF261.20 B242.41   Or it is presumed they did   It is almost as if Pynchon mistrusts the reader's ability to recognize as deliberate the chapter's indeterminacies and so steps in as the impersonal narrator, directing our attention overtly to the fact that nothing
is certain as far as Mondaugen's perceptions are concerned.

**PC277.16 PF261.23 B243.1   One could as well have been a stone-
mason**   Given the framing of the account that follows, Slade's claim
that "the episode is a surrealistic dream of Kurt Mondaugen" (65)
seems justified. The reader's relationship with the text is complicated however, by the fact that the incidents recounted are not
simply imaginative projections within the broad context of actual
historical events, but in some instances more or less a transcription
of portions of the document that Pynchon himself has identified as
his source, the 1918 *Report on the Natives of South-West Africa and
Their Treatment by Germany.* A passage cited by Sanders (albeit to
serve a more complex critical argument) provides a useful case in
point. The witness is a "Cape Bastard" interpreter: "On our return
journey we again halted at Hamakari. There, near a hut, we saw an
old Herero woman of about 50 or 60 years digging in the ground for
wild onions. Von Trotha and his staff were present. A soldier named
Konig jumped off his horse and shot the woman through the forehead
at point blank range. Before he shot her, he said, 'I am going to kill
you.' She simply looked up and said, 'I thank you'" (93). Sanders

has counted twenty-eight other borrowings from the report (fn 96). Mondaugen's "dream," in other words, has, at least in parts, a close congruence with accounts of events in a real 1904. The inextricably intermingled points of view that govern the telling of Mondaugen's story are complemented by this ontological fuzziness.

PC277.17 PF261.24 B243.2   you were in no sense killing   "With this attitude the natives are reduced to objects, automata, in the act of perception which conceives them only in terms of an ideologically inscribed function: the function of the victim" (Madsen 43).

PC278.11 PF262.16 B243.34   a mural of the Dance of Death "The Dance depicted here functions in a Christian *metaxy* to encourage the maintenance of moral vigilance, not its relaxation, while death itself is a terrifying presence but also a natural, inevitable, and universal one. Gnostic surrogation on the part of the genocides systematically subverts and inverts this symbolism to produce a Death that is itself the ultimate religious agent, rather than the enemy and spur to that agency" (Eddins 68).

PC279.29 PF263.30 B245.7   an odd sort of peace   "This moment of mystical ecstasy is the apprehension of a unity, one based upon a *telos* of murder" (Eddins 68).

PC280.4 PF264.5 B245.19   Things seemed all at once to fall into a pattern   Van Delden finds in the passage that follows "an overwhelming evocation" of the modernist epiphanies of Joyce, Proust, and Woolf (123). Structurally, he argues, the passage echoes moments in Proust ("the contrast between the boredom and futility of daily existence lived under the rule of habit and the ecstatic fullness of this other experience is highly reminiscent of Proust's concept of *mémoire involontaire*") and in Woolf. He cites a passage from *To the Lighthouse* in which Mrs. Ramsay is serving one of her guests and notes,

> The syntax brackets together . . . two very different levels of experience, and leaves us with a striking juxtaposition of a vision of eternity, of stability and permanence, with the representation of commonplace, unremarkable actions.

Pynchon's re-writing of the epiphany retains this paradoxical structure. Although the event that leads into the epiphany—the killing of the blackman—can obviously not be described as "trivial," Firelily's rider's experience does follow the modernist pattern in that it takes the form of a mental fusion of the universal and the particular. (125–26)

PC280.19 PF264.19 B245.35   different from the official language "This is, on one level, an almost perfect mimicry of the modernist/ New Critical vision. The contrast Pynchon sets up here may easily be inserted into the oppositions between history and epiphany, life and art, the mechanical and the organic, prose and poetry that were central to this tradition. On another level, however, Pynchon has clearly made the notion of an escape from history highly delusive. . . . Instead of the detached intellectual observer often placed at the center of modernist texts, the protagonist of these scenes from *V.* is a dedicated participant in a historical crime of appalling magnitude" (Van Delden 132).

PC280.32 PF264.33 B246.7   I thank you "The native Hereros and Hottentots . . . welcome death, not because they seek escape from colonial oppression, but because they contract the Europeans' disease, 'the Inanimate'" (Kharpertian 80).

PC282.25 PF266.21 B247.35   It offered life nothing Haarhoff notes that the desert terrain beyond Foppl's estate is "depicted . . . as an extension of the psyche of the castle inhabitants" (35). A similar relationship exists between the coastal wasteland of Foppl's postgenocide period and the white administrators who occupy it.

PC282.26 PF266.22 B247.37   the great Benguela An ocean current that flows northward along the west coast of southern Africa.

PC283.19 PF267.10 B248.21   Schachtmeister Foreman.

PC283.33 PF267.23 B248.33   this ash plain Both Eliot's wasteland and Fitzgerald's valley of ashes are evoked here.

PC284.11 PF267.36 B249.7   Väterliche Züchtigung "Under German law masters were authorized to punish their servants under the authority of the *Väterliche Zuchtigungsrecht*—the paternal right of correction. The punishment was presumed to be moderate and no official record or notification to any judicial authority was required.

Amongst the settlers in the [Protectorate] this institution became the pretext for flogging and assault on men and women to the point of death" (Soggot 7). Soggot goes into considerable detail in recording individual acts of brutality by German farmers.

PC284.32 PF268.20 B249.31   the cry of the brown hyena   The "image repeated through the chapter . . . provides a link between Melville ('The Hyena') and Camus (the laugh in *La Chute*), and relates them both to the laughter in *Steppenwolf*" (Dugdale 92).

PC285.33 PF269.18 B250.31   iridescent with flies   "The 'gaudy dream of annihilation' associated with 'iridescent' spider monkeys and Antarctic wastes is the one literally realized in a desolated Sudwest washed by Antarctic currents and heaped with native corpses" (Eddins 67).

PC286.8 PF269.27 B250.38   anything like that happening   The extent of Pynchon's dependence upon his sources can be estimated from the way he has used an eyewitness account of the broken leg incident which appears in the *Report:* "I personally saw a gang of these prisoners, all women, carrying a heavy double line of rails with iron sleepers attached on their shoulders, and unable to bear the weight they fell. One woman fell under the rails which broke her leg and held it fast. The Schachtmeister (ganger), without causing the rail to be lifted, dragged the woman from under and threw her on one side, where she died untended" (South Africa 102).

PC288.2 PF271.14 B252.21   Bight of Benin   That portion of the Atlantic Ocean bordering on the countries of Ghana, Togo, Benin, and Nigeria.

PC289.1 PF272.11 B253.15   Woman's perversity   While Foppl's stereotypical explanation for Sarah's apparent change of attitude serves (rather unnecessarily) to maintain the moral distance that has long opened up between reader and character, it also glosses over the need for a real explanation.

PC289.8 PF272.17 B253.23   Community may have been the only solution possible   In this instance, however, the solution is much worse than the problem, since it appears to reinforce behaviors that drain all semblance of humanity from those who indulge in them.

PC289.30 PF273.1 B254.2 Jackals had eaten her breasts This detail is drawn directly from testimony of a witness cited in the *Report:* "One corpse, I remember, was that of a young woman with practically fleshless limbs whose breasts had been eaten by jackals" (102).

PC290.2 PF273.8 B54.10 If a season like the Great Rebellion ever came to him again "This intricate narrative structure . . . casts doubt on the integrity of the experiences described. In making us uncertain as to whether these experiences actually belong to a particular individual, Pynchon seems to be moving away from the modernist belief that the power to contain and transcend the world's barrenness and disorder belongs to the individual, isolated mind" (Van Delden 129). Noting that Foppl's nostalgia for the days of von Trotha are a yearning for a kind of virtù—however dangerous, Berressem asserts that "Pynchon's point is that the possibility of such acts of virtù has died out. The mechanization of every aspect of life has taken from us this relation; we are living in an age of annihilation and mass-murder by remote-control, and we live by a press-the-button philosophy" (13).

PC290.20 PF273.25 B254.30 the year after Jacob Marengo died That is, 1908. Jacob Marengo was one of the Nama leaders who vigorously opposed German incursions into his homeland. He was killed in September 1907 (Hartwin Gebhart, cited by Ware).

PC293.24 PF276.17 B257.15 to run amok It is possible that Pynchon adapts this incident from the description of the fatal wounding of Abraham Morris by Lieutenant Prinsloo, who had pursued Morris and his men after their escape from the hillside where the bombing incident took place. Prinsloo's testimony was as follows: "I had personally the day of the fight effectively fired, at 800 yards on a big Hottentot, whom I had marked all through the fight as Abraham Morris, owing to his bravery that day in exposing himself to fatal rifle fire while he was conducting the fight" (*Report of the Commission Appointed to Enquire into the Rebellion of the Bondelzwarts.* Cape Town: Cape Times Limited, Government Printers, 1923. In Dewaldt 23–24).

PC293.29 PF276.22 B257.21 Now the planes could be heard It seems that Pynchon is here referring to the first engagement with the Bondels by the forces of the Union administration, which occurred on the afternoon and evening of May 29. The explosions that the guests hear in the days that follow would be from the Union planes, which assisted Prinsloo in his harassment of the fleeing survivors of the engagement at Guruchas. The fighting lasted from May 29 until June 7 or 8.

PC293.31 PF276.24 B257.23   the sun caught suddenly the three canisters   "The sardonic parody here is of the description of an air raid in 'Little Gidding' as a torment devised by Love:

> The dove descending breaks the air
> With flame of incandescent terror
> Of which the tongues declare
> The one discharge from sin and error.

Pynchon further twists the screw by returning to the poem in the next Stencil chapter, in which Fausto, the disciple of Eliot, is unable to view the relentless bombing of Malta and the loss of his wife in a raid as the work of Love" (Dugdale 113–14).

PC294.18 PF277.10 B258.4   Achphenomenon   This appears to be a coinage (of Pynchon's?) and probably means something like "epiphany," or "revelation." Literally, an Ah!-phenomenon.

PC294.19 PF277.11 B258.5   that his voyeurism had been determined purely by events seen   Patteson reads this as "an early variation on Fausto's 'fiction of cause and effect'" (38).

PC295.14 PF278.4 B258.38   GODMEANTNUURK   "Is this a scrambled reflection of Mondaugen's own introspection (the anagram of his name?) or a sign that God is babbling nonsense: 'God meant "nuurk"'? Or perhaps it is a subtle reference to 'New York,' where Stencil is telling this entire story to Eigenvalue?" (Porush 124). See also Stark (42): "However, if one makes some spaces in the sequences of letters and allows for eccentric spelling, one gets "God meant New York." In other words, Pynchon has arranged the code to show that Weissmann's interpretation of it goes astray because it is too ingenious."

**PC295.19 PF278.9 B258.43 DIEWELTISTALLESWASDER-
FALLIST** According to Weissmann, the sferics are quoting the
opening proposition of Wittgenstein's *Tractatus:* "The world is all
that is the case," an assertion that has considerable bearing on Stencil's undertaking as well as on the reader's effort to make sense of the
events of the novel. "Wittgenstein defines reality as the sum total of
all facts. By defining reality in this way he excludes the following
concepts as illusory: (1) the idea of a transcendence, a world beyond
the world of facts; (2) the idea of a realm of 'absolute values' which
could guide human behavior in a binding way; (3) the idea of a comprehensive ('holistic') order of reality which composes the individual facts into the kinds of system constructed by Aristotle, Hegel,
Marx, or other thinkers. Reality, in other words, is a conglomerate of
nothing but facts. These facts are without metaphysical meaning . . .
without value . . . and essentially isolated from each other. . . . It is a
world which to the thinking individual must appear as profoundly
senseless, strange, and incoherent as the kind of shattered cosmos
that emerges in the works of modern artists" (Bramann 4). According
to Cain, this glimpse of life's randomness is what finally provokes
Mondaugen into leaving the "insular security" of Foppl's farm (76).

McHoul and Wills read in the sferic's message the implication that
the world which we believe is accessible through language is in fact
nothing *but* the word. It is "the *case:* the boards and back of a book,
the tray in which the compositor has his types before him" (167).
Eddins suggests that "the sferic utterance can be read as the affirmation of an *Ur*-nature—a given, a *fait accompli* of accident that is the
only primordial truth in a wild whirl of projections, interpretations,
and modifications" (72), but he also notes the irony that such a message should be "no message at all, but random noise twisted into
meaning by human mental processes" (72). New strikes a similar
note: "The modern writer . . . is inhibited by the perception that constructs are human creations, and that the maze may well be all that
there is. It is the message that Weissmann finds in Mondaugen's recordings. . . . From outer space we receive a message that there is no
message in outer space. The music of the spheres that Dryden heard

so clearly in 1687—'From harmony, from heavenly harmony / This universal frame began'—in 1963 has become not silent but the paradoxical assertion of silence" (98). The reader who seeks to decode Pynchon's text is obliged to confront the possibility that a similar message lies at the heart of the tantalizing combinations and permutations of imagery and motif, which it generates like the marks on Mondaugen's oscillograph.

PC297.8 PF279.27 B260.18　his cheek against the Bondel's scarred back　The accidental intimacy, coupled with the fact that Mondaugen is leaving the domain of the oppressor, suggests his alignment with the doubly preterite survivors of the uprising.

PC297.15 PF279.34 B260.26　Mondaugen couldn't understand it "Having left the castle, and rejected its compulsive ethos, but lacking in the knowledge and linguistic competence needed to be part of an African community, Mondaugen appears to have no other place to go" (Sanders 84).

CHAPTER TEN

This highly fragmented chapter explores a number of relationships in a series of interleaved vignettes. It begins as McClintic Sphere takes refuge from condescending college-type jazz enthusiasts in the arms of a prostitute named Ruby (who turns out to be Paola Maijstral). Sphere later worries about Roony Winsome's mental health and speculates about the binary flip-flops of contemporary culture, while at the same time arguing with Ruby/Paola over her anxiety about her father. While out of town for the summer, he goes to a party on Cape Cod, where he resists the advances of one of the party-goers, citing his attachment to Ruby. Returning for a weekend to New York, he is just in time to prevent Ruby from leaving. A second thread follows Slab and Esther, who were once lovers. They discuss his latest Cheese Danish painting and Slab rejects Esther's advances. Esther returns to her lover, Schoenmaker, who attempts to persuade her to undergo more cosmetic surgery. Roony Winsome has become preoccupied with Paola Maijstral but is unable to ask Rachel Owlglass to set him up. At a party, Pig Bodine and Roony fight over Paola, though the spectators believe it to be over Roony's wife, Mafia, whom we see the next day attempting unsuccessfully to seduce Profane. Profane converses with the two test dummies at the research facility where he has recently become the night watchman. SHROUD unnerves Profane by invoking the history of the Holocaust. Various members of the Whole Sick Crew are seen rollicking; the dentist Eigenvalue speculates about the likely consequence of their decadence, and Paola gives Stencil the Confessions of her father, Fausto.

PC298.14 PF280.37 B261.35   Night Train   Jimmy Forrest's 1951 composition based on Duke Ellington's "Happy Go Lucky Local."

PC299.5 PF281.11 B262.4   Matilda Winthrop   Safer notes the association with John Winthrop, governor of the Massachusetts Bay Colony, inferring a comment on the distance that separates the Street of the twentieth century from the ideals of that original settlement (85).

PC300.16 PF282.19 B263.11   an ornate bird   Lense is reminded of the golden bird of Yeats's "Sailing to Byzantium," suggesting that, "as an allusion to Yeats's image . . . the partridge is a parody of the old man's dream of a machine-like state of perfection. . . . Slab's allusive parody of these approaches to life [V.'s and the old man's desire to avoid aging] suggest their futility, and warns that becoming a machine, even an ornate bird, is no proof against mortality" (60–61).

PC302.17 PF284.11 B264.39   SHROUD   The Pynchon Files web site (www.pynchonfiles.com/shock.htm, in March 2000) cited a 1965 *Cavalier* magazine article in which Jules Siegel identifies as the source for SHROUD and SHOCK a profile in the *New York Times*, April 9, 1959, of the work of Alderson Research Laboratories. The Alderson figures were known as REMAB (Radiation-Equivalent Man, Absorption) and REMCAL (Radiation-Equivalent Man, Calibration). "With her myriad identities V. suggests the condition of twentieth-century identity—elusive, plastic, diffused, defined by its appurtenances and accessories, by the ease with which it can fragment, in short, by its lack of soul. . . . Thus the mannequins SHOCK and SHROUD have as much character as any other characters in the novel, their level of existence being on about a par with that of Fergus Mixolydian" (Campbell 62). Kharpertian identifies the two figures as "symbolic victims of the dehumanizing effects of accident and violence, two of *V.*'s principal themes" (65), while McConnell finds a "darkly brilliant contemporary inversion of the Frankenstein motif: the fear that in our Faustian dedication to controlling and manipulating the physical world we might well be transforming ourselves into the insensate, automatized stuff of that rocky universe, that the arrogant independence of the modern, postromantic intellect may well be its own curse, its own damning judge" (168).

PC304.27 PF86.17 B266.41   Me and SHOCK are what you and

everybody will be someday   Profane is here projecting onto the mannequin the fears that find another outlet in his dream of disassembly (PC35).

PC306.22 PF288.6 B268.24   like a bundling board or Tristan's blade   Bundling, with or without an actual board as a barrier, was the practice whereby couples of the opposite sex in various cultures would sleep together without sexual contact. "Tristan's blade" is a reference to the legend of Tristan and Isolde, in which two fugitive lovers are discovered sleeping in a forest separated by a sword.

PC307.12 PF288.30 B269.7   To be quoted Thesis 1.7   Pittas-Giroux points out that there is no Thesis 1.7 in Wittgenstein's *Tractatus.* He suggests that Charisma is revealing a typical ignorance of the real nature of the philosophical system he invokes, and notes that the parody may refer obliquely to propositions 1 and 7, which open and close the *Tractatus:* "The world is all that is the case," and "Whereof one cannot speak, thereof one must be silent" (203). "What is being joked about here is Wittgenstein's theory that love is a meaningless concept and cannot be talked about but only demonstrated" (Bianchi 9). Bianchi cites as a parallel case the moment when Profane draws hearts and arrows in the sawdust on the floor of the Sailor's Grave (PC3.3). "The use of the proposition . . . aligns Wittgenstein with existentialism and absurdism which, whatever their other differences, start from the same negative basis. It is another example of the novel's strategy of locating precursors of the post-war mentality in earlier periods" (Dugdale 93). See also PC295.19n.

PC308.24 PF290.2 B270.10   The world started to run more and more afoul of the inanimate   "This points to perhaps the most inclusive theme of the book: not that man returns to the inanimate, since that is the oldest of truths, but that twentieth-century man seems to be dedicating himself to the annihilation of all animateness on a quite unprecedented scale, and with quite unanticipated inventiveness" (Tanner, "V2" 22).

PC309.21 PF290.37 B271.3   a congruent world which simply doesn't care   The narrator here asserts what Stencil has earlier projected onto the person of Gebrail, the farmer turned taxi driver in Cairo—"no treachery in the wall, no hostility in the desert" (PC80.32).

PC310.16 PF291.27 B271.33   Either the street or all cooped up Ruby/Paola comes up with her version of the hothouse/street metaphor articulated by Sidney Stencil (PC506). Her sense of the limited choices that face her as a woman in midcentury America parallels the constrained political options that Sidney envisages almost half a century earlier.

PC311.28 PF292.37 B272.41   stochastic music   Music composed according to probability models using a computer to program the score.

PC312.22 PF293.29 B273.28   what happened after the war? "The shift is from an art of 'crazy' emotion to one of indifference or casual amusement; from one in which the artist is involved with his surroundings through narcissistic identifications to one in which he imitates the alien vision of 'a being from another world,' from Romantic humanism to an absurdism in which the individual is viewed as dwarfed by impersonal forces; from an insistence on order and pattern to an embracing of, or recognition of the extent of, chaos, accident, randomness; from 'a sense of grand adventure about it all' [PC328] to a sense of the futility of all major gestures; from a world which has depth, latency, 'more behind and inside' [PC49] to one which is merely 'all that is the case'; from one in which people, places and objects have secret essences to one in which there is nothing but surface and contingency. The opposition between the two types of artist, and the two corresponding visions of the world, is illustrated throughout the novel, but is exhibited most clearly in Chapter 11, through the contrasts between early and late Fausto Maijstral, pre-war and war-time Malta" (Dugdale 102).

PC314.16 PF295.18 B275.9   stacked up like those poor car-bodies This equating of piles of human corpses with stacked cars is a stark illustration of the novel's central theme.

PC314.19 PF295.19 B275.10   Eichmann   Adolf Eichmann (1906–62), Nazi war criminal who was hanged in Israel in 1962.

PC314.19 PF295.19 B275.10 Mengele Josef Mengele (1911–79), Nazi doctor who conducted experiments on inmates at Auschwitz.

PC314.21 PF295.21 B275.14 now that it's started "What the 'it' is that has started (if there is an 'it'), what common process links remote imperialist incidents with a contemporary automation, tourism, Hitler, and the Whole Sick Crew (if there is any linking common process)—this is what the whole book is about" (Tanner, "V2" 22).

PC315.16 PF296.14 B276.3 harangued him with the Great Betrayal Slab's friend is presumably citing the views of the French intellectual Julien Benda, whose work *La Trahison des Clercs*, also known as *The Great Betrayal*, was published in 1927. Benda "denounced as moral traitors those who betray truth and justice for racial and political considerations" ("Benda, Julien," *Britannica Online*).

PC315.17 PF296.14 B276.3 the Dance of Death See PC212.18n.

PC315.22 PF296.19 B276.8 the same leprous pointillism of orris root Orrisroot, an oil derived from the roots of irises, is used in the manufacture of perfumes and was once used as a flavoring for candies and soft drinks. The reference here may be to the allergic reactions that have led to the decline of this latter use.

PC316.17 PF297.10 B276.40 Your own skill Esther is accusing Schoenmaker of something closely resembling that "obvoluted breed of self-aggrandizement," which leads Victoria Wren to believe in her own skill at manipulating events (PC209).

PC317.15 PF298.4 B277.31 they're bound to run out of arrangements someday The theme of the exhaustion of intellectual energy is a familiar one. As Tanner points out, "the Whole Sick Crew seems to be hastening the entropic decline of language as a vehicle for the transmission of significant information, by playing with all its permutations irrespective of what reference any of the permutations may or may not have to reality" ("V2" 25). Golden offers a less pessimistic view: "The dentist Eigenvalue realizes that the art of the Whole Sick Crew lacks true originality, but he also realizes that even this exhausted striving for the new has value" (10).

PC318.18 PF299.4 B278.30 Give me back my eye Although the reference appears to invoke the Gorgon's sisters, whose one eye Perseus stole, it seems likely that little more is intended here than a comically literal allusion to the fact that Sphere's "eye was taken by a little girl in dungarees" (PC318.15).

PC321.14 PF301.23 B281.6 what goes on underground Profane's speculation, based on his own experiences beneath the street, carries over from the earlier narrative description of his and Rachel's faulty timing over the phone, as a result of which their voices "collided somewhere underground . . . came out mostly noise" (PC321.3). The implication seems to be that the world under the street may be a place for self-analysis/discovery, but it is also a place where desires conflict with one another and communication fails.

PC322.17 PF302.24 B282.1 yo-yoing See PC2.7n.

PC323.8 PF303.10 B282.28 Vertical corpses Stencil's vision here is in direct contrast to the earlier description of the commuting crowds as "all manner of affluent [who] have filled the limits of that world with a sense of summer and life" (PC32.14). There is an echo here of the image of stacked Jewish corpses recalled by Profane during his "conversation" with SHROUD (PC314.16).

PC323.17 PF303.19 B282.37 a print of di Chirico's street "The cryptic reference is to Mystery and Melancholy of a Street (1914) which shows the shadow of a girl running along a yellow street towards an invisible source of light, past a carnival wagon, an arcade and the shadow of a statue of the previous century. . . . The Chiricesque scene is reinterpreted as evoking the baulking of romanticism in modern life. The particular pertinence of de Chirico for Pynchon is that in his world the mystique of the other or the object is recoverable only through projection, through regression to infantile narcissism. It survives in the urban environment only in the form of the 'enigma' . . . that is, as a sense of menace and the uncanny" (Dugdale 81).

CHAPTER ELEVEN

Paola's father has sent his daughter a newly completed manuscript in which he traces his progress through a succession of versions of himself, numbered Fausto I–IV. The manuscript quotes from Maijstral's earlier journals, building up a many-layered portrait of their author. The youthful Fausto is portrayed as a potential priest, enjoying life as a student in Malta during the years before World War II. His life-course changes with the news that he has impregnated Elena Xemxi, whom he marries despite a reluctance on her part that is engendered by her having come under the influence of a mysterious "Bad Priest." The second Fausto comes into being with the birth of Paola and the onset of the constant air raids that were to define Maltese experience for the next few years. Fausto III emerges gradually during the course of the war, as life on the island becomes increasingly defined in terms of the bombs that fall and the rock that shelters the inhabitants from them. This Fausto is the closest of all the personae to a state of non-humanity, identifying as he does with the rockhood of his island home. During this period, Elena is killed and Fausto is witness to the disassembly of the Bad Priest by some of the children of Malta, among them, it would seem, his daughter Paola. Only gradually does Fausto III regain his sense of humanity and modulate into the Fausto IV who presumably is narrating the story of all their lives.

PC324 PF304 B284　Confessions of Fausto Maijstral　"Since *V.* is a study of dual degeneration—that of a symbol and of the civilization it symbolizes—our best point of entry is Fausto's confessions, which contain an overview of the combined process. Born on Malta, and reared as a Catholic, Fausto has had immediate experience of a feminized transcendental, both as the anima of the island and as Adams's Virgin. The first three stages of his life, as set down in his diary, reflect the degeneration of this composite symbol from unifying Mother to inert matter, while the fourth suggests some vestige of spiritual power that brings him back toward humanity" (Eddins 56). "Fausto Maijstral represents, in Pynchon's novel, an advance point in the colonial ascent to awareness which counterpoints the picture of the decline of Imperialist culture" (Inglott, "Faustus" 40). Inglott also sees a parallel between Pynchon's chapter 11 and book 11 of the *Odyssey.* "In Maijstral's 'Confessions,' the 'hero' takes over from the narrator to describe in the first person his real poetic descent into an existence-language close to that of Homer's kingdom of the dead, 'Nekyia.' Maijstral, like Ulysses, inbuilds into his narrative a critique of his own poetic journey" (Inglott, "Faustus" 40). Dugdale claims that Fausto is a composite of the Provençal poet Frederic Mistral and "the genuine Maltese priest-poet, Dun Karm" (93).

PC324.5 PF304.28 B284.22   The room simply is   The Fausto who serves as the medium of the confessions of all his predecessors owes something of his manner and his beliefs to Alain Robbe-Grillet. The meticulous description of the physical orientation of the room is strongly reminiscent of the opening of *La Jalousie,* while the stain on the ceiling may recall a similar stain in "La Chambre secrète." Fausto's later observations on the subject of metaphor reinforce the connection (see PC349.22n).

PC324.7 PF304.30 B284.25   Let me describe the room   Inglott is reminded of M. C. Escher's print *An Exhibition of Prints,* in which a man looks at a print of Valletta harbor ("Faustus" 41).

PC325.15 PF305.22 B285.16   Fausto himself may be defined in only three ways   "As Paola's father, he assumes here the role of the loving authority. As a given name, he is identified with Faust, Godolphin, and Stencil, all of whom have the restless heart of the explorer. As an occupant, he is somewhat more sinister. Living in Malta, he inhabits a matriarchal island that is both British and Maltese; as a man and a priest, he is the colonizer whose presence subdues the natural mysteries of this ancient place—Venus's Malta" (Chambers

84). Inglott points out that "occupant" is an evocative word in the context of a memoir of the war years ("Faustus" 41).

PC325.19 PF305.26 B285.21   the room . . . is a hothouse   The relationship between the hothouse motif and the past that is here made explicit is given a more political dimension in Sidney Stencil's journal entry (PC506.20).

PC325.29 PF305.35 B285.32   Dnubietna   The name means "Our sins" in Maltese (Cassola 330).

PC325.30 PF305.37 B285.34   the Generation of '37   Chambers identifies Pound, Eliot, and Yeats as models (86).

PC326.7 PF306.11 B286.5   a successive rejection of personalities "Like Stencil [Fausto] also refers to himself in the third person, as Fausto I–IV. His third person references serve a purpose similar to Henry Adams' and quite different from Stencil's: like Adams, Fausto does not deny his own subjectivity with them, but rather reflects the fragmented nature of his subjective perspective. Stencil aims at credibility and the aura, at least, of certainty; never denying the limits of 'Fausto's' vision, Fausto underscores the unreliability of any account based on 'the false assumption that identity is single'" (Strehle 48).

PC326.15 PF306.18 B286.13   the fiction of continuity   Fausto's commitment to seeing past the various fictions that define the way the majority of his contemporaries (and ours) contrive to bring a sense of order to their lives is shared by his creator, who keeps his readers always conscious of the problematic status of the fiction they are reading. The novel eschews continuity, muddles the relationship between cause and effect, and calls very much into question the tendency to seek evidence of the operation of reason in the events out of which historical accounts are fabricated.

PC326.24 PF306.28 B286.22   Elena Xemxi   Inglott suggests that Elena is an inevitable name for the wife of a Faust ("Faustus" 51). Xemxi means "sunny" in Maltese (Cassola 330).

PC327.3 PF307.4 B286.38   auberges   The auberges of Malta were the lodges built for the various different nationalities of the Knights of Saint John.

PC327.12 PF307.11 B287.3 *Hebdomeros*   The 1929 novel by Giorgio de Chirico. "*Hebdomeros* . . . foreshadowed [the surrealists'] literary endeavors with its dreamscapes, its journey motif, its structure that reads like a picaresque of the subconscious and thus is so suggestive of the automatic writing to which the surrealists were so attached. The point here, however, is that, if Pynchon read *Hebdomeros* (and there is reason to believe he did), he read it either in an obscure 1929 French edition, and this seems unlikely, or in *View*, where it was published in two parts in a translation done by Paul Bowles in 1944" (Vella 31).

PC327.14 PF307.14 B287.6   Mount Ruwenzori   Ruwenzori is in fact the name not of a single mountain but of a mountain range that borders on Uganda and Zaire.

PC327.15 PF307.15 B287.7   our linguistic brothers the Bantu An inexplicable reference. According to anthropologist Lee Bickmore, "there is no known historical connection between Maltese and Bantu. Maltese is basically a variety of Arabic, . . . at its roots it is a Semitic language, and part of the Afro-Asiatic family. Bantu, on the other hand, is a group of languages which is ultimately part of the Niger-Congo family" (Personal correspondence).

PC327.21 PF307.21 B287.14   the false assumption that identity is single   "Fausto complicates his meditation on time and history by announcing the chimerical nature of memory. To him, memory has no reality because it depends on an immutable identity. That is, the rememberer must be identical with the person whose actions he remembers; otherwise the memory becomes distorted beyond recognition. Fausto does not have a consistent identity because dramatic changes in his personality divide his life into distinct periods; and he thus generalizes that memory has no validity for anyone. If he has reasoned correctly, time may exist but no one can accurately understand it, and thus history is real but also hopelessly jumbled" (Stark 112).

PC327.32 PF307.31 B287.25   St. Giles Fair   Saint Giles Fair was held in the English city of Winchester from the twelfth through the nineteenth centuries.

**PC327.32 PF307.31 B287.25   Her rhythms pulse regular and si-
nusoidal**   Stark identifies this as one among a number of ways in
which history's events are graphically visualized by various characters. "[Fausto's] graph depicts history as a series of rising and falling
periods that repeat the same movements but not the same content.
According to this theory, civilizations lying at the same point on different curves resemble each other in the level of their development
but differ in details" (112). Stark cites Dnubietna's description of history as a "step-function" (PC355.33n) and Mantissa's cyclical theory
(PC166.35). He also cites Wasson's claim that the whole point of *V*. is
to expose the inadequacy of all models of history (119).

PC328.14 PF308.8 B288.1   St.-John's-bread   "It is noteworthy
that carob is referred to as St. John's bread in Mark 1:6, hence underscoring Fausto's role as a forerunner of a figure of salvation" (Newman 11).

**PC328.23 PF308.16 B288.11   Shakespeare and T. S. Eliot ruined
us all**   Inglott notes that Pynchon is extremely accurate in his depiction of prewar Anglo-Maltese poetry and cites some examples of
work published during the period ("Faustus" 45–46).

PC329.3 PF308.31 B288.26   Strada Reale   Tanner notes the
irony of the idea of a royal street ("V2" 30).

PC330.13 PF309.33 B289.27   a new sort of being, a dual man
"Speaking and thinking in both languages, Fausto conceives of himself as 'a dual man, aimed in two ways at once,' torn between two
cognitive modes. As a result, Fausto describes the development of
his personality (through four stages to the time of writing his 'con-
fession'), in terms of his changing attitude towards, and use of, language. Fausto I is characterized by a love of high-flown rhetoric,
Shakespeare and Eliot; whilst Fausto II, a product of the siege of
Malta, is 'more Maltese and less British'; he is a 'young man in retreat,' a retreat into religious abstraction and poetry. 'Moving towards that island-wide sense of communion. And at the same time
towards the lowest form of consciousness' [PC336]. It is a communion in 'Purgatory,' and a retreat into non-humanity. As Fausto III
begins to emerge, abstraction gives way to a 'sensitivity to deca-

dence' or inanimation" (Madsen 35–36). Slade suggests that "Herbert Stencil is the second half of this dichotomy, too humorous a figure to qualify as a Faust" (52).

PC330.20 PF310.2 B289.33   Not even a word for mind   "Fausto might also have noted that there is no common word in Maltese to mean 'body' in the general sense in which it is used, say, in the formulation of the law of gravity; the word ';isem' is only used for living bodies. Thus, a radical dichotomy is established between the animate and the inanimate a point which is clearly relevant to Pynchon's interests" (Inglott, "Faustus" 43).

PC330.29 PF310.11 B290.1   ten raids per day   "The bombings are precisely that humanly controlled energy that in turn controls us by destroying our integrated symbols" (Eddins 57).

PC331.13 PF310.29 B290.22   Malta of the Knights of St. John   The Knights of Saint John, also known as Knights Hospitallers, originated as a religious order caring for the sick in the Holy Land and grew into a military organization that combined its caregiving with implacable enmity toward Islam. The Knights were given a base in Malta in 1530.

PC331.15 PF310.30 B290.24   Giaours   Infidels, those outside the Islamic faith.

PC331.16 PF310.30 B290.25   L'Isle-Adam and his ermine arm   "Philippe Villieres de L'Isle Adam was elected Grandmaster of the Order of St. John in 1521. Under his leadership, the Knights of St. John resisted for six months against the Turks in Rhodes. They were defeated in 1522 and for seven years the Knights of St. John were deprived of a permanent home. In 1530 L'Isle Adam and his knights were given Malta by Charles V. L'Isle Adam died in 1534" (Cassola 327).

PC331.16 PF310.32 B290.25   maniple   A long narrow strip of silk worn at mass over the left arm by clerics of or above the order of subdeacon (Merriam Webster's *Collegiate Dictionary*).

PC331.17 PF310.33 B290.26   M. Parisot   "Jean Parisot de La Valette, Grandmaster of the Order between 1557 and 1568, will always be remembered among the Maltese people as the greatest of all the Grandmasters. Under his able leadership the Maltese defeated the

impressive Turkish Armada which besieged Malta in 1565. La Valette laid the foundation stone of Valletta, the new capital city which
was named after him, on 29 March 1566" (Cassola 327).

PC331.19 PF310.34 B290.28 Great Siege "The 1565 Siege.
Thirty thousand Turks landed in Malta with the intention of ousting
La Valette and the Knights of St. John from the island" (Cassola 331).
The siege lasted for four months before the Turks withdrew, believ-
ing that a large relief force was on its way. Cassola suggests Themis-
tocles Zammit's *Malta: The Islands and Their History* (Malta: "The
Malta Herald" Office, 1926) as the source of Pynchon's knowledge
about the siege (316).

**PC331.29 PF311.5 B290.37 this God-favoured plot of sweet
Mediterranean earth** "The Great Mother, as a composite of the
Virgin and Venus *genetrix*, has certain functions: unifiying, nourish-
ing, regenerating, protecting, inspiriting. These are perceived as real
and effective by the Fausto of stage II, who also finds in the island a
timeless identity with his ancestors and their fertility rituals. The
sacred, transcendental nature of Malta as Virgin is sealed by [this]
description" (Eddins 56).

PC332.1 PF311.12 B291.3 somehow boring Chambers notes
that Fausto "shares the mentality that Firelily's rider in Southwest
Africa describes—the tedium and routine of destruction" (86).

PC332.20 PF311.27 B291.21 gregale The wind that brought
Saint Paul to Malta in the year A.D. 60 (Inglott, "Faustus," 51 [Acts
27:14]). The gregale, which is also called Euroclydon (PC345.25), is
a "strong and cold wind that blows from the northeast in the western and central Mediterranean region, mainly in winter. Most pronounced on the island of Malta, the gregale sometimes approaches
hurricane force and endangers shipping there; in 1555 it is reported
to have caused waves that drowned 600 persons in the city of Valletta" ("gregale," *Britannica Online*). The other wind of note in the
novel is of course the maijstral, which blows from the northwest.

PC335.14 PF314.2 B293.35 black slug "Since Elena's principal
'sin' has been the conception of a child outside wedlock, it is easy
enough to find a life-negating analogy here between embryo and slug.

Another priestly simile comparing sin to 'spirit's cancer' has a similar application so that Elena's frightened search for 'the metastasis she feared was in her' is really horror at the natural growth of new life" (Eddins 72).

PC335.17 PF314.4 B293.37   Christ was her proper husband The Bad Priest's advice to Elena is somewhat ironic in the light of Victoria Wren's ultimate rejection of the sisterhood because she is unwilling to stand for the "competition" of the "great harem clad in black" (PC69.31).

PC337.26 PF315.34 B295.29   Here on our dear tiny prison plot, our Malta Cf. "this God-favoured plot of sweet Mediterranean earth" (PC331.29n).

PC338.5 PF316.9 B296.1   gilded with an illusion of honour "This older, more personal form of violence largely disappears with the advent of mob violence, large-scale aerial bombing, and genocide. Most of the important violence of V.—the extermination of the Blacks in South Africa, the siege of Malta, the concentration camps of Germany (which SHROUD refers to), and the potential violence of nuclear radiation—is massive and impersonal" (Golden 7).

PC338.32 PF316.32 B296.28   Even the radical Dnubietna "Pynchon's description of Dnubietna accords with factual details of his own life and probably furnishes a clue to his artistic credo" (Stark 18).

PC339.24 PF317.21 B297.13   the most real state of affairs "It is noticeable that Fausto also uses Wittgensteinian terms, such as 'state of affairs' and 'accident' [PC343.24], suggesting that Robbe-Grillet's world that simply is corresponds to Wittgenstein's world that is the case; and that the novelist's attack on fraudulent metaphor corresponds to the philosopher's critique of language games" (Dugdale 94). See also PC349.22n.

PC340.15 PF318.7 B297.39   in the sense of attainable accuracy Strehle characterizes Fausto's definition of truth as that of an "actualist," who sees reality as "relative, discontinuous, energetic, statistical, subjective, uncertain, or contingent" (33,48).

PC341.6 PF318.32 B298.25   June Disturbances "These have gone down in Maltese history as the *Sette Giugno*. On 7 June 1919

British troops opened fire on the thousands of people demonstrating in Valletta. Three people were killed and a fourth victim died on 8 June as a result of injuries" (Cassola 331).

PC341.13 PF319.3 B298.32 a mysterious being named Stencil Fausto thus becomes in some sense Herbert Stencil's brother.

PC341.31 PF319.18 B299.7 One "plot" "German planes bomb the island's capital, Valletta. Those planes fly over in 'plots,' Maijstral's word for the formations, picked up by the 'scatter' of the searchlights, another word suggestive of V., since the narrator will laconically observe that the object of Stencil's search is 'a remarkably scattered concept'" (Slade 83).

PC343.10 PF320.26 B300.12 peeling paint . . . palsied stick Maratt's poem takes as its central metaphor the popular glove-puppet show Punch and Judy, typically performed in a tall narrow booth decked with fringed velvet hangings. A consistent feature of the show is Punch's belaboring of his wife and any other character who attracts his wrath.

PC343.23 PF320.37 B300.25 there is more accident One of many references throughout the novel to the difficulty we have in facing up to the possibility that life is without fundamental meaning or order. See in particular PC80.32, where Stencil, through the persona of the cab driver Gebrail, faces head-on the truth of the world's indifference to its human inhabitants.

PC343.34 PF321.9 B300.34 the same Maltese timelessness Inglott associates this timelessness with the Maltese language itself, which "reflects the dominant Muslim occasionalism—the view that, apart from God's will, there is no historical continuity in the sense of a causally connected chain between one event and another, but only a sequence of critical moments or atomised mosaic of happenings" ("Faustus" 43). The "near tenselessness" of the language is reflected in the way events associated with Malta reveal a degree of synchronicity that is at odds with our conventional notions of time. "The Great Siege of 1565 . . . is fused with the Second Great Siege. . . . The Grandmaster of the sixteenth-century patrols the streets during a twentieth-century air-raid; a dog-fight . . . is described in terms of a duel between knights" ("Faustus" 44). Mehemet's claim to have traveled through a rift in time and his mythic explanation of events during the Great Siege afford other instances. "Ultimately, Pynchon wants us to recognize that Malta itself . . . has something to do with Fausto's regeneration. . . . it is a place curiously untouched by time whose people . . . are not forced into patterns of history and so perhaps can avoid the decadence that usually accompanies the progress of time" (Olderman 141).

PC344.2 PF321.12 B300.38   There are always elephants to be made drunk   This seems to stand for the fact that a Maltese mother believes she always has something to teach her son.

PC344.22 PF321.31 B301.16   that connection between mother-rule and decadence?   "[Fausto's] rationale for this association takes us right to the heart of the link between the degeneration of the Virgin symbol and the growth of existential gnosticism" (Eddins 57).

PC344.34 PF322.3 B301.27   a mechanical and alien growth "Fausto's explicit association of this accidental and initially soulless 'zygote' with the Virgin Birth represents an explicit desecration of the Virgin symbol" (Eddins 57).

PC345.3 PF322.7 B301.31   the pelvic frontiers   "Over against the accident of death, then, there is the accident of birth and regeneration, also a kind of imperial conquest of 'the pelvic frontiers'" (Cooley 318).

PC345.17 PF322.21 B302.5   machines that are more complex than people   "Fausto's transvaluation of the machine is indeed 'apostasy' and of a particularly gnostic variety. It is a falling away from the 'true' religion centered upon the spiritual potential of the animate as manifested in humanity, and an embracing of the Inanimate heresy" (Eddins 58).

PC345.18 PF322.22 B302.6   hekk ikun   So be it (Cassola 330).

PC345.25 PF322.29 B302.14   Euroclydon   See PC332.20n.

PC346.29 PF323.24 B303.9   everything civilian and with a soul was underground   Reinforcement of the novel's consistent indication that the world beneath the surface is more likely to provide the means for the survival of the human self than the surface world, which is being taken over by the inanimate.

PC346.33 PF323.27 B303.13   not to change the truth of the "impressions" by the act of receiving them   Fausto's loss of subjectivity, occasioned by his descent into an inanimateness akin to that of his bombed island home, seems temporarily to place him outside the normal conditions dictated by physical law. The passage seems obliquely to invoke some of the broader epistemological inferences drawn from the century's discoveries in the realm of particle physics, notably the relationship between experimental design and results obtained in the case of the wave-particle duality of light, and Heisenberg's demonstration that the very act of observation of a subatomic particle introduces uncertainty into our picture of it. An experiment designed to measure the wavelike properties of light will succeed admirably; but so will an experiment designed to determine its particulate character. In Fausto's terms, then, the "truth" is shaped by the observational process chosen by the observer, whose subjectivity, one might thus say, determines what is observed, what impression is received.

PC347.7 PF323.36 B303.33   The street of the 20th Century   The street whose corner Profane is always turning, to find himself once more "in alien country" (PC13.33).

PC347.12 PF324.4 B303.28   It is the acid test   One that Stencil clearly fails. His compulsion to populate the street of the twentieth century with participants in a grand conspiracy reveals him to be, in Fausto's estimation, one of the "false-animate or unimaginative [who] refuse to let well enough alone" (PC347.1).

PC347.15 PF324.7 B303.32   a row of false shop fronts   "The mystery of V. is the mystery of why we pursue our destruction; it is the mystery of fact in the twentieth century, which points repeatedly to the madness of annihilation—not to the hope of love, but to the waste land after the holocaust" (Olderman 124). Dugdale identifies this passage as another instance of Pynchon's use of the de Chirico painting *Mystery and Melancholy of a Street*, which he claims is here "adapted and presented as a general metaphor for a fallen world" (81).

PC347.25 PF324.17 B303.43   Schultze   A Prussian military officer, Major E. Schultze, who invented a nitrocellulose propellant suitable for use in shotguns ("Explosives: nitrocellulosic explosives," *Britannica Online*).

PC347.25 PF324.17 B304.1 Nobel Alfred Nobel, the inventor of dynamite and Ballistite (a nitrocellulosic propellant).

PC348.28 PF325.11 B304.36 But in dream there are two worlds The novel's most explicit expression of the street/under the street motif that runs throughout. Fausto's claim is borne out particularly in Profane's dream of disassembly (PC35.3), which takes place at street level, and in its mirror image, the disassembly of the Bad Priest, which takes place in the cellar of a house (PC368.4).

PC349.22 PF326.1 B305.23 metaphor has no value apart from its function "The principal influence on Fausto's attitude to poetry would seem to be the Robbe-Grillet of the essays translated as 'A Path for the Future Novel' (1956) and 'Nature, humanism and tragedy' (1958). Robbe-Grillet's idea of adjectival 'camouflage' and statement that 'the world is neither meaningful nor absurd. It simply is' are closely reproduced by Fausto" (Dugdale 94). (See also PC379.24n.) Dugdale also equates Fausto's "Great Lie" with Robbe-Grillet's "metaphysical pact," which he identifies as "the myth that there is a communion between man and nature and that 'the universe and I share a single soul'" (93). See also PC324.5. According to Campbell, "Fausto's—and Pynchon's—metaphors do not signify some absolute, but assert the need for an operational metaphysics, for a 'transcendental function,' for a faith to give us the will to continue. . . . The poet's role in the twentieth century is to revitalize the mindless inanimate constructively. Pynchon performs this role by not continuing to deceive readers about 'the Great Lie' . . . but by admitting the artifice" (66–67). Kharpertian notes Fausto's problematizing of Eliot's belief in the capacity of metaphor to impose order on disparate experiences (305).

PC350.11 PF326.25 B306.6 catenary The shape made by a perfectly flexible chain suspended from its ends and acted upon by gravity. "Through the substitution of an inanimate hanging cable for the once-human smile of the poet, Dnubietna provides the theme of metaphor as a necessary delusion for humanity; and the poet, through his magic cloaking device of the catenary, resembles the weaver of dreams, one of the 'fairy folk' from [Mondaugen's song in] chapter 9" (Davis 2). See PC269.31n.

PC352.14 PF328.18 B307.35 his hairy stomach "Fausto also reject[s] the tourist's mode of vision, in which only things listed in Baedeker can be perceived. . . . in wartime Malta, Fausto sees a wine merchant scratch his hairy stomach" (Strehle 48).

PC352.14 PF328.19 B307.36 singlet A sleeveless undershirt.

PC354.18 PF330.13 B309.28 Somehow the street—the kingdom of death—was friendly A reminder that Fausto's vision of the street is not confined to the dream world.

PC355.16 PF331.7 B310.30 balloon-girl See PC63.30n.

PC355.29 PF331.20 B310.35 Can you still look both ways Lhamon (76) answers in the affirmative, claiming that Paola is the only character in the novel who can maintain this vantage point, which is mirrored in Sphere's "keep cool but care" dictum (PC393.25).

PC355.33 PF331.24 B310.40 History . . . is a step-function "This curve, which looks like the horizontal component of a staircase, represents a discontinuous function. Such a conception would be attractive to a resident of Malta who knows that his island's history has been a series of unpredictable invasions and resulting periods of submission to foreign conquerors" (Stark 112).

PC357.6 PF332.26 B311.40 Accordingly we made our ablutions . . . just such a contingency The pastiche nature of the language, which invites but does not receive Fausto IV's wry commentary, is so broad as to suggest that Pynchon is playing games with the reader, as well as reinforcing the distance that separates Fausto II from the concrete circumstances of his world.

PC359.6 PF334.9 B313.16 Elena and I rose at last "The passage evokes the two sides of Fausto and, through allusion, the two corresponding literatures. The main sources appear to be Eliot's 'Burnt Norton' and two episodes in the memoirs of Rilke's patroness, with details derived from de Chirico, Rilke, Stevens, Fitzgerald and perhaps Crane's 'Marriage of Faustus and Helen.' On the other hand, the friction between the couple has a distinctly modern quality, recalling the tortured male-female relationships in Sartre, and Fausto's philosophical questions (how do I know the other is real, experiences pain?) are those of the later Wittgenstein" (Dugdale 95).

PC361.35 PF336.17 B315.19 vibrating like a shadow in some street Dugdale suggests that this is another allusion to de Chirico (82).

PC362.27 PF337.3 B315.43 Missierna li-inti fis-smewwiet, jit-qaddes ismek. . . . "Our Father, who art in heaven, hallowed be thy name . . ." (Cassola, 330). Cassola indicates that "li-inti" should appear as "li-int."

PC363.21 PF337.28 B316.28 no epiphanies on Malta Another reminder that Fausto's sensibility has moved beyond the legacy of the modernists, whose use of the epiphanic moment served as a means of transcending their intuitions of disorder (van Delden 122).

PC364.11 PF338.16 B317.13 Manichaean Pertaining to the dualistic doctrine of the third-century Iranian prophet Mani, which regarded the present world as a mixing of the originally separate forces of good and evil.

PC364.27 PF339.31 B317.30 Fortune's Wheel "Although a crossroads of history, Malta also promises—however fitfully—an escape from the vicissitudes of inexorable change. The rock at the center may be a refuge or the hope of a rebirth, an escape from history into sacred eternal time such as the 'eternal return' of which Mircea Eliade writes [in *Cosmos and History*]" (Henderson 283).

PC368.20 PF342.11 B321.1 an ivory comb A typical instance of the indeterminism that governs the novel's use of details. Although we are bound to connect this comb with the one depicting the crucified soldiers, which appears in the possession of Victoria Wren and Paola Maijstral, nothing in Fausto's description absolutely confirms the association. His apparent coyness in identifying the recipient of the comb only as "the little girl" makes our assumption that she is Paola similarly uncertain. See also PC481.2, where Fausto claims not to have recognized any of the children.

PC369.34 PF343.20 B322.10 the disassembly of the Bad Priest "The ending of the chapter . . . involves an odd conjunction of sources. The famous vision of the 'familiar compound ghost' in 'Little Gidding,' which also occurs in a city damaged by bombs, is blended with the scene in *Le Temps Retrouvé* where the narrator, sheltering in a hotel during an air raid, sees into the next room where Charlus is being beaten. In Proust a 'bad priest' appears later at the hotel. Other possible influences include the epigraph to [the *Waste Land*], describing the caged Sibyl tormented by children, and Rilke's 'Birth of Venus' (1904), with its itemisation of a new female body now grimly applied to one being taken apart in death" (Dugdale 95–96). "In the Western Rose Window of Chartres, Adams had seen 'a confused effect of opals, in a delirium of color and light, with a result like a cluster of stones in jewelry' [p. 472]. This epiphany of transcendental hope in the name of the Queen of Heaven stands in parodic contrast to the brutal end of V. on Malta. Transformed by this point into the Queen of the inanimate, the spokeswoman of death, she has literally *become* artificial gaudiness and bedizenment. Her dismemberment . . . symbolizes the sterile crucifixion of a false god, a violent death without hope of resurrection" (Eddins 61). According to Kemeny, "the whole passage can be read as the literal deconstruction of a text; the Bad Priest, after all, is textualized for and by the children through war-time rumours" (263). The children themselves are variously regarded as a symbol of "pure evil, the complete loss of innocence" (Chambers 89), as "single-minded scientists" (Chambers 89), as the ironically appropriate agents of the destruction of someone who has preached an "antithetical gospel" (Eddins 74), and as representatives of a "motley of races" who take apart the woman who "has come to be identified with a particularly evil form of reified racist colonialism" (Holton 332). Campbell (61) notes that the false teeth and the star sapphire "seem like displaced parts from earlier sections of the novel," linking the teeth to Ploy's (PC4.5) and the sapphire to the golden navel-screw of Profane's recalled story (PC34).

PC370.18 PF344.2 B322.30   drawn-out wails   Lhamon links this with other pentecostal imagery in the novel, claiming that "her last voice is that of tongues" (80).

PC371.5 PF344.23 B323.11   so used her own blood   "In his own priestly preparation of the Bad Priest for death, Fausto symbolically confirms the transition from the realm of the inanimate to the realm of the animate. Instead of using oil from a chalice to anoint her sense organs, he dips blood from her navel. Out of the wound, caused by the children's removal of the inert star sapphire, comes the latent healing impulse that marks the return from the province of the plastic to the domain of the human" (Newman 61).

PC372.25 PF346.3 B324.25   V. or sleep   "The attempt to establish that everything is part of one big 'plot' might result in a realization that everything is simply 'accident.' We stay awake by vigilantly maneuvering between the two extreme and intolerable possibilities" (Tanner, *TP* 47).

CHAPTER TWELVE

Roony Winsome walks out on a row with Mafia and instead of going to the latest Crew party, which is just getting under way, he wanders down to the V. Note, where he meets McClintic Sphere. The two of them decide to go to Lenox and head over to Matilda Winthrop's to pick up Ruby/Paola. Roony tries to find Rachel Owlglass to take her with them but can only talk to her on the phone. Rachel is looking for Esther, who is upset at the discovery that she is pregnant. Slab's solution is to collect money from the guests at the party to pay for her to go to Cuba for an abortion. Rachel attempts to recruit Profane in an effort to thwart Esther's plan, but they are forced to wait until McClintic returns with Roony's car. Roony, meanwhile, has determined to commit suicide by jumping out of Rachel's apartment window; he is prevented by his own ineffectualness and by the intervention of Pig Bodine. At Idlewild, the attempt to intercept Esther goes awry amid a riot caused in part by the Crew and in part by the family and friends of a departing Puerto Rican child and her father. Among the latter group is Fina Mendoza, who is returning to Puerto Rico herself. Police raid Winsome's apartment, where Mafia appears to be holding an orgy. Paola and McClintic Sphere head for the Berkshires.

PC374.4 PF348.8 B326.1   Accidental art   The open refrigerator as art reminds Vella of Robert Rauschenberg's 1955 "Interview," a "collage-sculpture consisting of an open cupboard door with various banal objects exposed—family photographs, a baseball" (33).

PC376.26 PF350.25 B328.13   nobody knows what a Maltese is Paola's hybrid background is symbolic of her capacity to avoid the constraints of a single perspective—her capacity to "keep cool, but care."

PC378.8 PF352.1 B329.23 Alden John Alden (1599?–1687), one of the *Mayflower* pilgrims.

PC378.8 PF352.1 B329.23 Walden Walden Pond, in eastern Massachusetts. Setting for Thoreau's *Walden; or, Life in the Woods.*

PC379.14 PF353.2 B330.22 Little Willie John . . . singing Fever Little Willie John's recording of "Fever," by Otis Blackwell and Eddie Cooley, was a million-seller by May 1956.

PC380.1 PF353.22 B331.2 Battista Fulgencio Batista (1901–73), a Cuban dictator.

PC380.19 PF354.3 B331.21 Botticelli Not of course the painter, Sandro Botticelli, whose *Birth of Venus* is the focus of much of the activity in the Florence chapter, but the guessing game in which players try to earn the right to ask direct questions about the identity of a historical or fictional thought up by one of them. "[The Crew] know Botticelli only as a game whose object is the guessing of those proper nouns that constitute the whole substance of their conversation" (Cowart 22).

PC380.20 PF354.4 B331.22 Liguorian tracts The teachings of Saint Alphonsus Liguori (1696–1787), founder of the Congregation of the Most Holy Redeemer, also known as the Redemptorists.

PC380.20 PF354.4 B331.22 Galen "Greek physician, writer, and philosopher (129–c216) who exercised a dominant influence on medical theory and practice in Europe from the Middle Ages until the mid–17th century" ("Galen of Pergamum," *Britannica Online*).

PC380.20 PF354.4 B331.23 David Riesman American sociologist. Co-author with Reuel Denney and Nathan Glazer of *The Lonely Crowd* (1950), a study of the urban middle classes. Pittas-Giroux notes Riesman's use of the gyroscope and the radio dish as images for two of the social types he identified, the inner-directed and the other-directed, and argues that Pynchon "assimilates and perverts both emblems" (6).

PC382.2 PF355.18 B332.37 neo-Wobbly The Wobblies were members of the labor organization known as the Industrial Workers of the World. Joe Hill was one of its organizers until he was executed for murder in 1915.

PC382.3 PF355.18 B332.38 Joe Hill Joel Emmanuel Häglund (1879–1915), known as Joe Hill. "Swedish-born American songwriter and organizer for the Industrial Workers of the World (IWW); his execution for an alleged robbery-murder made him a martyr and folk hero in the radical American labour movement" ("Hill, Joe," *Britannica Online*).

PC382.5 PF355.21 B332.41 Westbrook Pegler Conservative newspaper columnist (1894–1969).

PC383.10 PF356.21 B333.43 shivaree A corruption of "charivari," meaning a confused babel, derived from the practice of serenading an unpopular marriage with "music" played on saucepans, kettles, trays, etc. (*OED*).

PC383.33 PF357.6 B334.25 Hank Snow Pittas-Giroux points out that the country-and-western singer's 1954 number-one hit was called "*I* Don't Hurt Any More" (230).

PC385.4 PF358.8 B335.24 like you love the dispossessed But Profane is soon seen to be "unwilling to convict himself of love for bums" (PC386.2), once again revealing his inability to risk connection with other human beings.

PC385.27 PF358.29 B336.5 rotated our 90° Rachel describes the end of her affair with Slab by reference to Profane's earlier reminder that she and Slab "were . . . horizontal once" (PC385.10).

PC386.14 PF359.12 B336.28 one hand moved to automatic McHoul and Wills invoke the image of Rachel fondling the MG's gearshift (PC22.29), claiming that "there is little wonder that the eventual description of their sexual intercourse is a peculiar combination of the biological and the mechanical" (174).

PC386.34 PF359.32 B337.7 defenestration Technically, Winsome's dream is of *self*-defenestration, the action of throwing himself out of a window.

PC387.23 PF360.17 B337.31 the Grand Climacteric The sixtythird year of one's life, reckoned by some to have particular numerological significance. "Climacteric" is defined as a critical period in human life. Here it is clearly used as the male equivalent of menopause.

PC387.28 PF360.22 B337.35 **a man who spent millions** A reference to Henry Ford, who published anti-Semitic charges in his newspaper, the *Dearborn Independent,* often citing as evidence the fraudulent *Protocols of the Learned Elders of Zion,* disseminated first in 1903 by the Russian secret police in an attempt to foster anti-Jewish sentiment by "proving" that Jews were involved in a conspiracy to dominate the world. Fausto Maijstral refers obliquely to the same document (PC487.4n).

PC391.34 PF364.14 B341.21 **I did it** "This admission of responsibility is a departure from the schlemiel stance, or at least a modification of it. Benny does not give up the schlemiel stance, as is clear from the conversation with Rachel (PC413–14) but he nevertheless asserts the possibility of actively initiating something. This means that he rejects the concept of complete determination by society, a concept which is embodied in the yo-yo feature" (Matthijs 130).

PC393.19 PF365.31 B342.37 **She talked to him straight** "The pastoral sequence validates the credentials of Paola as a goddess for the waste land. She is not the prostitute with the heart of gold, nor a reincarnation of the Earth-Mother; she is a new and fragile Venus, not so much an archetype as a wholly human figure" (Slade 109).

PC393.25 PF366.1 B342.43 **keep cool, but care** Golden notes that this "ethic of temperance . . . is the only golden mean found in *V.*" (Golden 14). In a similarly positive reading, Andrew Dinn notes "the suitability of McClintic Sphere's advice . . . to both Stencil's and Profane's diseases. Stencil needs some cool to stop the random Brownian motions induced in his mind by his paranoia. Profane needs some cool as a damper on the reinforcing yoyo flicks of fate which would otherwise serve to increase the amplitude of his simple harmonic motion. In both cases what they need most of all to do is care about what is going on around them—not ignore or fight against the forces which perturb them but watch them, sidestep them, route round them carefully, purposefully and attentively in order to achieve something" (Pynchon List archives, "pynchon-196-08.txt"). Other critics are more ambivalent. Olderman, who describes Sphere's sentiments as "simple but affirmative," nonetheless points out that their articulation is immediately followed by the information that "somebody had run over a skunk" (139). Seed regards the echo of Sphere's words supposedly uttered by SHROUD a few pages later as an ironic commentary on the difference between Sphere's enactment of his love for Paola and his attempt to "[generalize] his behaviour into a statement" (81). Tanner's mixed response is evidenced in the fact that at one point he defends Sphere against the charge of being "slick and glib," suggesting that this may be "a result of the problem of finding 'right words' in a world in which language seems to be declining like everything else." He goes on to argue that Sphere's catchphrase "gestures towards some form of maintained humanity in a world in which . . . an increasing number of people seem to be moving, or have moved, to the extremest states of flop and flip which . . . can seem to end up being the same thing: a very distinct symptom of increased entropy. Both are ways of 'retreating' from humanity; and it is at least *something* to begin to 'retreat from retreat' [PC339.20]" (*TP* 50). Elsewhere, however, Tanner insists that "You cannot render great emotions in comic-strip, and 'keep cool, but care,' is just such bubble talk or the sort of slogan-jargon mongered by advertisements. In proximity to the multiple parodic references which the book contains, any potentially serious emotion is bound to turn into its own caricature and join the masquerade as a costumed sentimentality" ("V2" 25).

PC394.2 PF366.11 B343.12 Malenkov Gregory Maximilianovich Malenkov (1902–88). Russian Prime Minister, 1953–55.

PC394.2 PF366.11 B343.12 Khrushchev Nikita Sergeyevich Khrushchev (1894–1971). First secretary of the Russian Communist Party, 1953–64; Russian premier, 1958–64.

CHAPTER THIRTEEN

Profane, Stencil, and Paola are off to Malta. Profane, who has taken up residence with Rachel after Esther's departure for Cuba, has lost his job at the research facility after oversleeping. He reestablishes his connection with Paola when he prevents Pig Bodine from raping her by calling in a favor from their days together in the navy. Profane had saved Pig's life inadvertently and is now able to capitalize on Pig's sense of obligation. Stencil asks for Profane's help in "handling" Paola during their trip to Malta, and despite his misgivings, he seems inclined to go, in part to extricate himself from his relationship with Rachel. After he has helped Stencil to steal Eigenvalue's precious set of false teeth, the two of them drift through Central Park.

PC402.15 PF374.3 B350.26 Teledu "A properization of the name of a 'small dark brown mammal' found in the mountains of Java, Sumatra, and Borneo. It ejects 'a fetid secretion when alarmed or in danger'" (Harder 73).

PC408.32 PF379.36 B356.10 making bits and pieces of it animate Profane's consumption of some of the food is an attempt to make up for the fact that the apartment is empty, affording no human connection.

PC409.7 PF380.6 B356.18 the Forked Yew Hite suggests that the name invokes Lear—the bar's patrons are "the twentieth century's poor 'forked' creatures" (55). Most readers are more likely to hear another of Pynchon's somewhat labored puns.

PC409.30 PF380.28 B356.43 Varèse Edgard Varèse (1883–1965). Franco-American composer of innovative electronic music.

PC411.14 PF382.3 B358.12 Wherever I am This recalls Pig's response to Profane's question earlier in the novel: "'Where we

going,' Profane said. 'The way we're heading,' said Pig" (PC10.3).
"Benny's 'profanity', in spatial terms, is not denied by his trip
through the sewers; he retains the essential characteristics of the
profane view: he has no orientation, because he lacks a centre, a fixed
point" (Matthijs 137).

PC413.6 PF383.28 B359.34   a Universal Principle   "But as Rachel points out, once even a flabby clumsy soul is amplified into a
Universal Principle . . . it merely assumes the function of a tautology. And tautologies work like clockwork. There are no surprises"
(McHoul and Wills 174).

PC414.1 PF384.20 B360.21   isn't this . . . enough   "The conversation questions the validity of the schlemiel stance. Rachel sees it
as a way of avoiding reality. Here we are confronted with the question whether the escapist quality of the schlemiel is not simply another way of avoiding the conflict between intention and reality"
(Matthijs 129).

PC414.2 PF384.21 B360.22   an inanimate schmuck   The phrase-
ological point of view here is somewhat confusing. Given Rachel's
critique of Profane's capacity for true human commitment, the reference to Profane's penis as "inanimate" seems to establish an alignment between the narrator and Rachel. At the same time, however,
the word seems to belong to Profane, who, despite his fear of disassembly into a collection of inert parts, is here given over to an un-
characteristically mechanistic vision of human interaction. See also
PC227.9n.

PC414.24 PF385.6 B361.4   an all-electronic woman   The link
with the increasingly inanimate V. is inescapable. See Stencil's day-
dream of the fully mechanized V. (PC444).

PC415.10 PF385.25 B361.24   Time, gentlemen, please   "The
Crew are wastelanders right down to the bar they frequent, where
'Time, gentlemen, please' echoes from Eliot's waste land" (Older-
man 135).

PC416.30 PF387.7 B362.41   whose etiology was also her own
Stencil here states explicitly what the novel has adumbrated all
along: "V." is the individual embodiment of the currents of history

whose confluence gives rise to massive outbursts of violence. "V. is finally a symbol of pure inanimateness, of the nothingness of death. Her desire for death and nothingness is a desire which Pynchon sees as the hidden urge of modern history" (Golden 11).

PC416.33 PF387.10 B363.2   then now, of all times   "Now" is toward the end of September 1956, when the crisis over Egypt's nationalization of the Suez canal was coming to a head.

PC418.5 PF388.15 B364.5   take Sir Alastair Wren for a lover This repeats the speculation that Stencil-as-Aïeul includes in his list of possible scenarios regarding the gathering of tourists and spies at the cafe in Alexandria (PC61). The hint of a sexual relationship between Victoria and the man who appears to be her father anticipates Mélanie l'Heuremaudit's relationship with her father in the next chapter.

PC418.34 PF389.5 B364.36   a remarkably scattered concept "From one point of view Stencil has far too much to go on, since he is bound to find clues everywhere—a fact he recognizes, near the end. Indeed, as this 'concept' expands to include ever more manifestations of V., and as opposites such as love and death, the political right and left, start to converge in this inclusiveness, it points to that ultimate disappearance of differences and loss of distinctions which is the terminal state of the entropic process. If V. can mean everything it means nothing" (Tanner, "V2" 27).

PC422.34 PF392.29 B368.13   a sense of population and warmth Provided, ironically enough, by a gay man beating up an undercover cop, a band of juvenile delinquents and a woman built like a garbage-truck driver trudging along in the wake of a floating condom. The irony is presumably pointed—serving perhaps to reorient the reader whose instincts may be to see the nightscape of the park as threatening and dehumanized.

CHAPTER FOURTEEN

It is summer in Paris, 1913. Mélanie L'Heuremaudit has arrived in the city at the invitation of a group of avant-garde artists who are planning the premiere of a new ballet in which she is to be the star. Mélanie, who was the object of her father's incestuous attentions, has been more or less abandoned by her mother after her father has fled the country. In Paris, she becomes the focus of an intense erotic attraction for the lady V., the chief sponsor of the ballet. On the evening of the premiere a riot erupts at the theater and during the performance, Mélanie is killed when she is impaled on a sharp pole, having neglected to put on the metal plate that was intended to protect her. The lady V. disappears from Paris.

PC424 PF393 B369   V. in love   Berressem argues that the story of V.'s affair is designed to undermine Freudian psychoanalysis by demonstrating its inapplicability to "a subject completely determined by forces outside of psychoanalysis" ("Love" 6–7).

PC424.4 PF393.4 B369.23   the hands might have stood anywhere   "Mélanie's exact time of arrival in Paris is not her time, and can only be extrapolated by its relation to various time-systems operating simultaneously. . . . Her arrival time is the interface of various paradigms, its time not an instance in a general flow, but already colonized by differing forces and determinations and a specific historical moment ["By the cover of Le Soleil"]. Against these geographically, culturally and politically mediated times, Mélanie herself is explicitly undefined" (Berressem, "Love" 7).

PC424.10 PF393.34 B369.28   the Orleanist morning paper   The Orleanists had long been the supporters of the claims of the dukes of Orleans to the throne of France.

PC424.12 PF393.35 B369.34　current Pretender The great-grandson of King Louis-Philippe, Louis Philippe Robert (1869–1926) became recognized by royalists as the rightful heir to the French throne upon the death of his father in 1894 ("Orléans, Louis-Philippe-Robert, duc d'," *Britannica Online*).

PC424.13 PF393.35 B369.31　Sirius Alpha Canis Majoris, the Dog Star, 8.6 light years from the solar system. Associated with the so-called dog days of July and August.

PC424.15 PF394.2 B369.34　Black Mass Eddins sees V.'s participation in the Black Masses as an anticipation of the Bad Priest's "antireproductive obsession" (77).

PC424.17 PF394.3 B369.35　l'Heuremaudit "[Mélanie's] last name translates as 'The Cursed Hour,' a time that denotes both a historical and a cultural framework—for Pynchon a growing decadence" (Berressem, "Love" 7). "Mélanie is the often apocalyptic image of the dancer in Yeats; a merger of the dancer-doll of the Fourth 'Duino Elegy' with the girl acrobat who is raised aloft in the Fifth" (Dugdale 96–97).

PC425.19 PF394.23 B370.15　Papa! The Freudian connection is established at the outset (Berressem, "Love" 12). See also PC426.14n.

PC426.3 PF395.4 B370.34　Serre Chaude The estate's name means "hothouse," a fitting name for the site of an incestuous relationship and for the home of one destined to become the lover of V.

PC426.14 PF395.14 B371.3　She imagined the sensation often "A thinly disguised dream about incestuous sexual intercourse" (Berressem, "Love" 12).

PC426.30 PF395.30 B371.21　M. Itague Cowart identifies "the famous impresario Serge Diaghilev" as the model for Itague (75), while Dugdale claims that he is "a combination of two figures in Sartre, the waiter and the anti-Semite" (96).

PC426.31 PF395.31 B371.22　fétiche "For Freud, fetishism is related to the fear of castration and is thus first a male domain. . . . The fetish is . . . related to woman in her function as the object of male desire; for man, it serves as a circumvention of the fear of castration because it recreates from a material object associated with women's bodies a missing phallus out of the realm of the inanimate" (Berressem, "Love" 7-8).

PC426.35 PF395.35 B371.26 Satin "Nijinsky, who choreographed but did not perform in the original production [of Stravinsky's *Rites of Spring*, on which Satin's ballet is modeled] becomes Satin" (Cowart 75).

PC427.1 PF395.36 B371.27 Mlle. Jarretière Mélanie's stage name can mean a number of things. The primary meaning is "garter," but it can also mean "picketing rope" and, according to Berressem, "conductor-wire" ("Love" 18). Dugdale finds a trace of the name of the French writer Alfred Jarry, the creator of the farce *Ubu Roi*, a forerunner of the theater of the absurd, to which Yeats responded with the comment, "After us, the Savage God" (97).

PC427.13 PF396.11 B371.39 L'Enlèvement des Vierges Chinoises "It is often particularly difficult to judge the value of the difference between parody and parodied; to interpret whether the parody is pointed or merely playful; whether it has a critical content or simply represents comic opportunism. Is the 'Enlèvement des Vierges Chinoises' an unmasking of the essence of the *Sacré* [*du Printemps*, Stravinsky's ballet] or just a game, a grateful borrowing of a scene?" (Dugdale 107).

PC427.15 PF396.13 B371.41 Porcépic "Porcupine." The novel's version of Igor Stravinsky (Cowart 75). Cowart notes that this is the novel's second porcupine, the first being Porpentine (PC59.13n).

PC427.18 PF396.16 B372.1 Su Feng "Su Feng contains the Chinese for 'phoenix' which, with the phallic pole and the 'climax' in the ballet, relates her to Lawrence" (Dugdale 97).

PC427.27 PF396.25 B372.13 Not like machines at all Another instance of the putative transformation of the inanimate into the animate, like Profane's conversations with SHOCK and SHROUD. Berressem sees the transformation apparently borne out at the moment of Mélanie's death, when "one of the automata . . . runs amok and commits, it seems out of some sort of machinic solidarity with Mélanie, a symbolic suicide" ("Love" 19).

PC427.35 PF396.31 B372.20 would it ever rain? "That the prevailing sultriness can only be relieved by an extremely violent storm hints at the state of Europe itself, on the verge of a catastrophic war" (Cowart 74). The question invokes the threatening dryness of the Waste Land.

PC428.20 PF397.15 B372.42   the legs of a dancer   "In her taking the perspective of her father's desire in relation to herself, she already inserts herself firmly into a fetish-function" (Berressem, "Love" 9).

PC428.31 PF397.27 B373.12   She was not pretty unless she wore something   Unless, that is, she covers up the evidence of her animate flesh with inanimate cloth.

PC429.5 PF397.35 B373.20   the kimono   Dugdale sees this as the kimono of "the suicidal Madame Butterfly" (97), while Eddins claims that it clearly links her with "the congeries of iridescent Vheissu images and thus with the inanimate" (Eddins 74–75).

PC429.11 PF398.3 B373.27   The lay figure   Citing Baudrillard's assertion that "the mannequin is the model for [the] complete phallic instrumentalization of the body," Berressem identifies the lay figure as "the perfect surrogate and substitute, especially because it is 'without a head' and thus has no identity: it is the truly phallic (and already machinic) body" ("Love" 11).

PC430.20 PF399.11 B374.33   chiffonnier   Rag-and-bone man.

PC430.34 PF399.24 B375.5   La Libre Parole . . . Captain Dreyfus In 1894, a French army captain named Alfred Dreyfus was convicted of treason and sent to the penal colony on Devil's Island. The trial sparked a twelve-year-long battle between those who believed Dreyfus was the victim of an injustice and those who held up his conviction as an example of the disloyalty of French Jews. *La Libre Parole* was the leader of the press campaign against Dreyfus.

PC431.8 PF399.31 B375.15   the color of a Negro's head   "The watershed configuration of the feminization of the Other is V.'s textualixed body. . . . This portrayal of V. highlights the heavily intertwined processes of feminization and the colonization of the body. The foregrounding of the color of V.'s dress as 'the color of a Negro's head' functions as a statement on the inscription of black skin in imperialistic discourse as 'pure signifier,' a husk, a covering, if you

will, that constitutes the western notion of the 'feminine principle'"
(Kemeny 260–61).

PC431.16 PF400.4 B375.24 Who knew her "soul" Following as
it does immediately upon a description of V.'s shoes, this question of
Itague's seems to be prompted in part by a rather obvious pun.

PC432.4 PF400.27 B376.5 The German could build another
Itague's identification of V. with the automata from the ballet suggests the extent to which she has figuratively already become what
she almost literally is when the children disassemble her in Malta
over twenty years later.

PC432.22 PF401.7 B376.25 a Poiret dress Paul Poiret (1879–
1944). French couturier who designed the hobble skirt.

**PC432.32 PF401.15 B376.34 a cocktail whose name you have
never heard** Itague's train of thought here is somewhat hard to follow. His recognition of V.'s desire to attend the Black Mass at Porcépic's house seems to have caused him to doubt his own expertise as
a judge of character (like a bartender stumped by a customer). Having
argued that V. is essentially inert, like a mannequin, he now sees that
she is moved by human desires.

PC433.22 PF402.4 B377.19 find a small key "The mechanical
'arousal' of the automata by the winding of the key between their/
her shoulderblades figures as a displacement of a more direct sexual
arousal: her whispered 'Between my thighs' denotes her desire to
change the place of arousal from the back to her genitals. . . . the
dream . . . is . . . a 'quotation' of psychoanalytical theory. . . . Mélanie's
desire (to be a phallic automaton) *mirrors the desire of psychoanalysis itself for its latent wish,* the implied (phallic) structuration behind
the scenarios of the dream-work" (Berressem, "Love" 13).

PC433.34 PF402.14 B377.31 Gerfaut French for "gerfalcon," a
large falcon.

PC434.14 PF402.28 B378.5 Doucette Reminiscent of Nabokov's *Lolita* (1955).

**PC434.28 PF403.5 B378.19 an exhausted yellow light . . . rain-
clouds which refused to burst** Once again the weather suggests the
Waste Land—in this case its "final entropic stasis" (Eddins 77).

PC435.21 PF403.32 B379.9 Isadora Duncan American dancer (1877–1927) famous for her free-floating expressive style.

PC436.17 PF404.23 B379.39 A chaos of flesh "The repressed image of the female body as a chaos of flesh is transformed by artificial light effects and costumes into a phallic performance" (Berressem, "Love" 14).

PC436.35 PF405.4 B380.16 Bakunin Mikhail Aleksandrovich Bakunin (1814–76). Russian anarchist and agitator.

PC436.35 PF405.4 B380.16 Ulyanov Vladimir Ilyich Ulyanov (1870–1924), better known as Lenin.

PC437.11 PF405.15 B380.28 a falling-away from what is human Itague's definition of decadence sums up the central thematic preoccupation of the entire novel, and he goes on to describe as one of the consequences of the loss of humanity precisely that tendency which Fausto Maijstral identifies in his disquisition on metaphor (PC349.22n).

PC437.24 PF405.28 B381.1 with the basic rhythms of History Kholsky's statement of basic Marxist dogma resonates with some of the other historiographies espoused by characters in the novel and defined in terms of cycles or rhythms (PC327.33n).

PC437.28 PF405.31 B381.5 metaphysical bedspring "To gloss this figure, we have only to compare Mondaugen's sferics. . . . In the case of both . . . the medium is the message in all its opacity and randomness" (Eddins 78).

PC440.2 PF407.35 B383.6 La Vie Heureuse, Le Rire, Le Charivari Popular magazines. Toulouse Lautrec published lithographs in *Le Rire. Le Charivari* was the forerunner of the famous English humor magazine, *Punch* (the London Charivari).

PC440.11 PF408.7 B383.16 64 different sets of roles Berressem regards this passage as evidence of Pynchon's having fun at Freud's expense ("Love" 17).

PC441.3 PF408.32 B384.3 world . . . at least described to its fullest by Karl Baedeker of Leipzig Via the connection between Leipzig and Freud's paranoid patient Schreber (PC47.35n), Dugdale makes the case that Pynchon here brings together "the ideas of fiction and the city, to envisage the latter as if it were the construction of an individual paranoid" (119).

PC441.29 PF409.21 B384.32   They are the Street's own   "The religious parallels only serve to enforce the fact that the 'tourist country' lacks any religious or spiritual dimension (what Henry James called 'the fourth dimension')—not to mention an emotional, human third dimension" (Tanner, *TP* 51).

PC441.31 PF409.23 B384.36   the null-time of human love   On the basis of Mélanie's last name ("cursed hour"), Campbell notes "the danger of living in this temporal zone" (64). Perhaps some comparison is intended with that moment in Florence when Evan and Victoria are temporarily removed from time (PC212.12n).

PC441.35 PF409.27 B384.39   on the authority of Porcépic himself   Unlike Mondaugen's story, the story of V.'s affair with Mélanie is not explicitly called into question as the Stencilized version of someone else's narrative. Indeed, in this case, the narrator steps in to editorialize not on Stencil's transformation of the original source material, but on the source material itself, as if "he" had read it: "[Porcépic's] description . . . is a well-composed and ageless still-life of love at one of its many extremes."

PC442.28 PF410.17 B385.28   the Porpentine theme, the Tristan-and-Iseult theme   Cowart insists that the "Porpentine theme" can be recovered only by reference to "Under the Rose," the earlier story version of chapter 3 (74). The novel certainly provides very little access to Porpentine's inner life, while the story's details come to us almost wholly from Porpentine's point of view, but in the end, the novel's Porpentine seems to be motivated by very much the same impulses as the story's. He is caught up in the conflict between his professional instincts, which teach him of the potentially deadly consequences of surrender to emotions such as love and compassion, and his personal inclination, which leads him somehow to become complicit in Goodfellow's affair with Victoria. In a somewhat superficial sense, then, his thinking is linked with the explication of the Tristan and Iseult theme that immediately follows, in that love and death do indeed go hand in hand. As Graves notes, however, this is not exactly the same connection identified by de Rougemont in his *Love in the Western World:* "Love and death, a fatal love—in these phrases is summed up, if not the whole of poetry, at least whatever is popular, whatever is universally moving in European literature.... Romance only comes into existence when love is fatal, frowned upon and doomed by life itself. What stirs lyrical poets to their finest flights is neither the delight of the senses nor the fruitful content-ment of the settled couple; not the satisfaction of love, but its pas-sion" (quoted in Graves 64).

PC443.5 PF410.28 B385.38   if she were in fact Victoria Wren This proviso serves as a salutary reminder of the uncertainties which govern assumptions about character in a novel that embodies Fausto's dismissal of "the false assumption that identity is single, soul continuous" (PC327.21). Like Stencil, the reader tends to favor the assumption that Victoria and Mélanie's lover are one and the same, even though precious little evidence exists to support it.

PC443.9 PF410.32 B386.1   her girl's faith   "The suggestion here seems to be that V.'s attempts—however self-defeating—to order and control the chaotic unfolding of events are giving way, by the time of Paris, to an increasing identification with this chaos in the guise of the apeirontic Inanimate toward which it tends.... It would thus appear that the final stage of Stencil's theory, the Paracletian descent of tongues, is merely the apocalyptic fruition of gnostic ten-dencies already immanent in both V.'s virtù and V.'s love feast, and ironically subversive of the well-wrought polity" (Eddins 82).

PC443.12 PF410.35 B386.5   had as yet no name   "According to the OED, [the] term *fascist* and its derivatives were not current until 1919 and after. Furthermore, the first fascist party was organized in March 1919 in Italy, just three months prior to the time in *V.* of the June Disturbances on Malta" (Kharpertian 82). Cowart notes that Pynchon correctly identifies V. as "the fascist *Zeitgeist.* . . . Though we do not see her actually consorting with Hitler and Mussolini, they serve what she represents, and she is of their generation: V., 1880–1943; Mussolini, 1883–1945; Hitler, 1889–1945" (18).

PC443.15 PF411.1 B386.8   part of any conspiracy   "Is Pynchon really speaking of the twentieth century, with its enormous store of hope in its virtù? of the struggle to subdue and control nature that would lead to the fearful discovery of atomic energy, with its threat to all life? Is it specifically this that Pynchon has in mind when he wonders whether V. knew that her fetishism was part of some 'conspiracy' . . . ? If the author knows, he never tells: he is willing to let us imagine any form of apocalypse we please, so long as we understand V.'s love as some form of step towards Armageddon" (Richter 108).

PC443.17 PF411.3 B386.9 a colony of the Kingdom of Death The phrase prompts Dugdale to identify Baedeker land as "a scale model of imperialism" (118).

PC443.20 PF411.6 B386.14 the mirror's soulless gleam "Mélanie's narcissism is a measure of her longing for the inanimate; her look into the mirror is a look into the void of the self. Because a death-wish is at the root of Mélanie's attempts to freeze her image in a mirror, Freud's psychoanalytic version of the theory of entropy is in force here. Wylie Sypher has discussed this aspect of Freud in *Loss of the Self in Modern Literature and Art:*

> If, [Freud] says, the tendency of instinct is toward repeating or restating an earlier condition, then the desire to return to the inorganic is irresistible, and our instinct is to obliterate the disturbance we call consciousness. "The organism is resolved to die in its own way," and the path of our life is simply our own way of choosing our progress toward death. The ultimate pleasure is an untroubled security of not-being; therefore the drag toward inertia [Thanatos] is constantly behind that self-assertion we call living. "The inanimate was there before the animate"—a wisdom graven ineffaceably, though illegibly, within the unconscious self. Like Schopenhauer or Nietzsche, Freud assumes that the root of all our troubles is our individuality, which we would extinguish. (Slade 73)

PC444.8 PF411.27 B386.38 a vision of her now "The limit of fetishism, and also the limit of psychoanalysis, is man as fetish and man as pure object. . . . In a radical critique of humanistic patterns of explication, psychoanalysis is the first to fall. Appropriately, the last image is, again, of V. standing metonymically for the new scene" (Berressem, "Love" 21). Stencil's vision of the seventy-six-year-old V. is of course congruent with the descriptions of SHOCK and SHROUD (PC302) and with Profane's fantasy of an "all-electronic woman" (PC414.25)

PC444.18 PF411.37 B386.7   Wheatstone bridges   A Wheatstone bridge is an apparatus used to measure electrical resistance.

PC444.33 PF412.15 B387.23   a beast of venery   A creature, that is, whose sole purpose is to be hunted. Yet Stencil is not quite ready to "let her die," since her death would bring to an end the quest that is maintaining his sense of his own animateness.

PC445.5 PF412.21 B387.31   Orientalism   Part of what Holton calls "a profusion of references to race and imperialism probing the 'erotic and aesthetic fascination with "the Orient"' that [Andreas] Huyssen (and, of course, [Edward] Said) has characterized as a 'deeply problematic' element of European culture" (333).

PC446.11 PF413.20 B388.29   the Norman dervish   Dugdale associates Mélanie via this phrase with the Virgin of Adams's *Mont-Saint-Michel and Chartres* (97).

PC447.25 PF414.29 B389.29   the one inanimate object that would have saved her   "Within this catastrophic moment, the inanimate and the animate implode, and the scene tumbles out of the psychoanalytical framework into a machinic one, which cannot be read in 'human' parameters (Lacanian or otherwise) anymore, but only in machinic ones, and in which the law-of-the-father is replaced by the 'law-of-the-machine'" (Berressem, "Love" 19). "The heavy symbolism of this scene—her death, so utterly phallic a destruction—puts sex back into its violent but heterosexual place, freeing V. of the lesbian alliance and making her available to men again, her life cleansed. The cruel and symbolic punishment of Mélanie for her failure to preserve her chastity—more important, to preserve it for men—is a powerful indictment of V. as the aggressor in love, as it is to all lesbianism" (Allen 45). "This particular act relates back to the mythic significance of Victoria Wren's name, the wren being described in *The Golden Bough* as 'the Lady of Heaven's hen.' Frazer notes the custom of hunting the wren which is killed and then carried aloft on the end of a pole. Pynchon conflates Frazer and Stravinsky to produce a work which travesties both and which contains neither mythic meaning, solemnity nor transcendence" (Seed 107).

PC447.29 PF414.34 B390.1   a mad Irredentist   See PC256.15, "Italia irredenta." V. shows up shortly after this episode in Malta accompanied by Sgherraccio (PC511.15n). The name Sgherraccio vaguely echoes "sgherro," a hired thug.

PC447.31 PF414.35 B340.3   the Butte   Montmartre. "Butte" = "knoll, hillock."

CHAPTER FIFTEEN

The prelude to the departure for Malta continues as events seem to conspire to propel Profane toward the Mediterranean. He and Stencil and Pig Bodine go to Washington, where Profane and Pig end up in jail after a period of drunken rollicking. Pig is recognized as a Navy deserter, and Profane is obliged to bid him farewell. Stencil makes his peace with Eigenvalue and Profane his with Rachel. In late September, Profane, Paola, and Stencil set sail for Malta on the Susanna Squaducci.

PC448.4 PF415.29 B391.22   the Whitney   Art museum in Manhattan.

PC448.4 PF415.29 B391.22   Kisch mein tokus   Yiddish—"Kiss my ass."

PC448.5 PF415.30 B391.23   Mene, mene, tekel, upharsin   These are the Aramaic words that appeared on the wall at Belshazzar's feast and that Daniel interpreted as a forecast of the destruction of Babylon (Daniel 5:25). Stencil is thus invoking the catchphrase "The writing on the wall" and, perhaps somewhat manipulatively, suggesting obliquely that Profane's relationship with Rachel may have run its course.

PC448.18 PF416.4 B391.37   what glittered in Stencil's hand   The teeth from Eigenvalue's office.

PC449.4 PF416.10 B391.43   Malta never showed me anything   And, as it turns out, it doesn't show him anything on his next visit, either (see PC491.1n).

PC449.28 PF416.33 B392.27   Bellevue   New York psychiatric hospital.

PC451.4 PF418.4 B393.32   the Gut   Kingsway in Valletta—once known as Strada Reale.

PC451.25 PF418.21 B394.12   Dali's Last Supper   A 1935 painting by the Spanish surrealist Salvador Dalí (1904–89).

PC452.29 PF419.20 B395.8   in attendance   The list is reminiscent of Fitzgerald's gently satiric enumeration of the partygoers on Long Island in *The Great Gatsby*.

PC453.3 PF419.29 B395.18   the only Manx monoglot in the world   Manx was the Gaelic language of the inhabitants of the Isle of Man. It was supplanted by English in the nineteenth century. As the last surviving speaker of nothing but Manx, the lady pathologist is likely to spend many an evening speaking to no one.

PC453.5 PF419.31 B395.19   Petard   Harder (73) points out that petard, which means "blast," or "explosion," may also be etymologically linked with "péter," to "break wind," and may thus be a particularly suitable name for a kazoo-playing musicologist.

PC455.23 PF422.5 B397.30   things never should have come this far   "Benny Profane's late feeling . . . is appropriately ominous if you allow the first word sufficient emphasis" (Tanner, "V2" 21)

PC456.25 PF423.4 B398.27   Sahha   Maltese for "hello" and "good-bye."

CHAPTER SIXTEEN

The crew of Profane's old ship, the *Scaffold*, are enjoying liberty in Valletta, where the 1956 Suez crisis is in full swing and British troops are enjoying their last night on the town before heading for Egypt. After an evening of drinking and fighting, Pappy Hod meets Paola and Profane as he stumbles back to his ship. Paola promises to wait for Pappy back in Norfolk. Stencil meets up with Maijstral and reluctantly follows up the meager clues that Malta affords. Unwilling to believe that his quest came to an end with the disassembly of the Bad Priest, Stencil leaves Malta in pursuit of yet another tenuous lead. Profane meets Brenda Wigglesworth and we last see him running with her in the direction of the sea.

PC459.24 PF426.22 B401.15   for the benefit of any Egyptian bomber pilots   Even though America's refusal, along with Britain, to honor a promise to finance construction of the Aswan Dam had originally provoked Egypt into nationalizing the canal, Britain and France were the military aggressors in the attempt to regain control of the canal, and hence an American ship would not be the target of an Egyptian bomber.

PC460.17 PF427.12 B402.4   a crown   A five-shilling piece, worth about seventy cents in 1956.

PC461.8 PF427.36 B402.31   Gitmo Bay   Guantánamo Bay in Cuba, where the United States has a large naval base.

PC462.14 PF429.1 B403.32   The Ark   Royal British aircraft carrier.

PC462.17 PF429.3 B403.34   AKA   Attack Cargo Ship.

PC462.20 PF429.6 B403.37   Yoko   Yokohama, Japan.

PC463.7 PF429.26 B404.15   Parliament . . . issued a resolution late this afternoon   It would appear that Pynchon is indulging in creative license here, since Parliament was never in a position to issue any "resolution." On October 30, 1956, the British Prime Minister, Sir Anthony Eden, announced to Parliament that his government had issued an ultimatum calling upon Israel and Egypt to cease hostilities and warning that Britain and France would intervene forcibly to protect the Suez Canal if the ultimatum were ignored. On October 31, after the deadline set by Eden had gone by with no concession from Egypt, the Commons were informed that British and French bombers were attacking military targets in Egypt and narrowly approved an amendment expressing support for the government policy. On November 1, Eden's government only just survived a vote of censure, which would effectively have brought it down. On November 3, he told an emergency session of Parliament (presumably the one referred to here) that his government intended to continue military intervention in Egypt. At no point was the house invited to debate and pass or vote down anything resembling a "resolution" on Suez. See also PC465.23n on the U.N. Security Council's involvement.

PC464.14 PF430.30 B405.19 Jayne Mansfield is getting married The *New York Times* did not appear to know this, though it did report on October 24, a week before the crew of the *Scaffold* head for the bars of Valletta, that Mansfield had obtained a divorce from her husband Paul. The divorce would not be final for another year.

PC465.5 PF431.18 B406.4 Contango "The percentage which the buyer of stock pays to the seller to postpone transfer to the next or any settling" (*OED*).

PC465.23 PF431.36 B406.23 We voted in the Security Council with Russia The United States and Russia had found themselves in agreement on three separate occasions over the previous three or four days. On October 30, as Eden was announcing the Anglo-French ultimatum to Parliament, the Council debated a motion calling on Israel to withdraw its troops from Egypt. Both the United States and Russia voted for the resolution, which was vetoed by Britain and France. Britain and France again vetoed a Russian resolution, and protested strongly a Yugoslav call for an emergency session of the U.N. General Assembly. During an overnight session of the Security

Council on November 1–2, John Foster Dulles introduced an American resolution calling for the withdrawal of British and French troops. "I doubt that any representative ever spoke from this rostrum with as heavy heart as I have brought here tonight," he said. "We speak on a matter of vital importance where the United States finds itself unable to agree with three nations with which it has ties of deep friendship, of admiration, and of respect, and two of which constitute our oldest and most trusted and most reliable of allies" (quoted in Kyle 402). It is presumably this latter event to which Contango is referring.

PC467.12 PF433.18 B407.43   Nasty Chobb "The ship's baker who does such a nasty job that he puts salt instead of sugar into the morning pies to discourage thieves" (Harder 73).

PC467.16 PF433.22 B408.4   Route 66 The 1946 Bobby Troup song celebrating America's most famous highway.

PC467.18 PF433.24 B408.6   corpsman striker A corpsman is "an enlisted man trained to give first aid and minor medical treatment," and a striker is "a junior enlisted man in the U.S. Navy who has declared an occupational specialty" (Merriam-Webster's *Collegiate Dictionary*).

PC467.19 PF433.24 B408.7   alum Potassium or ammonium aluminum sulfate, used as an emetic.

PC468.29 PF434.32 B409.11   Every Day I Have the Blues The Memphis Slim song made popular in 1955 by Joe Williams with the Count Basie Orchestra.

PC469.3 PF435.5 B409.20   Sam the werewolf "Mannaro" is Italian for "werewolf."

PC469.9 PF435.11 B409.27   Nasser Gamal Abdel Nasser (1918–70) had become the president of Egypt in June 1956, a month before the beginning of the Suez crisis.

PC470.9 PF436.9 B410.23   The foolish nose "Profane's sign is in the ascendant, but it is not a promising omen. His virility, i.e., his potential for redeeming the wasteland, is precarious indeed, since it turns on the degree to which he himself is vulnerable" (Slade 123).

PC470.17 PF436.17 B410.32   It was a masterful disguise: a meta-

phor   Cf. Fausto's observations about metaphors' ability to endow the inanimate with the illusion of animacy (PC349.21n).

PC470.19 PF436.18 B410.33   a band-pass filter   "A filter that transmits only frequencies within a certain band" (Merriam-Webster's *Collegiate Dictionary*).

PC470.26 PF436.27 B410.41   Bobbsey Twins   Characters in juvenile novels that came from the same stable as the Hardy Boys and Nancy Drew.

PC471.17 PF437.15 B411.24   They entered the Metro   "Contrasting Benny's initial movement to the Sailor's Grave, this journey is of a return to the source of love and, through the Greek root of the bar's name (Metropole, usually shortened to Metro from *meter* = mother), to the genuine mother" (Hawthorne 81).

PC472.18 PF438.12 B412.21   Dick Powell   Powell starred in the 1937 movie musical *Singing Marine*.

PC478.1 PF443.12 B417.12   I will sit home in Norfolk, faithful, and spin   Paola clearly casts herself as Penelope, the faithful wife waiting at home for the return of her seafaring husband, a comparison that Graves recognizes as incongruous, given "Paola's promiscuity and Pappy's brutality." She goes on to argue, however, that "the appropriateness of the allusion . . . is apparent when it is considered in the context of De Rougemont's arguments. It echoes De Rougemont's claim that a man and a woman, however imperfect, can create new identities for themselves as they create a life together" (71). Cooley takes issue with Graves's claim, suggesting that it "seems . . . to fly in the face of nearly everything the book has implied about empire and about narrative. . . . When Paola promises to spin a yarn we should perhaps be alert not for the promise of coherence . . . but for the incoherence and falsification beneath those strategies. The reconciliation of the American sailor to his Maltese child bride is a reconciliation between colonizer and colonized that looks equally suspicious" (321).

PC478.7 PF443.18 B417.19   She handed him an ivory comb   Hawthorne suggests that "the passing of the ivory comb signifies that she has learned to combine the freedom of V. with the ability to play the wife" (90). If we believe that Paola's promise to sit home and wait for Pappy is sincere, this view may be justified. However, we might equally suppose that Paola's use of V.'s comb as a token of her feelings is a warning to the reader (though not to Pappy) that her promise is tempered by the same provisional overtones that attend all of V.'s love affairs.

PC478.27 PF444.1 B417.41   Fenice   In a posting to the Pynchon discussion list (February 3, 1996), Paul Mackin speculates that Pynchon may have been thinking of the Venetian opera house, La Fenice.

PC478.30 PF444.3 B418.1   the poet Cinoglossa   An etymological stretch might find "empty-tongued" in this name (by analogy with "cenotaph"), while a rather labored and not altogether tasteful pun might allow for "see no tongue"—the poet is epileptic.

PC479.11 PF444.19 B418.21   at 2/8 per day   Two shillings and eightpence in pre-decimal British currency. At the exchange rate current in 1956, this would have been about thirty-seven cents.

PC481.2 PF446.2 B419.41   I recognized none of the faces   A somewhat disconcerting claim, since Fausto's account of the disassembly of the Bad Priest includes the detail that the little girl who was given the comb "smiled" (PC368.21), indicating that he was looking at her face. If he didn't recognize her, it seems unlikely that she was his daughter, so Paola's presence at the death of V. is at least called into question, despite the fact that she comes to own the comb.

PC483.8 PF448.1 B421.37   Mounting crisis in . . . Hungary and Poland   A student march in Budapest on October 23, 1956, was greeted by police gunfire and escalated into full-scale revolution. The "Polish October" period of apparent liberalization had been ushered in by confrontations between the Polish government and the Soviet Union in the wake of a viciously suppressed strike ("Hungary," "Poland," *Britannica Online*).

PC483.14 PF448.7 B422.1   such an obsession is a hothouse   "Stencil lives in a hothouse of hermetically-sealed fantasy where the past is arrested, as in a museum, immobilized in memory pictures to create an inner climate impervious to the inclemency of outer weather" (Tanner, "V2" 29).

PC484.6 PF448.31 B422.29   the Ghallis Tower murder   "A no-
torious murder carried out in 1955. A clerk [identified by Cassola as
having the last name Aquilina, the name Pynchon gives to the shipfitter who tells Stencil about Mme. Viola (PC487.23)] carrying a sum
of money and checks was murdered by a bank employee who later
disposed of the body by dumping it into the well of the Ghallis
Tower, situated on the Southeastern coast of Malta. The trial by jury
started on 23 July 1956 and was given wide coverage in the local papers" (Cassola 331).

**PC484.31 PF449.17 B423.15   Events seem to be ordered into an
ominous logic**   "One of two conclusions seems to follow from this
logic. Either the lady V. exists, in which case the Plot Which Has No
Name dominates the fictional present, or the lady V. does not exist,
and Stencil has hypothesized or even hallucinated relations between
random events" (Hite 47). Tanner notes the difference between Herbert Stencil's formulation of this insight and his father's—"events
would fall into ominous patterns" (PC520.5). "In writing out the notion in many different styles and hands, Stencil is doing in little what
Pynchon is doing throughout the book, so that the text is marked by
a constantly shifting calligraphy, as it were, and we can read it in
different ways with differing degrees of certainty and dubiety about
whether or not events *are*, or *seem*, 'to be ordered into an ominous
logic'" (Tanner, "V2" 42).

PC485.13 PF449.34 B423.37   APC's   Aspirin, phenacetin, and
either caffeine or codeine in combination.

**PC485.20 PF450.4 B423.39   a country of coincidence, ruled by a
ministry of myth**   New suggests that "country of coincidence" is
applicable to fiction itself (107), while Dugdale notes that "'ministry
of myth' . . . could equally be a figure for Modernism or a bureau-
cracy" (117).

PC485.25 PF450.10 B424.1   something far more appalling   From
Stencil's point of view, the absence of meaning implied by the possibility that he has been tracing nothing more organized than a series
of startling coincidences is much more threatening than the conspiracy theory legitimized by alternative explanations.

PC486.17 PF450.32 B424.30   She possesses him   "Certain images in the text . . . go further in making the undeniable power of Modernism seem actively malignant" (Dugdale 109). Dugdale associates this version of the image with the story Mehemet tells of Mara's enchantment of the Sultan's wives and eunuchs (PC500) and with Itague's (PC430) and Maijstral's (PC482) references to haunting.

PC487.4 PF451.16 B425.11   Thirteen of us rule the world in secret   Maijstral mocks Stencil's conspiracy-theory reactions in this reference to the fabricated *Protocols of the Learned Elders of Zion* (PC387.28n), which purported to be proof of the fact that thirteen rabbis were secretly in control of world events.

PC487.23 PF451.34 B425.33   one Mme. Viola, oneiromancer   A diviner of dreams. "It is suitable that the last clue he picks up, which will keep him moving on (approaching and avoiding), this time to Stockholm, is about a certain Mme. Viola. . . . She will not only be able to divine his dreams, but also induce and prolong them" (Tanner, "V2" 33).

PC488.7 PF452.15 B426.9   suede jacket   See PC1.1 "black levis."

PC488.9 PF452.17 B426.11   Brenda Wigglesworth   "A comic contrast to the devout Puritan poet Michael Wigglesworth" (Safer 85). Wigglesworth is best known for his long poem on the Day of Judgment, *The Day of Doom.*

PC490.12 PF454.13 B428.2   I am the twentieth century . . .   "In this parody of Whitman, Brenda's free-verse assertions of identity have become a cliché, showing the result of the dangerous tendency, the contradiction, always inherent in American democratic idealism. To be 'all' is to feel superior to everyone else, while paradoxically losing one's identity. . . . Such bodily plasticity can lead, according to Lawrence, and has led, according to Pynchon, to the purely mechanical and its deification" (Campbell 58).

PC491.2 PF454.37 B428.27   I haven't learned a goddamn thing   A remark that, as Hite notes, "sums up the experience of all the major characters" (Hite 51).

PC491.12 PF455.8 B428.39   toward the edge of Malta, and the Mediterranean beyond   "V. is whatever lights you *to* the end of the street: she is also the dark annihilation waiting *at* the end of the street" (Tanner, "V2" 36).

EPILOGUE

In the winter of 1919, Sidney Stencil arrives in Malta aboard a vessel captained by Mehemet, who claims to have sailed into the twentieth century through a rift in time. Mehemet tells Sidney the legend of Mara, the embodiment of the female spirit of Malta. Sidney makes contact with the shipfitter Maijstral, father to Fausto, who is his informant in the matter of the political unrest that is gathering force on the island. Maijstral is later seen in the company of Veronica Manganese, whose friends include the budding fascist, Mussolini. Sidney and his partner, Demivolt, encounter the disfigured Evan Godolphin at the villa occupied by Veronica Manganese. Carla Maijstral, Fausto's mother, comes to Sidney to ask him to terminate her husband's connection with the Foreign Office, threatening to kill herself if he does not comply. Sidney attempts to enlist the aid of Father Fairing, Carla's parish priest, and is interrupted by Veronica Manganese, whom he finally recognizes as the girl, Victoria Wren, with whom he had an affair in Florence twenty years before. Sidney leaves Malta shortly after the disturbances of June 7 and is aboard Mehemet's boat when it is destroyed by a waterspout.

PC493 PF456 B429   Epilogue   "To take the 'Epilogue' seriously is to see the novel as closed, all the plot lines drawn together, the enigmas fully explained, the order restored—providing at best a comic affirmation, and at worst a feeling that the explanations do not lead to any real understanding. To see the 'Epilogue' as a parody of an epilogue is to see the novel as open; it does not merely provide a shift in orientation, it is absolutely discontinuous with what came before. The events described are so preposterous that they give us a perspective on the novel's disorder—on the impossibility of explanation, on plot lines that only multiply and never connect" (Pearce 147).

PC493.1 PF456.25 B429.15 Winter Most of the internal evidence of the epilogue is consistent with this opening indication of the time of Sidney's arrival. Some confusion is caused by a couple of early references, however, the first of which is to the sailors on H.M.S. *Egmont* "shivering for the Harbour wind though it was June" as Sidney sails into port (PC493.12). Shortly thereafter, we are told that "after seven months" Sidney has had his fill of the celebrations that followed the signing of the armistice that brought World War I to an end (PC494.35). The Armistice was signed on November 11, 1918, placing Sidney's arrival in Valletta in June 1919. There is no doubt, though, that he is present in Malta before February 3, since Maijstral predicts an attack on the Chronicle newspaper offices during their first conversation and no such attack has taken place by that date (PC515.20). The confusion is surely the result of an oversight on Pynchon's part, but there is an odd resonance to the coincidental implication that Sidney both arrives and departs on the same day.

PC495.4 PF458.5 B430.38 Armistice, ha! Sidney's dismissive response to the Armistice is consistent with his world-weary cynicism over the human capacity to cloak the most unpleasant truths in comforting conceptual disguises that often, as in this case, take documentary form. See also PC496.11n.

PC495.16 PF458.17 B431.6 Viscount Grey Sir Edward Grey (later Viscount Grey of Faloddon) was British foreign secretary from 1905 to 1916. At the start of World War I, he made the comment, "The lamps are going out all over Europe; we shall not see them lit again in our lifetime" ("Grey, Sir Edward," *Britannica Online*).

PC495.27 PF458.27 B431.20 E. Mizzi "Enrico Mizzi (1885–1950). The seventh Maltese Prime Minister. A staunch defender of Malta's 'Italianity,' he very often clashed with His Majesty's representatives on the island" (Cassola 327).

PC495.28 PF458.27 B431.20 Major General Hunter-Blair Malta's Lieutenant-Governor during the June disturbances (Cassola 327).

PC496.11 PF459.8 B431.38   this loathsome weakness . . . the Great Tragedy   Sidney's cynicism at the spectacle of Europe retreating from the horrors of the trenches into misguided dreams of an end to warfare is expressed in terms of a plea for a clarity of vision not unlike that which Fausto invokes in his observations on the effects of metaphor (PC349.22). "Nameless Horror," "sudden prodigy"— these are the figurative devices that hide the hard facts ("Ten million dead. Gas. Passchendaele").

PC496.32 PF459.28 B432.18   Bizerte   Town on northern coast of Tunisia.

PC496.34 PF459.29 B432.19   a world taken from him   "Mehemet . . . claims to be from the past, from 1300, to be exact—the parameter of Henry Adams's survey of history—when the Virgin reigned supreme" (Slade 76).

PC497.6 PF459.37 B432.28   the Moslem calendar   The Islamic calendar is reckoned from July 16, 622, the date of the prophet Mohammed's flight to Medina. Each Islamic year differs from the Julian year by about eleven days.

PC497.11 PF460.3 B432.32   the Peri   A "peri" is "a supernatural being in Persian folklore descended from fallen angels and excluded from paradise until penance is accomplished" (Merriam-Webster's *Collegiate Dictionary*)

PC497.33 PF460.26 B433.13   A peasant . . . painting the side of a sinking ship   This somber and haunting image resonates at a number of levels, suggesting, among other things, that we the inhabitants of a postmodern world are uprooted peasants, torn from our erstwhile stable connection to a known and knowable culture and driven to cover up the fact of our impending destruction under layer after thin layer of protective delusion. Sidney makes the connection explicit when he later equates the Peri with "society" (PC498.24). Another reading would equate the fellah with the artist who, like Fausto's poet, takes on the task of preserving our illusions until the ship finally sinks beneath the waves.

PC498.5 PF460.32 B433.20   Levantine lanterloo   According to the *OED*, "lanterloo" was originally the meaningless refrain of a popular French song. "Levantine" refers to the Levant, the countries on the eastern shores of the Mediterranean.

PC498.13 PF461.3 B433.30   sometime between 1859 and 1919 "David Richter has identified the significance of 1859 as the year in which both Marx's *Critique of Political Economy* and Darwin's *Origin of Species* were " (Madsen 51).

PC498.20 PF461.9 B433.37   Is old age a disease? As Mehemet's response indicates, and as Sidney himself clearly understands, the disease metaphor is simply convenient protection against the stark indifference of a universe tending toward entropic decline. As Cain points out, "any theory (or for that matter any narrative), constitutes a kind of intellectual imperialism: an attempt to make the world conform to a single vision" (Cain 316).

PC498.32 PF461.21 B434.6   no gift of tongues The Paracletian reference harks back to Sidney's musings on the delusions of the postwar period (PC496.11). Despite vociferous claims to the contrary, Sidney is aware that nothing has been learned from the conflagration that has just died down—no revelation has been delivered, no wisdom that might stave off the next instance of human self-destruction.

PC498.35 PF461.24 B434.9   Mehemet told him of Mara "[An] animistic sense of existence has been preserved in Mehemet, the xebec captain who continues to recognize the viability (the V-ability) of the transcendental female symbol in the form of Mara. . . . Mehemet is the possessor of a centuries-old wisdom that marks him as the Jungian 'wise old man,' an archetypal figure who represents in turn the male psyche's successful assimilation of the archetypal anima, i.e. Mara. 'Mara' is Maltese for woman, and this apotheosis of woman is a love deity, closely related to Astarte, the goddess who provides the xebec's figurehead and is the Syrian counterpart of Aphrodite" (Eddins 58–59). "The legend of Mara is a composite spoof of some of the great Modernist sea-stories, relegating them to the status of yarns in Conrad. The manipulation of detail in the passage enables the parody to take in the cult of the Mediterranean goddess (Pound): the use of the myths of Odysseus (Joyce, Pound) or Orpheus (Rilke, cf. the severed head); the trope of the sea voyage (*The Waste Land*, the Byzantium poems, cf. Constantinople); the appeal to the poetry of Dante and the troubadours (Pound, Eliot); and the ambivalence towards the female prevalent in Modernist writing" (Dugdale 99).

PC499.14 PF462.1 B434.23   Lampedusa   The largest of the Italian Pelagie Islands between Malta and Tunisia.

PC499.16 PF462.3 B434.25   Early in your 1565   Which would be the year 979 in the Moslem calendar used by Mehemet.

PC499.24 PF462.11 B434.35   ragusy   A large merchant vessel (*OED*, "argosy").

PC501.24 PF464.6 B436.24   Dragut   The corsair Dragut, King of Tripoli, was in fact killed by a rock thrown up by a cannon aimed too low (Balbi 86).

PC501.26 PF464.8 B436.26   tied the corpses to planks   Francesco Balbi, who fought during the siege, gives the following account: "The Turkish barbarians . . . secured to planks and pieces of wood the bodies of the Christian dead—some mutilated, some without heads, and others with their bellies ripped open—and threw them into the sea so that the current would wash them over to Birgu. Their intention was to terrify us with so revolting a sight and to cow us into submission" (93).

PC502.1 PF464.17 B436.37   because of a rumor   The rumor was not so much about the impending arrival of Don Garcia's forces, but about the size of the relief force. Don Garcia had landed half of his force (eight thousand men) with remarkable secrecy, and had taken ship to fetch the other half when the Turks began their retreat, mistakenly thinking they were confronted with a much larger influx of fresh opponents (Balbi 142).

PC502.17 PF464.32 B437.12   Falconière   "The parallel between [Falconière's] lyric for Mara and the verses produced by medieval troubadours for Mary is inescapable, and leads us back once again to the metacontext that [Henry Adams's] *Mont Saint Michel and Chartres* provides for V. . . . [The content of the Marian songs] is a paradigm of miraculous intervention that clearly covers Mara's su-

pernatural feats and further links Pynchon and Adams in a common
value locus, nostalgia for a feminized transcendental" (Eddins 59).

PC502.23 PF465.2 B437.18 Janissaries Soldiers of an elite corps
of Turkish troops (Merriam-Webster's *Collegiate Dictionary*).

PC503.3 PF465.16 B437.34 galiot "A small swift galley for-
merly used in the Mediterranean" (Merriam-Webster's *Collegiate
Dictionary*).

PC503.8 PF465.20 B437.38 Beware of Mara "It is clear that
Mehemet has moved from revering an image of benevolent deity like
the Maltese Gaea-Tellus whom Fausto II espoused, to fearing an
image of cosmic menace—Venus *genetrix* declined to a capricious
demiurge who is finally indistinguishable from the goddess of fortune" (Eddins 59–60). According to Eddins, this change is reflected
in the contrast between the "living figurehead" (PC499.26) of Mara
and the Astarte figurehead on the xebec. The former is a heroic sav-
ior, while the latter is a succubus (PC494.1). "The disorder and violence of Malta at this period are symptomatic of just such a ravishing
and reflect the degeneration of the feminine life principle into the
Jungian archetype of the Terrible Mother—the Medusan opponent,
as Erich von Neumann puts it, of 'the mobility of the life stream that
flows in all organic life,' the advocate of 'petrifaction and sclerosis'"
(Eddins 59–60).

PC505.7 PF467.11 B439.23 What of the Dockyard people Cassola notes that the information Maijstral supplies is drawn directly
from the report of the Commission appointed to look into the disturbances. Cassola quotes at some length from the relevant portion of
that document:

A1—*Unrest among Dockyard people*
60. The Dockyard workers allege that they have grievances
against the imperial Government, the local Government and
also against the well-to-do classes of the population.
61. They complain of differences in the pay and in the advan-
tages between the English and the Maltese workmen. We have
ascertained that the difference is not as between English and

Maltese workmen, but between workmen sent out from England under an agreement and those locally employed. They admit that English workmen sent out from England should receive extra remuneration in the shape of colonial allowance, but their grievance is that for identical work and equal hours the English workman gets much more pay, and that the English workers are kept quite separate from their Maltese fellow workmen.

62. They were under the impression that the Daily Malta Chronicle had not taken up their cause, and a letter published in the Chronicle in 1917 condemning the strike which was just over, caused offense especially as they thought that the Chronicle had refused to publish a protest against that letter. In fairness to the Chronicle we have ascertained that the protests never reached the Chronicle Office.

63. Before the war the number of workmen at the Dockyard was about 4,600. During the war it went up to about 12,000. It was perfectly understood that that number could not be maintained and that discharges would soon take place, and that the local market could not afford employment to the men so discharged.

64. A rumour which gained considerable credence was spread that passports were being refused by the local government in order to keep the workmen in Malta should their services be again required at the Dockyard, at any time.

The Lieutenant-Governor has made a statement before this Commission to the effect that the rumour was unfounded and that His Excellency the Governor was doing his utmost to delay the discharges from the Dockyard. (quoted in Cassola 314)

PC506.20 PF468.19 B440.31   an intolerable double vision   Critics tend to agree in their association of the twin poles of Sidney's characterization with the "hothouse" of the past and the "street" of the future. "The implication of this is that all political thinking— and by extension all man's mental projections—is either a dream of the past or a dream of the future. By this account, man himself can never properly occupy present time. The street and the hothouse are the dreams by which man avoids confronting that nothingness which is the shapeless truth behind the structured fantasy of human history. . . . The street is the zone of waking, planning consciousness which, unable to endure the meaninglessness of the absolute present, projects plans into the future or finds plans in the past. The hothouse is the realm of memory where the mind is sealed up in the secretions of its reveries over the past" (Tanner, "V2" 30–31). "The 'hothouse' is the assumption that time is static, without progress or change, and that the past exists only to be relived in the hermetic medium of memory. Stencil attempts to bring the 'hothouse' into relation with the image of the 'street' which is predicated on the idea that time is linear, that the present exists as a function of the future and consequently must be devoted to the realization of futuristic dreams. The 'street' is therefore a place of political revolution, of violent opposition to the present order and of death. Both time schemes constitute a rejection of the present, of the lived moment or 'real time,' in favour of illusions, memories, and dreams and as such are firmly situated within the V-metaphysic" (Madsen 41). According to Campbell, Herbert Stencil is the representative of the Right, the politics of memory, while Profane stands for a pale version of the future-oriented politics of the Left (63); his "symbolic Street is to [Sidney] Stencil's what Mrs. Buffo's Beatrice is to Dante's: a vestigial form of the original, a metaphor without a metaphysic" (Campbell 59).

PC506.27 PF468.27 B440.40   a highly 'alienated' populace "Stencil's alienated populace is a reality of our time. Wanting to live in either a mythic past or a utopian future, we have rejected the present. At least emotionally, we are all extremists, and the pre-Romantic ideal of the Golden Mean has gone the way of the Ptolemaic Universe and the Great Chain of Being" (Golden 6).

PC509.3 PF470.30 B443.3   The Situation as an N-Dimensional Mishmash   Pearce (23) finds the origin of this concept in Durrell's *Justine:* "Pursewarden on the 'n-dimensional novel' trilogy: 'The narrative momentum forward is counter-sprung by references backwards in time, giving the impression of a book which is not travelling from a to b but standing above time and turning slowly on its own axis to comprehend the whole pattern. Things do not all lead forward to other things: some lead backwards to things which have passed. A marriage of past and present with the flying multiplicity of the future racing towards one. Anyway, that was my idea.'"

PC510.3 PF471.27 B443.39   The poor would seek revenge against the millers   Cassola (315) confirms that Pynchon has obtained all but one of his dissident factions from the Official Report of the disturbances. Only the Bolshevists are absent from the original document. Eddins sees the list as a foretaste of an "anarchic melange" that signals "the growth of social and cultural entropy and the end of polity in a random political splintering" (78).

PC510.26 PF472.13 B444.21   The matter of a Paraclete's coming   Both Dugdale (98) and Eddins (79) trace Stencil's trinitarian metaphor back to Joachim of Fiore, whose vision of human history was structured by the persons of the Trinity. Citing Voegelin's association of National Socialism with the third stage of the trinitarian schema, Eddins argues that Sidney's version "becomes a historical theory in which the Father represents the transcendental charismatic figure who anchors the metaxy and incarnates virtù in the form of a history-determining Logos. The order of the secular state mirrors as best it can a projected City of God—the civitas Dei—and receives its progressive modifications from perceptions of this higher ordering. At a later, increasingly gnostic, stage, this projection and the metaxic tension that accompanied it gave way to what Stencil contemptuously terms 'the liberal love-feast,' democratic experiments in human self-sufficiency that produce violent revolution in the name of social harmony and brotherly love. The final era of history—terminal, perhaps—is symbolized by the descent of the Holy Ghost, whose gnostic analogue inaugurates a politics of demonic anarchy similar to that described in Yeats's prophetic poems. All notion of an authoritative center quite lost, the humanizing polity dissolves into a riotous chaos of movements, each claiming the sanction of some divine voice that is incomprehensible to the others, and to the world that must suffer the fanatical ravagings licensed by the assumed mandate" (80). In political terms, the first two stages of the schema correspond to the Right and the Left of Sidney's hothouse/ street metaphor, while the third stage corresponds to the fascistic blending of Right and Left that was beginning to emerge in 1919 (Kharpertian 83).

PC510.32 PF472.19 B444.28 which had produced 1848 Revolutionary fervor reached its peak in Europe that year, bringing political upheaval to France, Italy, Germany, Austria, Bohemia, and Hungary.

PC511.10 PF472.31 B444.40 Veronica Manganese Inglott suggests the ingenious "True-Icon-In-Dark-Metal" as a gloss on the name ("Sette" 59). See also PC123.33n.

PC511.11 PF472.32 B444.41 Gustavus V is ruler of Sweden Sidney's sarcasm is probably based on nothing more significant than the fact that Gustavus had been king for twelve years at this point.

PC511.15 PF472.36 B445.2 Sgherraccio, a Mizzist See PC495.27n, PC447.29n.

PC511.17 PF473.1 B445.4 D'Annunzio the poet-militant See PC265.15n, PC262.27n.

PC511.17 PF473.2 B445.5 Mussolini See PC265.15n, PC262.26n, PC443.12n.

PC512.14 PF473.31 B445.37 level of elevation above the jumble Cf. Eigenvalue's musings on historical perspective (PC161.30).

PC514.26 PF475.33 B447.36 Both of you then Evan Godolphin recognizes both Sidney and Demivolt from their meeting in Florence.

PC515.8 PF476.13 B448.11 give it twenty years Demivolt's prescience as to the timing of the next world war may seem startling until we remember that Stencil's history of V. begins in 1898, twenty years before the end of World War I.

PC516.9 PF477.12 B449.7 La Bella Gigogin A patriotic Italian song dating back to the mid–nineteenth century at the height of Italian resistance to Austrian rule.

PC517.5 PF478.6 B449.42 Dr. Mifsud "In 1919 Dr. Ugo Mifsud was appointed secretary of the National Assembly. He served as Prime Minister for two terms (1924–27; 1932–33)" (Cassola 327).

PC518.12 PF479.10 B450.41 we do not control the world in

secret   Fairing's anticipation of Stencil's Church of England "leeri-
ness" toward the Jesuits echoes Fausto Maijstral's sarcastic response
to young Stencil's conspiracy-theory tendencies (PC487.4), which are
an extreme version of his father's nascent British distrust of Rome.

PC519.5 PF479.37 B451.29   his theory of Paracletian politics
See PC510.26n.

PC519.6 PF480.1   The Church has matured   Lhamon claims
that the reverse is in fact the case: "The church instituted hierarchy,
but the coming Paraclete will abolish its hierarchy and return 'promiscuity'" (77).

**PC520.5 PF480.33 B452.24   events would fall into ominous pat-
terns**   See PC484.31n.

PC520.17 PF481.7 B452.37   this stone fish   The island of Malta
itself.

PC520.18 PF481.7 B452.37   Ghaudex   The second largest island
of the Maltese archipelago.

PC520.18 PF481.8 B452.38   Cumin-seed and Peppercorn   The
islands of Kemmuna and Filfla. Cassola explains that Kemmuna's
Italian name is "Comino" or "cumin-seed," while Filfla derives from
"felfel" or "peppercorn" (329–30).

**PC523.20 PF483.31 B455.20   Don't act as if it were a conscious
plot against you**   Stencil's self-admonishment takes the same form
as the observations of his son in the guise of Gebrail, the farmer
turned taxi driver (PC80.32n).

PC527.3 PF486.35 B458.15   the hothouse of a Florentine spring
The "hothouse," we recall, is the domain of memory and is thus consistent with the sense of nostalgia that Demivolt claims hangs over
the whole Maltese operation.

PC527.3 PF486.36 B458.16   fayed and filleted   Joined and bound.

**PC527.23 PF487.19 B458.38   My employers must move in a
straight line**   "In contrast to the totalitarian controls envisioned
by V., Profane's society represents the chaotic capitulation to individualism and private eroticism which De Rougemont ascribes to
the Western democracies" (Graves 69).

PC527.32 PF487.28 B459.3   The street and the hothouse   "According to Sidney's meditations, Veronica shares with Mara the hermaphroditic quality that blends gender as well as the binaries that grow from male domination" (Hawthorne 78).

PC528.15 PF488.8 B459.24   a lovely rainbow   "It is the Vheissu syndrome once again, the concealing of the inanimate beneath seductive variegations and—in this case—beneath the pseudoanimation of memory" (Eddins 80).

PC528.18 PF488.11 B459.28   the same balloon-girl   This epithet is applied to Victoria Wren by Herbert Stencil in his guise as Yusef the factotum in chapter 3 (PC63.30) and by Fausto Maijstral to his daughter Paola (PC355.16).

PC528.20 PF488.12 B459.28   who'd seduced him   See PC49.24n for a discussion of the possibility that Victoria Wren is Herbert Stencil's mother.

PC529.9 PF489.1 B460.15   increasingly more difficult to live in the real present   To occupy, that is, the precarious middle ground between the nostalgia of the hothouse and the always deferred future of street-level desire for change.

PC529.17 PF489.9 B460.24   Treacherous pasture, this island   "The ending of the novel, the dénouement of the investigation into his fate, shows Old Stencil committing treason by being lured into a liaison with a Fascist agent. This is clearly intelligible . . . as a parable which concerns the collusion of Modernism with the monstrous forces of the century, given that Old Stencil is a parody of Yeats, and a father who in 1922 leaves a legacy of texts to a son who will dream fictions in the 1950s. The traitor is also the man who hands on the tradition: *traditor, traditio,* both from tradere" (Dugdale 110).

PC529.33 PF489.22 B460.39   a circle begun in England eighteen years ago   This takes us back to the earlier mention of the disappearance of Herbert Stencil's mother—"some way of vanishing painful enough to keep Sidney from ever referring to it" (PC48.14). The reference to adultery here suggests that "ran off with someone" may have been the accurate description of what happened eighteen years before.

PC530.10 PF489.34 B461.8   There were no more princes   The first age of Sidney's trinitarian schema has passed.

PC531.8 PF490.26 B461.41   He forced himself into the real present   Schaub describes the "real present" as "the proper relation to the extremes of [Sidney's] Situation. . . . This relation is not the absolute present refuted by relativity, but is "a switching point in the local time in which the participant remains poised at the personal nexus of the Situation's dimensions, rejecting the violent simplicity of a swing toward any single one, and integrating their competing claims in the interest of an equilibrium both expeditious and true" (12).

PC532.18 PF491.33 B463.6   one Board of Inquiry report   Identified by Cassola as *Reports of the Commission appointed to inquire into the events of the 7th and 8th June 1919 and into the circumstances which led up to those events—18th and 19th September, 1919*, in *Malta Government Gazette Supplement*, no. 26, October 7, 1919, pp. 167–80. A copy of the report was available online at http://www.pynchonfiles.com/maltapage1.htm. Inglott ("Sette" 58) quotes from a document that Pynchon may or may not have seen but that certainly aligns very nicely with the novel's preoccupation with hidden forces at work in the political arena. The extract comes from a note written by Henry Casolani, then the Principal Secretary in the Office of the Lieutenant-Governor, in the early hours of the June 7, 1919: "Their worst feelings have evidently been worked to white heat by some agency, which is not the 'Comitato Patriottico'—and which has been doing its work in a quiet and mysterious way, for, while apparently there is no organization whatever, yet everyone knows what he is to do. . . . All the hooligan elements have been drawn into the movement and carefully prepared for the occasion by this secret force; and it will not be the latter's fault if it fails."

PC533.3 PF492.16 B463.28   Draw a line from Malta to Lampedusa   Schaub asserts that Pynchon here reminds us of Sidney's earlier conversation with Mehemet, in which he warns the old diplomat about Mara, whose sphere of influence extends "as far as the fish-ing banks off Lampedusa" (462). The result is that we are "caught between two contradictory explanations of the same experience: either the waterspout is a freak accident, or Stencil's death is the result of another and simultaneous order of experience, in which the mechanical parody of the timeless goddess has reached out to destroy the 'obsolete' diplomat, no longer useful in the century she presages" (17).

PC533.4 PF492.17 B463.29 waterspout "It recalls most clearly the shipwreck suffered by the Phoenician sailor in *The Waste Land*, and the lines Eliot quotes from *The Tempest* on the drowning of the father; the sinking of the *Pequod* in *Moby-Dick*; and the white cataract at the end of Poe's *Pym*. Less obvious analogues for the mysterious fate of the ship and the waterspout include the legend of Fata Morgana, and Charybdis in *Odyssey*, xix, both of which are associated with the nearby Straits of Messina (cf. [PC465]); the drowning in a whirlpool of Dante's Ulysses (*Inferno*, xxvi); the wreck of the *Hesperus* (Hesper-Hester-Esther-Astarte), and of St Paul's ship off the coast of Malta (cf. [PC499]); and the myth of Icarus, since Evan Godolphin, the fallen airman who waves goodbye to Old Stencil, has been so described ([PC97]). Like the ending of *The Waste Land*, albeit with an entirely different technique, the paragraph is a miniature evocation of a whole tradition that is coming to an end—all literary history at once—a concentration given particular significance by its adumbration of nuclear catastrophe" (Dugdale 99–100). Chambers suggests that the scene originates from the disappearance of a ship called the *Victoria* off the coast of Malta in June 1893 (93). Tanner suggests that Sidney's death is "associated with the goddess Astarte, the Eastern equivalent to Aphrodite, suggesting perhaps that the sexual drive has been diverted—perverted—into a death-bringing and destructive force in our century" (Tanner, *TP* 54). Patteson notes that the V. of the spout is once again deceptive, having a vacuum at its core, "the point of expected closure" ("True Text" 301). Greenberg places Sidney's death in the midst of "the promiscuous Mediterranean that is the home of Venus/Aphrodite, 'the wave-borne,'" around which the novel has been circling from the beginning (65).

REFERENCES

Please note: Web addresses are subject to change, as is the text posted on Web sites. Web site addresses cited below were current as of February 2000.

Abulafia, David. *A Mediterranean Emporium: The Catalan Kingdom of Mallorca.* Cambridge: Cambridge University Press, 1994.

Allen, Mary. *The Necessary Blankness: Women in Major American Fiction of the Sixties.* Urbana: University of Illinois Press, 1976.

Baedeker, Karl. *Egypt and the Sudan.* Leipzig: Karl Baedeker, 1908.

———. *Ägypten und der Sudan: Handbuch für Reisende/von Karl Baedeker.* Leipzig: Karl Baedeker, 1899.

Balbi di Correggio, Francesco. *The Siege of Malta.* Translated from the Spanish edition of 1568 by Ernle Bradford. London: The Folio Society, 1965.

Begnal, Michael H. "Thomas Pynchon's *V.:* In Defense of Benny Profane." *Journal of Narrative Technique* 9, no. 2 (Spring 1979): 61–69.

Berressem, Hanjo. "Godolphin—Goodolphin—Goodol'phin—Goodol'-Pyn—Good ol' Pym." *Pynchon Notes* 10 (1982): 3–17.

———. "V. in Love: From the 'Other Scene' to the 'New Scene.'" *Pynchon Notes* 18–19 (1986): 5–28.

Bianchi, Petra. "The Wittgensteinian Thread in Thomas Pynchon's Labyrinth: Aspects of Wittgensteinian Thought in *V.*" In E. Mendelson, *Pynchon, Malta and Wittgenstein,* 1–13. Mgarr, Malta: Malta University Press, 1994.

Bloom, Harold, ed. *Thomas Pynchon: Modern Critical Views.* New York: Chelsea House Publishers, 1986.

Booker, M. Keith. "The Rats of God: Pynchon, Joyce, Beckett, and the Carnivalization of Religion." *Pynchon Notes* 24–25 (1989): 21–30.

Bramann, Jorn K. *Wittgenstein's Tractatus and the Modern Arts.* Rochester, NY: Adler Publishing, 1985.

Brewer, Ebenezer Cobham. *Brewer's Dictionary of Phrase and Fable*. Revised by Ivor H. Evans. New York: Harper and Row, 1970.

Bridgman, Jon. *The Revolt of the Heroes*. Berkeley: University of California Press, 1981.

Cain, Jimmie E., Jr. "The Clock as Metaphor in 'Mondaugen's Story.'" *Pynchon Notes* 17 (1985): 73–77.

Calendrillo, Linda T. "Cloaks and More Cloaks: Pynchon's V. and the Classic Spy Novel." *Clues: A Journal of Detection* 5, no. 2 (Fall–Winter 1984): 58–65.

Campbell, Elizabeth. "Metaphor and V.: Metaphysics in the Mirror." *Pynchon Notes* 22–23 (1988): 57–69.

Cassola, Arnold. "Pynchon, V., and the Malta Connection." *Journal of Modern Literature* 12 (July 1985): 311–31.

Celmer, Paul W., Jr. "Pynchon's V. and the Rhetoric of the Cold War." *Pynchon Notes* 32–33 (1993): 5–32.

Chambers, Judith. *Thomas Pynchon*. New York, NY: Twayne Publishers, 1992.

Clouzet, Jean. *Boris Vian*. Paris: Éditions Seghers, 1966.

Cohen-Stratyner, Barbara Naomi. *Biographical Dictionary of Dance*. New York: Schirner Books, 1982.

Conrad, Joseph. *Heart of Darkness*. London: Penguin Books, 1987.

Cooley, Ronald W. "The Hothouse or the Street: Imperialism and Narrative in Pynchon's V." *Modern Fiction Studies* 39 (Summer 1993): 307–25.

Cowart, David. *Thomas Pynchon: The Art of Allusion*. Carbondale: Southern Illinois University Press, 1980.

Delden, Maarten van. "Modernism, the New Criticism and Thomas Pynchon's V." *Novel* 23 (Winter 1990): 117–36.

Dewaldt, Franz. *Native Uprisings in Southwest Africa. Documents on the Armed Uprising of the Bondelzwart Tribe (1922) and the Bloodless Revolt of the Rehoboth Bastards (1925) in Ex-German Southwest Africa Administered by the Union of South Africa under Mandate*. Salisbury, N.C.: Documentary Publications, 1976.

Dietz, Mary G. "Machiavelli, Niccolò." In *Routledge Encyclopedia of Philosophy*, ed. Edward Craig. London: Routledge, 1988.

Dugdale, John. *Thomas Pynchon: Allusive Parables of Power*. New York: St. Martin's Press, 1990.

Duyfhuizen, Bernard. "A Long View of V 2." *Pynchon Notes* 5 (1981): 17–19.

Eddins, Dwight. *The Gnostic Pynchon.* Bloomington: Indiana University Press, 1990.

Fahy, Joseph. "Thomas Pynchon's V. and Mythology." *Critique* 18, no. 3 (1977): 5–18.

First, Ruth. *South West Africa.* Baltimore: Penguin Books, 1963.

Fletcher, Richard. *The Quest for El Cid.* Oxford: Oxford University Press, 1989.

Fowler, Douglas. "Story into Chapter: Thomas Pynchon's Transformation of 'Under the Rose.'" *Journal of Narrative Technique* 14, no. 1 (Winter 1984): 33–43.

Friedman, Melvin J. "The Schlemiel: Jew and Non-Jew." *Studies in the Literary Imagination* 9, no. 1 (Winter 1978): 133–78.

Gammond, Peter. *The Oxford Companion to Popular Music.* Oxford: Oxford University Press, 1991.

Giffen, Morrison B. *Fashoda. The Incident and Its Diplomatic Setting.* Chicago: University of Chicago Press, 1930.

Golden, Robert E. "Mass Man and Modernism: Violence in Pynchon's V." *Critique* 14, no. 2 (1972): 5–17.

Graves, Lila V. "Love and the Western World of Pynchon's V." *South Atlantic Review* 47 (January 1982): 62–73.

Greenberg, Alvin. "The Underground Woman: An Excursion into the V-ness of Thomas Pyncheon" [sic]. *Chelsea* 27 (1969): 58–65.

Greiner, Donald J. "Fiction as History, History as Fiction: The Reader and Thomas Pynchon's V." *South Carolina Review* 10, no. 1 (November 1977): 4–18.

Haarhoff, Dorian. "Bondels and Bombs: The Bondelswarts Rebellion in Historical Fiction." *English Studies in Africa: A Journal of the Humanities* 32, no. 1 (1989): 25–39.

Harder, Kelsie B. "Names in Thomas Pynchon's *V.*" *Literary Onomastics Studies* 5 (1978): 64–80.

Hausdorff, Don. "Thomas Pynchon's Multiple Absurdities." *Wisconsin Studies in Contemporary Literature* 7 (Autumn 1966): 258–69.

Hawthorne, Mark D. "A 'Hermaphrodite Sort of Deity': Sexuality, Gender, and Gender Blending in Thomas Pynchon's *V.*" *Studies in the Novel* 29 (Spring 1997): 74–93.

Hayles, N. Katherine. *The Cosmic Web: Scientific Field Models and Literary Strategies in the Twentieth Century.* Ithaca: Cornell University Press, 1984.

Henderson, Harry B., III. *Versions of the Past: The Historical Imagination in American Fiction.* New York: Oxford University Press, 1974.

Hipkiss, Robert A. *The American Absurd: Pynchon, Vonnegut, and Barth.* Port Washington, N.Y.: Associated Faculty Press, 1984.

Hite, Molly. *Ideas of Order in the Novels of Thomas Pynchon.* Columbus: Ohio State University Press, 1983.

Holton, Robert. "In the Rathouse of History with Thomas Pynchon: Rereading *V.*" *Textual Practice* 2, no. 3 (Winter 1988): 324–44.

Howe, Darcy E. "The Power of Love in Chimera and V." *Pynchon Notes* 30–31 (1992): 165–71.

Inglott, Peter Serracino. "The Faustus of Malta: Fact and Fiction in Pynchon's *V.*" In E. Mendelson, *Pynchon, Malta and Wittgenstein*, 39–54. Mgarr, Malta: Malta University Press, 1994.

Jardine, Alice. *Gynesis: Configurations of Women and Modernity.* Ithaca: Cornell University Press, 1985.

Karpinski, Eva C. "From *V.* to *Vineland:* Pynchon's Utopian Moments." *Pynchon Notes* 32–33 (1993): 33–43.

Kemeny, Annemarie. "The Female Machine in the Postmodern Circuit." In *Liminal Postmodernisms: The Postmodern, the (Post-)Colonial, and the (Post-)Feminist*, ed. D'haen-Theo and Bertens-Hans, 255–73. Amsterdam: Rodopi, 1994.

Kharpertian, Theodore D. *A Hand to Turn the Time: The Menippean Satires of Thomas Pynchon.* Rutherford: Fairleigh Dickinson University Press, 1990.

Knepler, Henry. *The Gilded Stage.* New York: William Morrow, 1968.

Kowalewski, Michael. "For Once, Then, Pynchon." *Texas Studies in Literature and Language* 28, no. 2 (Summer 1986): 182–208.

Kozlowski, Lisa M. "The Truth behind the Catenary in Pynchon's *V:* A Dream That Will Help You Not at All." *Notes on Contemporary Literature* 19, no. 4 (September 1989): 2–4.

Kyle, Keith. *Suez.* New York: St. Martin's Press, 1991.

Leca, Ange-Pierre. *The Egyptian Way of Death: Mummies and the Cult of the Immortal.* Trans. Louise Asmal. New York: Doubleday, 1981.

Lense, Edward. "Pynchon's *V.*" *The Explicator* 43 (Fall 1984): 60–61.

Levine, George, and David Leverenz, eds. *Mindful Pleasures: Essays on Thomas Pynchon.* Boston: Little, Brown, 1976.

Lewis, R. W. B. *Trials of the Word.* New Haven: Yale University Press, 1965.

Lhamon, W. T., Jr. "Pentecost, Promiscuity, and Pynchon's V.: From the Scaffold to the Impulsive." *Twentieth Century Literature* 21 (May 1975): 163–76. Reprinted in Levine and Leverenz (1976), 69–86.

McCarron, William E. "Pynchon and Yeats." *Notes on Contemporary Literature* 18, no. 3 (May 1988): 6–7.

McConnell, Frank D. *Four Postwar American Novelists: Bellow, Mailer, Barth, and Pynchon.* Chicago: Unversity of Chicago Press, 1977.

Machiavelli, Nicolo. *The Prince.* Trans. W. K. Marriot. London: J. M. Dent and Sons, 1908.

McHoul, Alec, and David Wills. *Writing Pynchon: Strategies in Fictional Analysis.* Urbana: University of Illinois Press, 1990.

Madsen, Deborah L. *The Postmodernist Allegories of Thomas Pynchon.* New York: St. Martin's Press, 1991.

Maltby, Paul. *Dissident Postmodernists: Barthelme, Coover, Pynchon.* Philadelphia: University of Pennsylvania Press, 1991.

Marsland, William David. *Venezuela through Its History.* New York: Crowell, 1954.

Matthijs, Michel. "Character in Pynchon's V." *Restant* 10, no. 2 (Summer 1982): 125–44.

Mendelson, Edward, ed. *Pynchon: A Collection of Critical Essays.* Englewood Cliffs, N.J.: Prentice-Hall, 1978.

———. Preface of *Pynchon, Malta and Wittgenstein.* Mgarr, Malta: Malta University Press, 1997.

Nericcio, William Anthony. "Autopsy of a Rat: Sundry Parables of Freddy Lopez, Speedy Gonzales, and Other Chicano/Latino Marionettes Prancing about Our First World Visual Emporium." *camera obscura* 37 (January 1996): 189–237.

New, Melvyn. "Profaned and Stenciled Texts: In Search of Pynchon's V." *Georgia Review* 33 (Summer 1979): 395–412. Reprinted in Bloom (1986), 93–109.

Newman, Robert D. *Understanding Thomas Pynchon.* Columbia, S.C.: University of South Carolina Press, 1986.

———. "Pynchon's Use of Carob in V." *Notes on Contemporary Literature* 11, no. 3 (May 1981): 11.

O'Connor, Peter. "The Wasteland of Thomas Pynchon's V." *College Literature* 3, no. 1 (Winter 1976): 49–55.

Olderman, Raymond. *Beyond the Wasteland: A Study of the American Novel in the 1960s.* New Haven: Yale University Press, 1972.

Orr, Leonard. "Pleasures of the Immachination: Transformations of the Inanimate in Durrell and Pynchon." In *Lawrence Durrell: Comprehending the Whole*, ed. Julius Rowan Raper, Melody L. Enscore, and Paige Matthey Bynum, 127–36. Columbia: University of Missouri Press, 1995.

Patteson, Richard. "What Stencil Knew: Structure and Certitude in Pynchon's V." *Critique* 16, no. 2 (1974): 30–44.

———. "Horus, Harmakhis, and Harpokrates in Chapter III of V. and 'Under the Rose.'" *Pynchon Notes* 6 (1981): 39–40.

———. "How True a Text? Chapter Three of V. and 'Under the Rose.'" *Southern Humanities Review* 18 (Fall 1984): 299–308.

Pearce, Richard, ed. *Critical Essays on Thomas Pynchon*. Boston: G. K. Hall, 1981.

———. "Pynchon's Endings." *Novel: A Forum on Fiction* 18, no. 2 (Winter 1985): 145–53.

Peirce, Carol Marshall. "Pynchon's V. and Durrell's Alexandria Quartet: A Seminar in the Modern Tradition." *Pynchon Notes* 8 (1982): 23–29.

Pittas-Giroux, Justin Arthur. "A Reader's Guide to Thomas Pynchon's V." Thesis (M.A.), University of South Carolina, 1995.

Poirier, Richard. "The Importance of Thomas Pynchon." *Twentieth-Century Literature* 21 (1975): 151–62.

Porush, David. *The Soft Machine: Cybernetic Fiction*. New York: Methuen, 1984.

Pynchon, Thomas. *Slow Learner*. Boston: Little, Brown, 1984.

Pynchon List. http://waste.org/pynchon-l/

Richter, David. *Fable's End: Completeness and Closure in Rhetorical Fiction*. Chicago: University of Chicago Press, 1974.

Rosten, Leo. *The Joys of Yiddish*. New York: McGraw-Hill, 1968.

Safer, Elaine B. *The Contemporary American Comic Epic: The Novels of Barth, Pynchon, Gaddis, and Kesey*. Detroit: Wayne State University Press, 1988.

Sanders, Mark. "The Politics of Literary Reinscription in Thomas Pynchon's V." *Critique* 39 (Fall 1997): 81–96.

Schaub, Thomas H. *Pynchon, the Voice of Ambiguity*. Urbana: University of Illinois Press, 1981.

Schulz, Max F., *Black Humor Fiction of the Sixties*. Athens: Ohio University Press, 1973.

Scott, Nathan A., ed. *Adversity and Grace: Studies in Recent American Literature*. Chicago: University of Chicago Press, 1968.

Seed, David. *The Fictional Labyrinths of Thomas Pynchon.* Iowa City: University of Iowa Press, 1988.

———. "Pynchon, Joseph Heller, and V." *Pynchon Notes* 24–25 (1989): 127.

Seton-Watson, Christopher. *Italy from Liberalism to Fascism, 1870–1925.* London: Methuen, 1967.

Simon, Louis P., Jr. "Profane Illuminations: Benny Profane, Herbert Stencil and Walter Benjamin's Flaneur." *Pynchon Notes* 30–31 (1992): 172–78.

Simons, John L. "Pynchon on Household: Reworking the Traditional Spy Novel." *Pynchon Notes* 16 (Spring 1985): 83–88.

Slade, Joseph W. *Thomas Pynchon.* New York: Warner Paperback Library, 1974.

Smith, Marcus. "*V.* and *The Maltese Falcon:* A Connection?" *Pynchon Notes* 2 (1980): 6.

Soggot, David. *Namibia: The Violent Heritage.* New York: St. Martin's Press, 1986.

South Africa, Union of. *South-west Africa, Administrator's Office. Report on the Natives of South-West Africa and Their Treatment by Germany.* London: His Majesty's Stationary Office, 1918.

Stark, John O. *Pynchon's Fictions: Thomas Pynchon and the Literature of Information.* Athens: Ohio University Press, 1980.

Stonehill, Brian. *The Self-Conscious Novel: Artifice in Fiction from Joyce to Pynchon.* Philadelphia: University of Pennsylvania Press, 1988.

Strehle, Susan. "Actualism: Pynchon's Debt to Nabokov." *Contemporary Literature* 24, no. 1 (Spring 1983): 30–50.

Tanner, Tony. "*V.* and *V-2.*" In *Pynchon: A Collection of Critical Essays,* ed. Mendelson, 16–55.

———. *Thomas Pynchon.* New York: Methuen, 1982.

Theobald, A. B. *The Mahdiya. A History of the Anglo-Egyptian Sudan, 1881–1899.* London: Longmans, 1951.

Vella, Michael W. "Pynchon, V., and the French Surrealists." *Pynchon Notes* 18–19 (1986): 29–38.

———. "Thomas Pynchon's Intrusion in the Enchanter's Domain." *Twentieth Century Literature* 35 (Summer 1989): 131–46.

Vukmirovich, John. "Porter's 'Flowering Judas' and Pynchon's V." *Pynchon Notes* 22–23 (1988): 71–73.

Ware, Tim. *V. A Web Guide.* http://www.hyperarts.com/pynchon/v/v-novel-f.html

Wasson, Richard. "Notes on a New Sensibility." *Partisan Review* 36, no. 3 (Winter 1969).

Wentworth, Harold, and Stuart Berg Flexner, eds. *Dictionary of American Slang.* New York: Thomas Y. Crowell, 1960.

Wills, David, and Alec McHoul. "'Die Welt ist alles was der Fall ist' (Wittgenstein, Weissman, Pynchon)/'Le Signe est toujours le signe de la chute' (Derrida)" *Southern Review: Literary and Interdisciplinary Essays* 16, no. 2 (July 1983): 274–91.

INDEX